# THE SPIRIT SHAPED CHURCH

# THE SPIRIT SHAPED CHURCH

## A SPIRIT ECCLESIOLOGY IN INDIA

**Swarup Bar**

FORTRESS PRESS
MINNEAPOLIS

THE SPIRIT SHAPED CHURCH
A Spirit Ecclesiology in India



Cover image: © 2020 iStock; watercolor frame blue by Ekaterina Urvantseva

Cover design: Alisha Lofgren

Paperback ISBN: 978-1-5064-6689-7

eBook ISBN: 978-1-5064-6690-3

*To*

*my parents who taught me the value of learning*

*and*

*my loving wife Sonali and daughter Ayanna*

*who patiently endured the time I was abroad during my research.*

# CONTENTS

# ACKNOWLEDGEMENTS

The present work is a revised version of my PhD thesis at the University of Edinburgh, UK, for which I was awarded a PhD in Systematic Theology in the year 2017. The title of the thesis was *Towards a Permeable Spirit Ecclesiology in the Context of North India*. After revision, the present book is entitled as *The Spirit Shaped Church: A Spirit Ecclesiology in India.*

Before I acknowledge those who have been of assistance regarding publication of this book, I wish to acknowledge and thank those who have been of enormous help and assistance during my period of study and stay in Scotland in the School of Divinity, University of Edinburgh, UK, from 2013 to 2016 for finishing my PhD.

I wish to express my gratitude to several faculty members of New College, School of Divinity, beginning with my first supervisor, the late Prof. Michael Purcell whom I met only once before he sadly passed away in October 2013. Thereafter, I was skilfully guided by Dr. Nicholas Adams, who launched me into my project. I express my heartfelt thanks to him. I am profoundly grateful to my next primary supervisor Prof. David Fergusson, who patiently and painstakingly guided me to sharpen and refocus my thesis. He not only guided me academically but also provided me much moral support. I am also thankful to Dr. James Eglington, my secondary supervisor. Thanks go to Prof. Kirsteen Kim and Dr. Alex Chow for being my examiners during my viva and for their valuable suggestions thereafter. I am also thankful to Prof. K.P. Aleaz, former professor of Bishop's College, who gave suggestions regarding the portion on Indian theologies and the late Prof. Somen Das for his valuable suggestions. I am also grateful to Dr. Robin H.S. Boyd, alumnus of New College, who gave suggestions regarding my thesis. My sincere thanks go to Dr. Katie Bradley, also an alumna, who patiently browsed through my entire manuscript and gave valuable suggestions. Heartfelt thanks go to Catherine Meikle, one of my senior friends in Scotland, for going through my chapters and her critical suggestions. My thanks go to Margaret Acton for doing the proofreading for my thesis.

My grateful thanks go to the School of Divinity, University of Edinburgh, through which I received scholarships for study. I am grateful and thankful for the *Miller and Dalziel Scholarship* (2013–14) and the *John and Ian Baillie Scholarship* (2015–16), which catered towards my tuition fees. I wish to express my heartfelt thanks and gratitude to the Presbyterian Church, US, for considering financial support till the completion of my studies. Here, I wish to particularly mention the recommendations of Mr. Alwan Masih, the then General Secretary of the Church of North India (CNI), during several stages of the process. He deserves my thanks for his recommendations for obtaining the Church of Scotland accommodation for my second and final year of studies. In this case, I wish to record my thanks and gratitude to the Church of Scotland for allowing me the needed accommodation. Thanks go to Mr. Sandy Sneddon, the Asia Secretary, and others at the World Mission Council office of the Church of Scotland who helped me in the process.

My profound gratitude and thanks go to the Rt. Rev. Ashoke Biswas, the then Bishop of Calcutta, Diocese of Calcutta, without whose help and support I would not have contemplated studying in Edinburgh. Bishop Ashoke has been instrumental through his valuable recommendations at different levels, for arranging financial support from the Diocese to launch me into my doctoral studies and for his encouragement throughout. I wish to thank the Rev. Dr. Sunil M. Caleb, Principal of Bishop's College, who encouraged and gave me advice from time to time. Thanks to him for allowing me to use the Bishop's College library during the course of my studies. I wish to gratefully acknowledge the Most Rev. David Chillingworth, the then Primus of Scottish Episcopal Church, who gave me opportunity to serve in his Diocese. Thanks go to the members of St. John's Church, Alloa, UK, who have been so kind.

I cannot thank enough Catherine and David Meikle, the friendly couple from Scotland, who have been a great source of strength in every way, including financial support, during my time in Scotland. I am deeply indebted to their contributions and shall be always grateful for their support from the beginning to the completion of my studies. I wish to express my heartfelt thanks to Val and Robert Nellist, Prof. Allen Werity, and Ingrid Jaeckel for their financial support throughout.

Apart from the above, I wish to especially thank Ms. Karoline Mclean at the Divinity Office for her hand of help always, the Library Staff, and my friends and colleagues at New College, and in my wider fellowships in Scotland, India, and beyond who have constantly encouraged me in different ways.

I wish to express my profound gratitude to my parents, whose prayers, moral support, and love from afar have encouraged me to study. Finally, I cannot express in words how grateful and thankful I am to my wife Sonali and my only daughter Ayanna who had endured the pain of separation for three long years while I did my studies in Edinburgh. I am indebted to my mother-in-law for being there with my family at this time. They deserve all my respect and love for their sacrifice to see me successfully complete this work.

For the present book, I am gratefully indebted to the principal of Bishop's College, Rev. Dr. Sunil M. Caleb, who had encouraged me and permitted me to use the library for turning my thesis into a book. I am also grateful once again to Prof. David Fergusson, professor of School of Divinity, University of Edinburgh, and Prof. Kirsteen Kim, currently professor of Missiology at Fuller Theological Seminary, US, for encouraging me to publish this in the book form and all their assistance.

I am also grateful and thankful to Prof. Jesudas Athyal, acquiring editor, South Asian Theology, Fortress Press, for approving my revised thesis for publication and the whole team at Fortress Press.

Over and above everything, all praise and thanks to God for making it all possible.

# INTRODUCTION

The present book is entitled *The Spirit Shaped Church: A Spirit Ecclesiology in India*. The book engages Western and Indian perspectives or paradigms to propose a particular type of ecclesiology which could be viable for the Indian context. The model of ecclesiology proposed here is that of a permeable Spirit ecclesiology.

Before we go further, the use of the word *permeable* needs clarification. The Merriam-Webster Dictionary definition of the word *permeable* is "having pores or openings that permit liquids or gases to pass through."[1] In other words, the meaning of the term suggests exchange or passage of materials through porous borders or boundaries. Although this term is used in the discipline of science or other similar fields, it could easily be used for explaining similar characters in other disciplines. When this term is interpreted in the context of the church, it could mean a church with porous boundaries or borders. What this essentially means is that the church, while having definite boundaries, will be porous in that it would allow the passage of different perspectives or people to flow in and out. In other words, it refers to how the church may relate to its surroundings.

Again, the term *Spirit ecclesiology* refers to understanding the church, its nature, ministry, and mission from a pneumatological perspective, while maintaining the christological dimension. Spirit ecclesiology is a term used rather sparingly by some contemporary authors. Sometimes, the term has been used in isolation, but at other times, it has been used interchangeably with similar phrases like *pneumatological ecclesiology* or *pentecostal ecclesiology*.[2] Clarke Pinnock, in his book, *Flame of Love: A*

1 Merriam-Webster Online, s.v. "permeable," accessed October 19, 2019, https://www.merriam-webster.com/dictionary/permeable.

2 There are others who have used the concept of Spirit ecclesiology but termed it differently as "Third Article Ecclesiology." For example, see Gregory J. Liston, *The Anointed Church: Toward a Third Article Ecclesiology* (Minneapolis, MN: Fortress Press, 2015).

*Theology of the Holy Spirit,* uses this term.[3] He uses this in the sense that the church is essentially a charismatic community guided by the Spirit, which continues the mission of Christ through the gifts that believers possess. Spirit ecclesiology appears also in the title of a book, *Towards a Relational Spirit Ecclesiology in Asia* (2009) by the Indian theologian Abraham Kadaliyil. This relational Spirit ecclesiology considers "Christ as the motivating centre and the Spirit as the guiding centre of the Asian church and mission and life in the Asian context of many religions, many cultures, and many poor."[4] Furthermore, pentecostal theologian Amos Yong, in his book *The Spirit Poured out on All Flesh: Pentecostalism and Global Theology* (2005), mentions the term Spirit ecclesiology in his discussion of the essential marks of the church from a pneumatological perspective.[5] Kirsteen Kim, in her book *Mission in the Spirit: The Holy Spirit in Indian Christian Theologies,* uses this term in reference to Samuel Rayan's pneumatological understanding of the church.[6] In an article written by Chia Roland, entitled *The Community of the Holy Spirit: A Spirit-Ecclesiology in Outline,*[7] it is noted that the Spirit enables Christ's death and resurrection and the hope of eschatological fulfilment. The Holy Spirit is the basis of the creation of the church and its continued existence. Another article by Laurenti Magesa, *Towards a Spirit Ecclesiology,*[8] written from an African perspective, seeks to propose how the church should be open in the Spirit and respect the religio-cultural diversity of Africa, and have meaningful dialogue as the mission of Christ.

Therefore, the term Spirit ecclesiology is a comprehensive one that signifies broad engagement of the church beyond its own confines in various contexts through the presence and action of the Spirit in the world. It signifies mutual engagement across borders for effective witness and establishment of the kingdom of God. We can find that this term has been used to signify interrelationships of the church and the Indian contexts

---

3 Clark H. Pinnock, *Flame of Love: A Theology of the Holy Spirit* (Downer's Grove, IL: IVP, 1996), 141.

4 Abraham Kadaliyil, *Toward a Relational Spirit Ecclesiology in Asia: A Study on the Documents of the Federation of Asian Bishops' Conferences* (Germany: VDM Verlag, 2009).

5 Amos Yong, *The Spirit Poured Out on All Flesh: Pentecostalism and the Possibility of Global Theology* (Grand Rapids, MI: Baker Academic, 2005), 151.

6 Kirsteen Kim, *Mission in the Spirit: The Holy Spirit in Indian Christian Theologies* (New Delhi: ISPCK, 2003), 161.

7 Roland Chia, "The Community of the Holy Spirit: A Spirit-Ecclesiology in Outline," *CGST Journal,* no. 29 (July 2000): 119–155.

8 Laurenti Magesa, "Toward a Spirit-Ecclesiology," in *Redemption and Dialogue: Reading Redemptoris Mission and Dialogue and Proclamation*, ed. William R. Burrows (Maryknoll, NY: Orbis Books, 1994), 173–182.

of poverty and plurality too. This term also represents the dynamics of the Spirit's leading and Christ's work in the church's engagement with the world.

Questions of developing a Spirit ecclesiology which is permeable are based on the particular context of India and in the following, we want to briefly outline the context delineated by its particular history so that a rationale for such an ecclesiology is drawn out.

The history of India is partly the history of colonialism by various peoples at different stages. One of the most influential colonising efforts was that of European and, particularly, British colonialism. The effects of centuries of colonialism have left deep marks in India's society, culture, and political life, which are still felt today. One of the most sustained effects has been on the nature of Christianity and churches in India. Though the missionary movement in India has been involved in education, healthcare, alleviating the plight of the masses, and bringing the gospel in various ways, the majority of the churches in India have continued to be Western in their theology, structures, and practice. In other words, Christian expansion in this land had been done with an attitude of supremacy, and a devaluation and demonisation of other religious backgrounds and cultures.[9] This has resulted in a Christian community with little interaction with communities and peoples of other faiths and backgrounds. Thus, culturally, the church has not been able to connect with Indian cultures on an equal footing as such and therefore has followed Western cultures and practices in its life and ministry as the norm. Religious and theological dialogue with other cultures and religions is still kept to a minimum in the life of the church. These aspects have given the impression that Christianity is a Western religion.[10]

However, there have been sincere attempts since the nineteenth century by some missionaries and converts to integrate and indigenise Christianity religiously, culturally, and nationally. Although these were significant ground-breaking attempts, the Western nature of the church largely continues. Thus, Christianity continues to be looked upon with suspicion and its missionary endeavours have been equated with imperialistic undertakings. The fundamentalist groups of different religions, especially Hindu fundamentalist groups, accuse Christianity of being an anti-national, anti-Hindu, and a foreign religion whose secret agenda is to spread Western culture and Western religion and to convert India into a

[9] John Parratt, ed., *An Introduction to Third World Theologies* (Cambridge: Cambridge University Press, 2004), 5.

[10] Kadaliyil, *Toward a Relational Spirit Ecclesiology*, 5.

Christian nation.[11] Under these circumstances, the church in India struggles to be both Indian and Christian.

On the other hand, there is a huge challenge in India concerning the condition of the marginalised, the poor, and the oppressed. The churches in India are mostly constituted by these people. The Dalits and tribals who constitute the majority of the members of the churches in India are oppressed both inside and outside the church. There is a significant issue about justice and liberation of the marginalised in India. The challenges of solidarity with the marginalised, standing for their rights within and beyond the church, and seeking to empower them socially, religiously, and politically, are some of the greatest challenges that the churches currently face.

Thus, broadly, the challenge is on two fronts: First, to secure the identity of the Indian church as both Indian and Christian in its nature, ministry, and mission; second, for the churches in India to wake up to the fact of justice and liberation of the marginalised. However, it will be seen that these two concerns are interrelated, as the issue of identity of the Indian church cannot bypass the issue of marginalisation. Therefore, the churches in India should be able to address both the above challenges integrally.

The import of this study is that it seeks to address these dual challenges in an integrated manner and it does so from within the context of India. The research claims that a particular type of ecclesiology with a strongly pneumatological perspective coupled with its christological dimension, in a dialectical relationship, can be a viable way forward for the Indian churches. Consequently, it is argued that the churches in India need to be relational with other communities and religions to counteract the alienation caused due to colonialism's impact while also being distinctive regarding their christological witness, and their critical nature and Indian identity with particular concerns for the marginalised. It is also argued that this relational-distinctive dialectic is played out in terms of the features of universality-particularity, the spiritual and the concrete, the unity and diversity, and so on in the church's relationship with the world, especially in the Indian context. In this research therefore, a permeable Spirit ecclesiology is expressed in its relational-distinctive dialectic which is upheld as a way forward for the Indian churches. This relational-distinctive dialectic is shown to be an integral feature of a permeable ecclesiology. The project also seeks to be practical in applying such a permeable Spirit ecclesiology to select issues of ecumenism, multiple religious belonging,

[11] See Sathianathan Clarke, "Hindutva, Religious and Ethnocultural Minorities and Indian-Christian Theology," *Harvard Theological Review* 95, no. 2 (2002): 197–226.

and interfaith relations, which are some of the major issues the church grapples with today. In other words, while we talk about permeability here, it is basically deliberating about what sort of borders the church can have with those who are outside, including communities, marginalised groups, people of other faiths and ideologies, especially in India.

The study depends on both Western and Indian theologians as conversation partners. Western theologians and perspectives are used here to situate Indian theological thinking into the framework of global conversation about Spirit ecclesiology. They are also used here to set the framework for the project and contribute in building up a paradigm for a permeable Spirit ecclesiology. The Indian theologians from their own perspectives contribute to problematise the project, basing on the particular context of India and thereby making it relevant.

At this juncture, brief introductions to our theological partners for the project are in order. Jürgen Moltmann, from the German reformed tradition who actually needs no introduction, can safely be regarded as contributing significantly towards broad ideas of a pneumatological orientation to ecclesiology. The broadness and relationality in the Spirit in Moltmann's theology and its trinitarian basis and his wider ecumenical engagement makes him a suitable conversation partner for launching a discussion of an ecclesiology with relational borders.[12]

On the other hand, Stanley Hauerwas, the American post-liberal ethicist and theologian, as a conversation partner is engaged to highlight the distinctive nature of the church. Hauerwas stands out for his distinctive and contrastive ecclesiology and serves as a foil to Moltmann's relational open ecclesiology in our project. His ecclesiology that stresses on the embodied character of the Christian community of witness is noteworthy for our purposes. Hauerwas represents an ecclesiocentric and distinctive ecclesiology in this project.

Kathryn Tanner from Yale is used as a foil and critique for especially Moltmann's social trinitarian project and as a response to Hauerwas. Tanner's critique of Social Trinity exposes the weaknesses of a solely relational view of the church and her stress on appreciation of diversity, otherness, and justice is a counterbalance to postliberal ideals. Tanner projects the christo-theocentric model of the human community or the church. Her perspective also brings home the importance of the christological dimension of ecclesiology or the human community at large

12 Veli-Matti Kärkkäinen, *An Introduction to Ecclesiology: Ecumenical, Historical & Global Perspectives* (Downer's Grove, IL: IVP, 2002), 127.

and reinforces the distinctive aspect of the relational distinctive dialectics we were talking about.

Another crucial theologian is engaged to arrive at a formative shape of a permeable Spirit ecclesiology. He is Amos Yong, a Malaysian-American pentecostal theologian. A pentecostal theologian is brought into this project because it is felt that any pneumatologically-oriented construction of theology should include the voice of the pentecostal/charismatic tradition which has a growing number of following throughout the world. Wolfgang Vondey and Martin W. Mittlestadt in the introduction to their edited volume, *The Theology of Amos Yong and the New Face of Pentecostal Scholarship*, acknowledge along with others that Yong is a pioneering and leading pentecostal theologian, a major representative of pentecostal scholarship.[13] Yong has engaged in various fields: ranging from "theology to neurobiology, from biblical interpretation to interreligious dialogue, from theological hermeneutics to theology of disability, from political theology to theology of creation, from pentecostal doctrines to philosophical debates."[14] It is said that both the Pentecostals and the non-Pentecostals alike see a fresh endeavour in Yong's works.[15] Yong helps to precipitate a workable foundation of a permeable Spirit ecclesiology developing on the relational-distinctive dialectics of unity and diversity, spiritual and concrete, universal and the particular, and so on.

The Indian theologians Pandipeddi Chenchiah, M.M. Thomas, and Samuel Rayan SJ are all prominent theologians in their respective fields. Chenchiah here represents lay Hindu converts, during the pre- and post-Independence era in India who were among the pioneers of Indian Christian theology. Also, Chenchiah, along with Vengal Chakkari from Madras (now Chennai) and others were part of the group *Rethinking Christianity* which was very prominent and influential in guiding Indian Christian thinking. Chenchiah represents a significant strand in Indian theological thinking along with others regarding his criticism of the Western nature of the church, his concept of decolonisation, and his rethinking of the shape or form of the Indian church in terms of community structures and spirituality of other religions, especially Hinduism. This seems to provide the borders of the Indian church much porosity and elasticity in terms of broader engagement and community building with people of other faiths. Moreover, one of the distinctive aspects of

13 Wolfgang Vondey and Martin William Mittelstadt, eds., *The Theology of Amos Yong and the New Face of Pentecostal Scholarship, Passion for the Spirit* (Leiden: Brill, 2013), 1–2.

14 Vondey and Mittelstadt, *Theology of Amos Yong*, 1–2.

15 Vondey and Mittelstadt, *Theology of Amos Yong*, 1–2.

his theology and ecclesiology is his strong pneumatological orientation which provides significant insights towards an Indian ecclesiology of the type we are seeking to establish.

M.M. Thomas, the Indian theologian from the background of the Mar Thoma Church, brings into the project significant insights on ecclesiology in India which relate to how the church can meaningfully relate to secular culture, religious faiths, and ideologies. He is one of the major voices in the Indian theological scene who have contributed deeply in terms of an ecclesiology with relation to the secular realm. His insights regarding salvation and humanisation and open secular fellowships, challenge the Indian church to go beyond, in determining what sort of borders the church should have in its engagement with those who are outside.

Finally, Samuel Rayan, the Jesuit Indian theologian, is crucial for the overarching argument of this book, i.e., in our bid to develop a permeable Spirit ecclesiology for India. Samuel Rayan fulfils the search for a theologian who has a sustained pneumatological perspective in his theology, together with a relational but distinctive approach, along with a decolonisation stance, an engagement with the religious other in terms of the Indian context, and a liberationist outlook for the marginalised. He is both christological as well as pneumatologically sensitive and has been able to balance these dialectics.

The book takes the approach of dialoguing critically with the theological conversation partners to develop a model of a permeable Spirit ecclesiology as well as identifying the theological stance of the most suitable theologian in this project. Subsequently, it also evaluates such a model of ecclesiology in some select contexts which are crucial for India. It takes a context-first approach in which the description of the Indian context comes first, against the background of which the critical dialogue with the theologians occurs to arrive at the proposed model.

The book consists of five chapters, apart from Introduction and Conclusion. A brief outline of the discussions that feature in the upcoming chapters will give a brief idea of the entire project.

The first chapter entitled "Plural Contexts, Marginalised Communities: Ecclesial Challenges in India" outlines the broader context of India. This chapter is devoted to a descriptive survey of the context of India, especially mentioning those which are considered as major challenges for the churches. It provides the contextual foundations for the arguments to follow. The second chapter is entitled "The Church and its Pneumatological Shape with Permeable Borders: Exploring Western Paradigms." This chapter includes an explanation of the concept of permeability and offers paradigms or models from Western thinkers. The goal of this chapter is to arrive at a proposed shape of the church with permeable borders which is pneumatologically conditioned, yet christologically defined. The third chapter is entitled "Shape of The Church: Overview of Indian Ecclesiological Conversations" which highlights briefly the historical-theological background of the Indian church and gives a brief overview of the various general models of the Indian ecclesiological thinking. The fourth chapter entitled "The Spirit Shaped Church: Ecclesiologies of Select Indian Thinkers" deals with the contributions of the Indian theologians who have theologised about the church in the background of the various challenges of the Indian church. Here, a suitable shape of a permeable Spirit ecclesiology is arrived at, in the background of the Indian context. The fifth and last chapter is entitled "Implications of a Permeable Spirit Ecclesiology for Select Issues in India" which seeks to bring out the implications of such an ecclesiology on select issues of ecumenism, multiple religious belonging, and interfaith relations. The book ends with a conclusion and directions for further research in this area.

# CHAPTER ONE

# PLURAL CONTEXTS, MARGINALISED COMMUNITIES: ECCLESIAL CHALLENGES IN INDIA

India's rich diversity and plural contexts is a well-known fact in terms of its languages, religions, cultures, and people groups. This is made enormously complex with the presence of communities which have been marginalised on the basis of religion, caste, ethnicity, education, economic status, and so on. In the midst of such diversity and complexity, the church in India struggles to witness to Christ and also seeks to be rooted in the land and among the people. The challenge of the church to relate to its plural surroundings yet keeping its Christian moorings is a veritable challenge to be reckoned with. This has been the acknowledged struggle of the Indian church: to be relational as well as distinct, to be truly Indian, and to be truly Christian. The following pages will therefore highlight various aspects of India's complex plurality along with the challenge of religious fundamentalism and paint a broad picture of the struggles of the marginalised communities that form the bases of the church's challenges.

## India's complex plurality

India has a population of over 1.2 billion people.[1] This vast population is characterised by great diversity and immense complexity, to say the least. To present a fair idea of India's complex plurality and diversity, we shall go into a bit of a detail in terms of ethnolinguistic and religio-cultural diversity. We shall also find that people in India often transcend these boundaries of religion, culture, ethnicity, etc., even unknowingly. It will be seen that while Indians managed to live together with various religions and

1 See "Census InfoIndia 2011, Our Census, Our Future," accessed October 7, 2019. http://www.dataforall.org/dashboard/censusinfoindia_pca/.

cultures through the ages, there have been significant conflicts between communities because of this plural complexity. All these pose tremendous challenges to the mission and ministry of the church in this land. Let us now delve into the kind of diversity and complexity we have in India so that we are able to gauge the challenges that the church faces.

### Ethnolinguistic diversity

India is home to a baffling array of ethnic and linguistic groups. The latest government census of 2011 threw up interesting facts about India's ethnolinguistic make-up.[2] The number of scheduled languages in India is 22. The non-scheduled languages are 99. The total number of languages are 121, and many are mother-tongues among them.[3] Indian people comprise of various ethnic groups with their own features, languages, and cultures. Some of the general classifications include: Negrito, Proto-Austroloid, Mongoloid, Dravidians, Mediterranean, Indo-Aryan, etc.[4] This gives a rough picture of India's complex ethnolinguistic composition. These baffling statistics presuppose numerous communities with their own cultures, languages, and ethnicities where the Indian churches are supposed to do their witnessing, ministry, and mission. The Indian churches therefore are faced with the challenge of being meaningful and relevant in such diverse ethnolinguistic communities and contexts. The church's struggle is to find out meaningful ways in this situation to relate to these communities, keeping in mind not to alienate them from their local cultures, languages, and contexts. This involves quite a bit of research and relearning how the life, ministry, and mission of the church could be relevant to these communities.

### Religio-cultural diversity

Apart from ethnolinguistic diversity, religious diversity adds to the complexity of the nation. Religious communities include Hindus (79.8 percent), Muslims (14.23 percent) and Christians (2.3 percent), as well as Sikhs (1.72 percent), Buddhists (0.7 percent), Jains (0.37 percent), and other religious or non-religious groups (0.9 percent).[5] Christian presence in India can be found in the form of various denominations, mainline and younger churches, and fellowships. Roman Catholics make up the

2 See "Census of India 2011," accessed October 7, 2019, http://censusindia.gov.in/2011Census/C-16_25062018_NEW.pdf.

3 See "Census of India 2011."

4 See "Ethnic Composition of Indian Population," accessed October 15, 2019, https://tinyurl.com/y3qwwx29.

5 See "Census and You," accessed October 7, 2019, http://censusindia.gov.in/Census_And_You/religion.aspx.

majority of Christians, followed by Church of South India (CSI),[6] Church of North India (CNI),[7] and other denominations. Other denominations include Orthodox, Mar Thoma, Lutheran, Baptist, Methodist, Church of God, Pentecostal, Presbyterian, Seventh-Day Adventist, etc., including younger churches. Most of these churches prefer to work on their own, each with its own mission strategy based on the background it draws from and the challenges of the mission-field.[8] Besides these, there are other "popular" and primitive religious expressions too.[9]

The religion-wise diversity also varies across different states. Few examples will suffice: while Hindus form the religious majority in India, Muslims are the majority in Kashmir but are in a minority in the state of Mizoram in the northeast region.[10] Muslims are the second largest minority population in the states of Assam, West Bengal, Uttar Pradesh, Kerala, and a few other states. Christians form the majority in Nagaland, Mizoram, and Meghalaya, all of which are northeastern states, and in Goa, Kerala, and others and are a minority in the states of Haryana, Rajasthan, Uttar Pradesh, Bihar, Madhya Pradesh, and Gujarat, which are eastern, western, and northwestern states. Sikhs form the majority in Punjab and have little presence in other states.[11] Buddhism is the second largest minority in Sikkim and Arunachal Pradesh with some presence in states like Jammu and Kashmir which includes the Ladakh region, Mizoram, and Maharashtra. There is a small minority of Jews in Rajasthan, Gujarat, and

---

6 "The Church of South India is the result of the union of churches of varying traditions, Anglican, Methodist, Congregational, Presbyterian, and Reformed. It was inaugurated in September 1947, after protracted negotiation among the churches concerned." Cf. "Church of South India: History," accessed October 3, 2019, http://www.csisynod.com/history.php.

7 The Church of North India (CNI), formed in the year 1970, is a merger of six denominations—namely, The Council of Baptist Churches in Northern India, The Church of the Brethren in India, The Disciples of Christ, CIPBC, The Methodist Church (British and Australian Conferences), the Methodist Church in Southern Asia, UCNI. See *The Constitution of The Church of North India and Bye-Laws* (as amended upto October 3, 2017) (Delhi: ISPCK, 2018), 183.

8 See the detailed discussion of different churches formed by different mission agencies that have arrived in India at different periods and which often led to conflicts with other denominations, in C.B. Firth, *An Introduction to Indian Church History*, Indian Theological Library, rev. ed. (Delhi: ISPCK, 1998).

9 Felix Wilfred, *On the Banks of Ganges: Doing Contextual Theology* (Delhi: ISPCK, 2002), 2.

10 For details of the distribution of religion in different states, see "2011 Our Census, Our Future," accessed October 24, 2019, http://www.censusindia.gov.in/2011census/c-01.html.

11 See "2011 Our Census, Our Future."

Maharashtra. Parsees can be found in Gujarat and Mumbai.[12] Culturally, in terms of food, dress, habits, and life-style, there is a wide variety among Indians: For example, the food habits in West Bengal differ considerably from the food habits of people in the state of Gujarat or Tamilnadu. The cultural norms, taboos, and customs also differ according to various communities. It is clearly evident here how challenging it is for the church to bear witness, do its ministry, and mission in this multireligious and multicultural context. There remains always a tension as to how Christianity ought to relate to the multi-religious-cultural climate of the nation. The issues of influencing other cultures or being influenced by other cultures and religions are all very challenging. Again, the issue of how we relate to these communities, how far Christianity can be accommodative of the various cultures while the Christian community's essence is preserved is always a difficult question. Moreover, the church's mission and ministry becomes more challenging in the context of conflicting cultures and religions, which is very true of India. For example, cultures and traditions which are forbidden among the Hindus could well be part of the tradition of the Muslim communities. These may cause continued misunderstanding and conflicts between communities of various faiths.

### Transcending of ethnolinguistic and religio-cultural boundaries

Apart from these complex dynamics cited, there are obviously instances of peoples, groups, and communities intermingling and transcending boundaries of religion, culture, language, and ethnicity. One of our prominent Indian theologians Felix Wilfred notes that in Asia, people do not generally hold to rigidly demarcated borders. There is a lot of fluidity between communities and religions and there is interpenetration and free crossing of boundaries.[13] For example, movements like the one founded by Kabir,[14] known as *Kabirpanth* (Saint Kabir's path) in north India, draw Hindu and Muslim principles together and propagate the brotherhood of all under the fatherhood of God. *Kabirpanth* opposes caste practices and declares that God is equally to be found in temples and mosques.[15]

[12] See "2011 Our Census, Our Future."

[13] Felix Wilfred, *Margins: Site of Asian Theologies* (Delhi: ISPCK, 2008),175.

[14] Kabir was a fifteenth century saint honoured throughout India. He was born in a Muslim weaver's family in Varanasi (Benaras in north India). He studied under a Hindu guru, probably Ramananda, and developed into a powerful preacher and poet. His legacy is acknowledged in the failure of any attempt to put him within the confines of either Hinduism or Islam or any particular religion for that matter. For a discussion of his life and work, see Kabir, *Bijak of Kabir*, trans. Linda Hess and Shukhdeo Singh (Oxford: Oxford University Press, 2002).

[15] Roger Hedlund, *Quest for Identity: India's Churches of Indigenous Origin: The Little Tradition in Indian Christianity* (Chennai/Delhi: MIIS/ISPCK, 2000),108.

Kabir's present-day followers, the *Kabir-panthis*, are active as they conduct inclusive *satsangs* (fellowships) and community events in various parts of India.[16] This shows the reality that Indian religious communities show intermingling and crossing of boundaries. Religious borders are porous[17] and religious practices are often intercommunity events. Similar crossing of borders can be found in the interrelation between Hinduism and Christianity. For example, communities such as Hindu devotees of Christ are found to exist where thousands of *Christbhaktas*[18] come together in Varanasi, Allahabad, and Lucknow, in the state of Uttar Pradesh in India for prayer meetings, and express their faith in Jesus without being baptised.[19] These instances show that in many parts of India, people experience religio-cultural intermingling and harmonious living.

While we see intermingling and movement across borders, these open up potential for conflicts. These conflicts may be due to caste or tribal discrimination, due to religion or ethnicity, or due to geopolitical and historical reasons. An example of this can be seen in the northeast, which consists of eight states as recognised by the government of India,[20] having a population of 45 million people.[21] Geopolitically, it is a strategic area as it shares borders with Bangladesh, Bhutan, Myanmar, and China. Different factors like language, ethnicity, tribal rivalry, feelings of exploitation, control of resources, and discrimination have resulted in conflicts and insurgencies in this region. Similarly, Jammu and Kashmir in the far north is a politically strategic area as it shares boundaries with neighbouring Pakistan, Afghanistan, and China. This area has remained tense and prone to violence[22] since Indian independence. Again, situations of

16 Hedlund, *Quest for Identity*, 108.

17 Wilfred, *Margins*, 175.

18 See a research about this community by Jerome Sylvester, *Kristbhakta Movement: Hermeneutics of Religio-Cultural Phenomenon* (Delhi: ISPCK, 2013).

19 Sylvester, *Kristbhakta Movement*.

20 The states are Arunachal Pradesh, Assam, Manipur, Meghalaya, Nagaland, Mizoram, Sikkim, and Tripura. See "Welcome to the Northeast," accessed October 24, 2019, http://northeasttourism.gov.in/.

21 For a study of northeast India, see K.R. Dikshit and Jutta K. Dikshit, *North East India: Land, People and Economy*, Advances in Asian-Human Environmental Research (Netherlands: Springer, 2014), 421.

22 The recent incident of the Indian government's crackdown on the special status of Jammu and Kashmir granted by Article 370 of the Indian Constitution on August 5, 2019 and on the bifurcation of the state, made headlines for its alleged treatment of the minorities and separatists. See Rana Ayub, "India's Crackdown on Kashmir has Paralysed and Silenced Entire Communities," *Washington Post*, October 23, 2019, accessed October 24, 2019; https://www.washingtonpost.com/opinions/2019/10/23/indias-crackdown-kashmir-has-paralyzed-silenced-entire-communities/.

conflict are common over water and land, and questions of religion and language in south India. The Cauvery water dispute among the states of Tamilnadu, Andhra Pradesh, and Kerala are well known.[23] On the other hand are disputes regarding efforts towards forcible imposition of Hindi as the national language by vested interests which are totally rejected by south Indian states. Situations of conflict like these pose great challenges for the Christian community and the church. These are essentially related to justice and peace issues which the Indian church is often either oblivious to or is at a loss how to respond to while willing to be witnesses of Christ.

Apart from this plurality and diversity, India is known for its poverty and marginalisation. These aspects will be dealt with in the following paragraphs.

## The Context of Marginalisation

According to the census in 2011, 21.9 percent or 260.3 million people of India live below the poverty-line.[24] This reveals that India's population is still overwhelmingly poor. This stark reality of poverty is very much connected with the socioeconomic, religious, and political marginalisation these people face. The immense diversity described earlier coupled with poverty and marginalisation present numerous challenges for India and the churches. This situation is rendered complex by the striking contrasts inherent in the Indian society. Felix Wilfred succinctly captures this reality. He notes that there is a huge gap between the rich and the poor. The reality of sophisticated technological, industrial, and nuclear capability stands in contrast to the lack of basic necessities of life and even cases of deaths by starvation. The richness of human resources contradicts the reality of illiteracy and child-labour. India is the largest democracy in the world, but sadly has a society stratified by a rigid caste system compounded with the challenges of religiopolitical conflicts.[25] In the following, we will try to highlight the situation of marginalisation with respect to Dalits, tribals and/or *adivasis*, and women. We will also briefly highlight the "marginalisation" of the earth, in other words, the ecological concerns which are very much related to the above-marginalised communities. We will begin with the context of the Dalits.

23 Narendar Pani, "Institutions that Cannot Manage Change: A Gandhian Perspective on the Cauvery Dispute in South India," *Water Alternatives* 2(3): 315–327, accessed October 25, 2019, https://tinyurl.com/y5hc9q4v.

24 Estimated distribution of population: 25.7 percent in rural areas, 13.7 percent in urban areas. See Planning Commission, Government of India, "Press Note on Poverty Estimates, 2011–12," July 2013, accessed October 25, 2019, http://planningcommission.nic.in/news/pre_pov2307.pdf.

25 Wilfred, *Banks of Ganges*, 2–4.

## The marginalisation of Dalits

### *A history of oppression, discrimination, and violence*

The origin of caste, untouchability, and the Dalit community is itself a debatable issue as there is little or no conclusive evidence about it. However, the Aryan invasion theory continues to be popular. Proponents of this theory argue that an invasion or a series of invasions occurred during 1500 BCE when the Aryans conquered the original inhabitants in India and initiated a process of caste system and untouchability.[26] The Aryan society is classified into four castes (more appropriately *varnas*).[27] They are the *Brahmins* (priests and teachers), *Kshatriyas* (rulers and warriors), *Vaishyas* (merchants or traders), and *Shudras* (labourers or servants). Those that fall outside this classification are known as the "untouchables," or outcastes, or Dalits. Dalits are discriminated against in many ways and find themselves outside the borders of the Hindu society.[28] Dalit oppression ranges from religious to social to economic deprivation. They are discriminated in the spheres of education and employment, forbidden to enter temples or use public vehicles, and are subject to violent atrocities.[29] For instance, it is reported that from 1995 to 1997, a total of 90,925 crimes against Dalits were allegedly reported and it continues to this day.[30] Dalits

---

26 The Aryan Invasion theory was first published by Herbert Risely, a British administrator, ethnographer, and anthropologist. There are of course suggestions of other theories based on Ambedkar and from Dalit local myths. See Philip Vinod Peacock, "In the Beginning Is Also an End: Expounding and Exploring Theological Resourcefulness of Myths of Dalit Origins," in *Dalit Theology in the Twenty-first Century: Discordant Voices, Discerning Pathways*, ed. Sathianathan Clarke, Deenabandhu Manchala, and Philip Vinod Peacock (New Delhi: Oxford University Press, 2010), 74–90. This theory has been used to their respective advantage by different groups of people—both Right-wing and the Left. See Peniel J.R. Rajkumar, *Dalit Theology and Dalit Liberation: Problems, Paradigms and Possibilities*, Ashgate New Critical Thinking in Religion, Theology and Biblical Studies Series (London: Routledge, 2010), 6–19.

27 Peniel J.R. Rajkumar contends that the understanding of the word *caste* is often simply equated with the *varna* system. But, he argues that the notion of caste involves the concept of *jati* also. The varna system involved the fourfold classification of Indian society which was based on function. *Jati*, on the other hand, referred to people from the same ancestry. Rajkumar, *Dalit Theology*, 4.

28 S. Clarke, D. Manchala and P.V. Peacock, "Introduction," in *Dalit Theology in the Twenty-First Century*, 2–3.

29 For a description of the plight of the Dalits, see Vidya Devi, *The Plight of the Indian Dalits* (New Delhi: MD Publications, 2009).

30 Chandran Paul Martin, "Globalisation and its Impact on Dalits: A Theological Response," in *Globalisation and its Impact on Dalits: A Theological Response*, ed. James Massey (New Delhi: Centre for Dalit/Subaltern Studies, 2004), 21–24.

often work as scavengers, sewage cleaners, and in other menial occupations, considered polluting jobs from the perspective of the high castes. The present Dalit population in India is 16.2 percent (STs).[31] Almost two-thirds of Dalits are illiterate, but those who are educated still suffer oppression. The incident in January 2016 of the suicide of a Dalit named Rohit Vemula, a research scholar in the University of Hyderabad, due to discrimination by the high caste Hindu establishment shows the seriousness of the oppression that does not spare even the educated and aspiring young people.[32] The plight of Dalit women is worse. They are often tortured, abused, gang raped, and subjected to inhuman treatment by the higher castes. Thousands of Dalit girls are sold into the commercial sex industry.[33] Globalisation, on the other hand, contributes further towards land alienation, unemployment, displacement, migration, acute poverty, starvation, and lack of food security for the Dalits.[34]

It will be insightful to note here the plight of especially the Dalit Christians not only with respect to the wider community of castes but within the church and Christianity. It will be interesting to see that many Dalits have tried to accommodate themselves within this social structure often by transcending boundaries of caste, religion, and culture.

### *The plight of Dalit Christians*

Christian Dalits form the majority of the Christian community in India (70 to 80 percent of Christians are from a Dalit background).[35] Jose Kalapura, in his article *Margins of Faith: Dalits and Tribal Christians in Eastern India*, shows that Bihar (east India) has the largest concentration

---

31 According to government classification, Dalits come under the Scheduled Caste category, "Total Population, Population of Scheduled Castes and Scheduled Tribes and Their Proportions to the Total Population," accessed October 25, 2019, http://censusindia.gov.in/Tables_Published/A-Series/A-Series_links/t_00_005.aspx.

32 For the full incident, see Manash Bhattacharjee, "The Clarity of a Suicide Note," *The Hindu*, January 25, 2016, accessed October 25, 2019, http://www.thehindu.com/opinion/op-ed/dalit-scholar-rohith-vemulas-suicide-letter-clarity-of-a-suicide-note/article8130703.ece.

33 Prasanna Kumari Samuel, *Dalit Women's Experiences: A Theological Imperative for Indian Feminist Theology* (Chennai: Gurukul, 2009), 133.

34 Chandran Paul Martin, "Globalisation and its Impact on Dalits," 21–24.

35 S.M. Michael, "Dalit Encounter with Christianity: Change and Continuity," in *Margins of Faith: Dalit and Tribal Christianity*, ed. Rowena Robinson and Joseph Marianus Kujur (New Delhi: SAGE, 2010), 52–54; cf. Julian Saldanha, "Patterns of Conversion in Indian Mission History," in *Mission and Conversion: A Reappraisal*, ed. Joseph Mattam and Sebastian Kim, Fellowship of Indian Missiologists (FOIM) (Mumbai: St. Paul's, 1996), 79–80.

of Dalit Christians. It is inhabited by three ethnic Christian communities: the *Bettiah* Christians, converted from upper and middle castes, *Santhals* (tribals), and Dalit Christians.[36] Dalit conversions have occurred due to mass movements as in Punjab (northwest India) and also due to kin-group ties and interfamily ties within different castes. The vast majority of Dalits in this region are known as *Chamars*. In terms of religious identity, a Dalit Chamar Christian is not regarded as a true Christian because of the factor of untouchability. According to some ecclesial data, there are around 50,000 Dalit (*Chamar*) Catholics in this region. Other churches, including Pentecostals, claim that Bihar has around 68,000 Dalit Christians from seventeen Scheduled Caste (SC) groups.[37] S.M. Michael, in his article *Dalit Encounter with Christianity: Change and Continuity*, points out that in Bihar, the majority of Dalit Christians work as agricultural labourers, cobblers, watchmen, cooks, carpenters, drivers, petty businessmen, and domestic servants.[38] In Tamilnadu, Dalit Christians are treated as outcastes by fellow Christians. It is quite common to have segregated seating arrangements in caste-oriented churches. The Dalit Christian community here reflects a deep social crisis within itself.[39] In states like Andhra Pradesh and Karnataka, Dalit Christians are discriminated by Other Backward Classes and sub-caste groups in the churches.[40]

The Dalit Christians face manifold discrimination: First, from the hands of the government; second, from the caste Hindus; third, the caste Christian community; fourth, fellow Hindu Dalits; and fifth, the subgroups of Dalit Christians themselves.[41] The discrimination by the government takes the form of negating Scheduled Caste (SC) status to Dalit Christians (and Dalit Muslims) as enjoyed by their Hindu, Sikh, or Buddhist counterparts. This issue has been a struggle for the church since

36 Jose Kalapura, "Margins of Faith: Dalits and Tribal Christians in Eastern India," in Robinson and Kujur, *Margins of Faith*, 77.

37 Kalapura, "Dalits and Tribal Christians," 78–79.

38 Michael, "Dalit Encounter with Christianity," 51–62.

39 Godwin Shiri, *The Plight of Christian Dalits: A South Indian Case Study* (Bangalore: Asian Trading Corp, 1997), 245.

40 The major groups in conflict in the churches in Andhra Pradesh belong to *sudra* caste Reddys and Khammas, Dalit sub-castes Mala and Madigas. In Karnataka, the converts belonging to the Madiga and Holeya subcastes are given stepmotherly treatment in the church both by the clergy and laity belonging to the *sudra* caste. See D.Y. Moses, "An Overview of Christians in Karnataka with a Special Focus on the Plight of Dalit Christians" (Bengaluru: NLSIU), 16–18, accessed October 25, 2019, https://tinyurl.com/y2bgxbu2.

41 L. Stanislaus, "Dalits and Mission of the Church," in *Liberative Struggles in a Violent Society*, ed. John Vattamattam, Forum Series-1 (Hyderabad: Forum Publication, 1991), 197.

1950 when the Presidential Order was passed that Christian Dalits are not entitled to constitutional provisions.[42] The argument behind this order presumed that once converted to Christianity, people are automatically released from caste stratification and discrimination, both social and economic, which is far from the reality. Dalit Christians have been campaigning for the SC category and churches of various denominations are at the forefront in this struggle.

*Dalit Christians living with fluid boundaries*

Due to the discrimination meted out to Christian Dalits by the government, many converts in various parts of India have reverted, or remained "non-practicing/non-professing" Christians, or live in "two worlds," to avail themselves of the facilities given to Hindu Dalits. The response to this situation, for example, by the Roman Catholic Church, has been in terms of efforts at "faith formation" through catechising, discourses, and seminars to teach people to be regulars in the churches.[43] Yet, in spite of such efforts, most of the Dalit Christians seem to live in two worlds. They switch between their identity of being a Dalit on the one hand and being Christian on the other. These two identities do not seem to sit comfortably with each other. On the one hand, being a Christian does not necessarily guarantee a socioeconomic uplift; at the same time, there is ambiguity regarding whether they should avail themselves of the special privileges awarded to their other faith counterparts by the government. Some Christians tend to reject any privilege that come along with caste while others seek it. In this situation of ambiguity, some are seen to either hide their Christian identity, while others assert their Christian beliefs depending on a particular situation. It has been seen that when Christian Dalits need admission in Christian schools, they assert their Christian identity, but when they look for government jobs, they uphold their Hindu identity. While this may be considered an opportunistic attitude and a lack of religious conviction, some have pointed out that governmental reservations or provisions are not only required socially or economically, but also required for prevention of violence against them.[44] The example of the Christian Dalit dilemma is witnessed in an incident where a Dalit

---

42 James Massey, *Roots: Concise History of the Dalits* (Bangalore: CISRS, 1991), 35–46. See also the Presidential Order in, "The Constitution (Scheduled Castes) Order, 1950, 1," accessed October 25, 2019, https://tinyurl.com/y5dnfgez.

43 Kalapura, "Dalits and Tribal Christians," 78–79.

44 Kalapura, "Dalits and Tribal Christians," 90. See the argument of Ashok Kumar M. and Robinson, in Rowena Robinson, "Legally Hindu: Dalit Lutheran Christians of Coastal Andhra Pradesh," in Robinson and Kujur, *Margins of Faith*, 149–165.

Christian carrying the dead body of a person shouted *Ram Naam Satya Hai* ("Rama's name is truth") on the road, but while in the vicinity of the church shouted *Jai Yesu* ("Praise Jesus").[45]

This phenomenon of transcending boundaries between Dalit and non-Dalit identities is seen in the encounter of Dalit culture and Christianity. Here, some socioreligious boundaries have become blurred and others have been redrawn. It is actually a process of change and continuity occurring simultaneously. Kalapura reports that in recent years, in the urban parish communities in Patna (Bihar), there has been a weakening of caste boundaries, and inter-caste, inter-ethnic Christian cooperation has arisen particularly around the issue of marriage. Some Dalit Christians do not like Christian restrictions on Christian-Hindu marriage alliances as Hindu grooms frequently opt for Christian girls who are better educated than their Hindu counterparts.[46] The transcending of boundaries thus continues between the Hindu and Christian cultural norms and traditions.

### *Attitudes and response of the churches*

John C.B. Webster shows that Dalit congregations have considerable diversities in terms of their background, nature, and visions. He writes that Dalit Christians

> differ in the length of their histories and in their denominational traditions; in their patterns of conversion and of worship; in the facilities at their disposal; in governance and organisation; in social class and occupation; in their leadership; and in the levels of harassment, discrimination, and opposition they face.[47]

The diversity so described also leads to a diversity of responses to the Dalit issue in the church. In one congregation with an Anglican background in New Delhi, Dalit identity is rejected, while it appears to be a taboo at a Catholic church in Punjab; however, this Dalit identity is acknowledged in a pentecostal church and a CNI church in the same state. In a church of Presbyterian background, in the state of Uttar Pradesh, Dalit identity is both taken for granted and used as a basis for inviting others to become Dalits.[48] Efforts at indigenisation, for example, by the Catholic churches in the region in question, have been in terms of liturgy and cultural practices. Kalapura shows that in certain churches,

---

45 Kalapura, "Dalits and Tribal Christians," 90.

46 Interview with Ramesh Robert, May 23, 1998, Ganj, cited in Kalapura, "Dalits and Tribal Christians," 83.

47 John C.B. Webster, "Varieties of Dalit Christianity in North India," in Robinson and Kujur, *Margins of Faith*, 113.

48 Webster, "Varieties of Dalit Christianity," 113.

Ganga *jal* (river water) is substituted with "holy water" and Lord Ganesh's statue replaced by one of Jesus Christ and Mother Mary.[49] Since 1989, the local *puja* (worship) of *Chhat Mata*, a Hindu celebration of the divine mother (in which women offered prayers for their children and husbands through fasting and rituals), is converted into a prayer to *Mata Mariam* (Mother Mary). These practices have been both accepted and rejected by Christians in various contexts.[50] Indigenisation covered music, folk songs, and story-telling in song (*Isayan*—Life of Christ in local dialect) replaced the epic of *Ramayana*. The adoption of the Hindi equivalent of Christian names was allowed from the 1950s. Kalapura notes that in spite of all the efforts at indigenisation, some former practices and beliefs persist, which conflict with Christian practices. The liminal world of the Dalits and transcending of boundaries is also seen in the practice of some Christians privately consulting *bhagats* and *pundits* (Hindu priests) to cure diseases and solemnise marriages in Bhojpur districts of Bihar.[51] The community here also retains certain cultural traditions such as the playing of drums and dancing.[52]

### *The challenge for the churches*

The struggle for the churches in this overall Dalit issue is, on the one hand, showing solidarity with the Christian Dalits to counteract discrimination in the churches and on the other, struggling with them against the upper castes and advocating with the government for Dalit rights. The ministry of the church becomes very complicated in this context. On the one hand, their struggle for Dalit justice can bring confrontation with upper caste Hindu society and the government. On the other hand, the church's message of peace and unity between all communities could be in jeopardy as there are no easy avenues of reconciliation between the oppressor and the oppressed. Moreover, the denominational diversity, along with diversity of opinions regarding Dalit identity and Dalit rights, further complicates the issue for the churches. Added to this is the suspicion of the wider Hindu community and the fundamentalist groups who accuse the church of conspiring with anti-nationalist or "Western" forces in addressing such issues. Thus, the church faces the dilemma of affirming its

---

49 See K.N. Sahay, *Christianity and Culture Change in India* (New Delhi: Inter India Publications, 1986), 165–169, cited in Kalapura, "Dalits and Tribal Christians," 80.

50 Kalapura, quoting interviews with Father Mani Thundathikunnel, January 15, 1998, Shahpur, and George Sakhichand, January 19, 1998, Ganj Shahpur, in Kalapura, "Dalits and Tribal Christians," 81.

51 Kalapura, referring to interview with Mohangu Baptist, April 21, 1997, Ganj Shahpur, in "Dalits and Tribal Christians," 81.

52 Kalapura, "Dalits and Tribal Christians," 81.

nationality and averting people's suspicion even as it struggles for peace and justice for and with the oppressed Dalits. Complicating the dilemma further is the wrongly projected elitist image of the church, which drowns its actual Dalit reality. The CNI recognises this fact in one of its synodical statements (1993), which states:

> Despite the majority of the membership of the church consisting of the marginalised, it has been primarily serving the interests of the elite and upper ten percent through the educational, medical, and other institutions . . .. The church also generally reflects the culture and values of the dominant systems.[53]

Another statement issued by the *Yesu Krist Jayanti* 2000 shows the caste-ridden church in India. It says, "The Christian community cannot shrug off its responsibility collectively and individually, because we too have tolerated caste discrimination within the church, in spite of the official statements of the church condemning it as sinful."[54] Over the years, there has been significant growth of Dalit theology as a means to respond to the challenges of the Dalit struggles but correspondingly, there have not been enough changes at the ecclesial level.[55]

Now let us deal briefly with the issue of marginalisation of tribal communities.

## The marginalisation of tribal and adivasi (indigenous) people

The following paragraphs will give a general picture of the condition of marginalisation of the tribals in central, east, and northeast India. Let us begin by a general description of the tribal demography in India.

### *Tribal demography in India*

According to the latest 2011 Census figures, there are 705 groups notified as Scheduled Tribes (STs). They represent 8.6 percent of India's total population.[56] It is to be noted that there are some common challenges that the tribal people face in different parts of India. The areas of common concerns are those of loss of land and livelihood due

---

53 CNI, "Towards a Holistic Understanding of Mission Consultation" in *Church: A Community in Mission for Justice, Peace and Integrity of Creation*, A Report, New Delhi (November 15–17, 1993).

54 Stanislaus, "Dalits and Mission of the Church," 197.

55 Peniel Rajkumar addresses this issue of the difference between Dalit theology in the academia and the Indian churches in his work. Rajkumar, *Dalit Theology*.

56 See "Total Population, Population of Scheduled Castes and Scheduled Tribes and Their Proportions to the Total Population," accessed October 25, 2019, https://tinyurl.com/y2ky9g8g.

to profitmaking groups and economic globalisation, discrimination by non-tribal communities, religious fundamentalist forces that disregard their particular identity seeking to co-opt them into their religion, and the discriminatory policies of the government. These issues will become clearer as we proceed further.

*Tribal discrimination and oppression pre- and post-Independence in central and eastern India*

The tribals in central and east India are usually called *adivasis* (or indigenous people) and theology concerning them is commonly known as *adivasi* theology. Theologians have been found to use "tribals" and "*adivasi*'" interchangeably and separately, but ironically, the tribals or *adivasis* themselves are not satisfied with such terminologies. Nirmal Minz, a tribal theologian for one, contends that "tribe" is an administrative concept and tribals often do not want to call themselves tribals, but prefer names like Mundas, Oraons, Bhils, etc., according to their particular group or tribe name.[57] Tribal oppression and discrimination started during different periods of colonialisation of India. Minz notes that the tribals were alienated by the Aryans and Moghuls who treated them with contempt. The British colonialists brought about a different administrative treatment. Actually, confusion of identity followed due to colonial dissection of ethnic groups with national and international boundaries.[58] The geographical boundaries did not correspond with the demarcation of different ethnic tribes. This led to the denial of constitutional and other rights for some tribes. For example, the *Oraon* tribe was split among the three states of Bihar and Orissa in the east, and Madhya Pradesh in central India. Tribal theologians consider this to be a great injustice to the tribals.[59] Post-Independence, the Indian government again classified

---

[57] Nirmal Minz, "Dalit-Tribal: A Search for Common Ideology," in *Indigenous People: Dalit Issues in Today's Theological Debate*, ed. James Massey (Delhi: ISPCK, 1994), 136. Also see Sumit Abhay Kerketta, *Adivasi Theology, Towards a Relevant Christian Theology for the Jharkhandi Adivasis* (Ranchi: ATCR/GTC,2009), xii.

[58] Vanlal Chhuanawma, "A Search for Tribal Identity in North-East India: A Challenge to Formation of Tribal Theology," in *Search for a New Society: Tribal Theology for North East India*, ed. Yangkahao Vashum, Peter Haokip, and Melvil Pereira (Guwahati: North Eastern Social Research Centre, 2012), 75.

[59] Nirmal Minz, "Missiology for Twenty First Century Tribal India," in *Missiology for the 21st Century: South Asian Perspectives*, ed. Roger E. Hedlund and Paul Joshua Bhakiaraj (Delhi/ Chennai: ISPCK/Mylapore Institute for Indigenous Studies, 2004), 399.

the Indian states into fifth and sixth schedule areas.[60] Following this in 1950, the terms Scheduled Caste (SC: Dalits) and Scheduled Tribe (ST: Tribals) were adopted as constitutional names, thus further classifying and branding Indian marginalised people.[61] This complicated the problems for the *adivasis*. For example, in some states such as Assam they still strive to get the constitutional provision of the ST status. Apart from this discriminatory treatment by the government, the tribals are often deprived of their land by non-tribals. There are the entrepreneurs and the political leadership who dispossess the tribals of their land in the name of developmental projects. Various religious groups again attempt to add to their number from among tribals through religious conversions. Such attempts contribute considerably to the disintegration of tribal society and cultural unity.

Due to conversion (especially to Christianity), a complicated process of interrelationship between the tribal Christians and tribals of indigenous religions and Hinduism continues to take place. The example of one of the states, Jharkhand, will make the point clear. This state can also be taken as representative of some of the other tribal states (in central India). Jharkhand state in east India has around 4.1 percent Christians. It consists of 27.67 percent tribals of whom the main ones are Santhals, Oraons, Mundas, and Hos. The majority of Christians belong to the above tribes. The advent of Christianity in this region with Lutheran (1845) and Jesuit missionaries (1869) was soon followed by more than a dozen other missionary bodies of different denominations in subsequent years. Tribal conversions hugely increased from 1880 under the Jesuit missionary Constant Lievens, who offered to help the tribals in land-related disputes with the upper castes.[62] All these changed the demography of the state.

### *Complex religio-cultural transcending of boundaries among tribal Christians*

Post conversion, the tribals however continued to oscillate between their old religion and Christianity. It is to be noted that conversion brought about several complexities in the lives of the tribals.[63] Particularly, the relationship of Christianity with tribal religion or religiosity can be characterised by that of considerable heterogeneity, change, assimilation,

60 The Fifth Schedule areas are found in the states of Andhra Pradesh, Bihar, Gujarat, Himachal Pradesh, Maharashtra, Orissa, and Rajasthan; Sixth Schedule areas are operational in Assam, Meghalaya, Manipur, Mizoram, and Tripura.

61 Chhuanawma, "Search for Tribal Identity, 67.

62 Kalapura, "Dalits and Tribal Christians," 85.

63 Kalapura, "Dalits and Tribal Christians," 85.

conflict, and reaffirmation. As Kalapura notes, before conversion a tribe was a relatively homogeneous group with shared socioreligious traditions. After conversion, Christianity brought about heterogeneity leading to, he cites Pandey,[64] "caste like groups" within the tribe. In terms of marriage, in the same tribe one can marry only people of similar religion where earlier tribal endogamy and clan exogamy existed. So, while it created intertribe solidarity on religious lines, it created a wedge within the tribe.[65] So, Christianity is seen to both unify and to disintegrate tribal communities. Further, tribal Christians seem to live in two worlds, that of the Christian and the *Sarna*[66] ones, transcending boundaries. This aspect, however, is not regarded in a favourable light by other Christians who try to strictly follow Christian practices. The latter look down upon the former and try to dissociate from them as much as possible. As a result, there is considerable intertribal, interreligious, and intercultural conflict going on in these areas.

### *Challenges of the churches in eastern and central Indian tribal belts*

The churches belonging to different denominations have been trying to assimilate, accommodate, or reject different cultural or religious elements in order to bring harmony. Kalapura draws attention to a work by Keshari N. Sahay, which characterised similar trends in terms of "oscillation, securitization, combination, indigenization, and retroversion."[67] The tribal peoples have often opted to oscillate between the Christian and the *Sarna* rituals and practices overtly or covertly. Baptised tribals are seen to oscillate between attending prayers at churches and also secretly or openly practising indigenous spirit worship, witchcraft, and the observance of *Sarna* festivals. This happens when they face a calamity or difficult situation. Fellow converts call them *kachcha* Christians (raw Christians) as "they have so called *mithyabiswas* (superstitious belief) in them."[68] As pointed out earlier, securitisation or scrutinisation regarding which

[64] As cited in Kalapura, "Dalits and Tribal Christians," 86.

[65] Kalapura, "Dalits and Tribal Christians," 86.

[66] The *Sarna* religion is the traditional tribal religion, for example, of the Munda tribes in the Chhotanagpur region. The visible mark of their religious identity is the *sarna*, the sacred grove where rituals for the gods are performed. For a detailed description of *Sarna* religion, see Koenraad Elst, "The *Sarna*: A Case-Study in Natural Religion," accessed October 25, 2019, http://koenraadelst.bharatvani.org/articles/chr/sarna.html.

[67] K.N. Sahay, *Under the Shadow of the Cross* (Calcutta: Institute of Social Research and Applied Anthropology, 1976), viii, ix, cited in Kalapura, "Dalits and Tribal Christians," 86.

[68] Pandey, *Christianity and Tribes in India*, 175–76, cited in Kalapura, "Dalits and Tribal Christians," 87.

*Sarna* tradition or practices to retain or what to reject have led to meaningful engagement and dialogue. On the other hand, any noncritical rejection has led to alienation and religious superiority complex in the tribal Christians.[69] There is also the aspect of cultural combination where both Christian and *Sarna* traditions have been merged or tolerated in the socioreligious schema. One example is how the dancing traditions of *Sarnas* for young people have been limited to festive occasions while it used to be held every night, with a consensus reached between Christian principles and *Sarna* cultures.[70] A retroversion process is also seen where previously discarded cultural elements are reintroduced by the tribal Christians. A case in point is the re-use of vermillion (a powder put on the forehead by women during marriage or during festivities) which now does not seem to essentially conflict with Christian principles.[71] Kalapura points out that tribal Christianity here does not smack of "foreignness," but as a rich and diverse religion which has the capacity of assimilating different compatible tribal elements in its fold. This has also been important as a challenge to the homogenising and hegemonising attempts by the fundamentalist Hindu forces who say that tribals converting to Christianity have lost their tribal identity.[72] Having shown the situation of tribals in central and east India, now let us turn particularly to northeast India. It will be seen that northeast Indian tribal Christians have several similar challenges in common with their counterparts in other parts of India, but at the same time, also face some different challenges.

### *Tribal Christianity in Northeast India*

This region is taken separately since the tribals here have their own particular challenges and struggles in addition to some that are similar to the tribals of central India.[73] Apart from the ethnolinguistic diversity, it has some of the major religions, like Hinduism, Islam, Christianity, and Buddhism in its midst. Christians form a majority in three of the eight states, namely, Nagaland, Mizoram, and Meghalaya. Others are Hindu or Buddhist majority states. This speaks much of the tribal ethnolinguistic plurality and religio-cultural complexity brought about by conversions, mainly to Christianity. Like the tribals in central and east India, the northeast tribals also have reservations about using the term "tribals," as it carries a connotation of backwardness and superstition; characteristics that are showing

69 Kalapura, "Dalits and Tribal Christians," 87, 88.

70 Kalapura, "Dalits and Tribal Christians," 88; cf. references no. 27, 94.

71 Kalapura, "Dalits and Tribal Christians," 89.

72 Kalapura, "Dalits and Tribal Christians," 89.

73 The issue of loss of land and livelihood and the discrimination of the government towards them are similar to the struggles of the tribals in central India.

signs of waning in recent decades.[74] The advent of Christianity via British colonialism, missionary endeavours in the nineteenth century, and revival movements[75] in the twentieth century impacted the tribal communities both negatively and positively. Some of the negative impacts have been the erosion of traditional customary laws and customs with British laws of governance which alienated them from the earth and community-centred customs; the shift from an agrarian economy to a monetary economy and urbanisation leading to individualism; and creation-centred to anthropocentric and other-worldly theology and ethos.[76] All these ultimately alienated the converts from their previous communities.[77] The positive aspects were that of educational and the social-moral uplift of the tribals. Many harmful practices such as "head-hunting"[78] and superstitious practices were given up in favour of "moral aspects" of Christianity.

*The challenges of the churches vis-à-vis Northeast tribals*

There are various challenges for the churches in this region which are outlined in the following:

First, there is the question of meaningful engagement with the distinct, rich tradition of myths, stories, and semantic worldview of each of

74 V. Xaxa, "Tribes, Conversion and the Sangh Parivar," *Jnanadeepa* 3, no. 1 (2000): 23–25; Also cited in Peter Haokip, "Tribal Theology: Sources, Methodology and Hermeneutics," in Vashum, Haokip, and Pereira, *Search for a New Society*, 30.

75 Lakshmi Bhatia, "Contradiction and Change in Mizo Church," in Robinson and Kujur, *Margins of Faith*, 169–182.

76 Wati Longchar, "Tribal Identity and Theology," in *Rethinking Theology in India: Christianity in the Twenty First Century*, eds. James Massey and T.K. John (Delhi: Manohar Publishers, 2013), 107–112. For a particular discussion on the tribal loss of self-identity and connectedness to the earth and nature due to colonial missionary thinking and globalisation, see Wati Longchar, ed., *Returning to Mother Earth: Theology, Christian Witness and Theological Education: An Indigenous Perspective* Series no. 4 (Taiwan: PTCA, 2012).

77 George E. Tinker, *Missionary Conquest: The Gospel and Native American Cultural Genocide*, (Minneapolis, MN: Fortress Press, 1993), 48–49, cited in Longchar, "Tribal Identity and Theology," 107–112.

78 Headhunting is a practice which preserved the heads of enemies as trophies after killing. The Naga tribes of India and Myanmar used to practise such a custom. The practice was common up to the twentieth century. Many of the Naga warriors still bear the marks (tattoos and others) of a successful headhunt. In Assam, in the northeast of India, the Garos, Khasis, Nagas, and Kukis used to be head hunters including the Mizos of the Lushai Hills, which was later abolished when Christianity was introduced in the region. For a study on headhunting practices, see Janet Hoskins, ed., *Headhunting and Social Imagination in Southeast Asia* (Stanford, CA: Stanford University Press, 1996).

the tribes.[79] Second, there is the hurdle of strong denominational disunity within the Christian churches.[80] Third, there is the challenge in the process of *Sanskritisation* carried out by Hindu fundamentalist groups through forceful denial of the tribal religious identity and language and their gradual assimilation into the Hindu fold.[81] Fourth, there is a genuine lack of interreligious dialogical relations between different religious communities. Fifth, there are intertribal conflicts to attain socioeconomic and political status and land.[82] Sixth, the impact of globalisation has taken away habitable and agricultural land for building megadevelopment projects leading to displacement of the tribals. Seventh, there is discontent regarding the so-called "step-motherly"[83] attitude of the central government—the allegedly irresponsible actions of its personnel (political, military, bureaucrats, business etc.), which tends to fuel insurgencies,[84] and violence and injustice in the region. Any sociopolitical movement for autonomy or self-determination is therefore seen as having anti-national, sectarian undertones. Eighth, there remain ideological differences among community leaders and intellectuals with regard to people's movements for liberation. Ninth, there is the sensitive issue of migrants from central India and neighbouring countries which takes a toll on the limited resources of land and employment opportunities.[85]

### *Tribal spirituality in India and Christian missions*

Traditionally, the tribals sought to face the above challenges with a spirituality that is interconnected and earth-friendly, one that stands in contrast

---

79 Haokip, "Tribal Theology," 35.

80 Alphonsus B. D'Souza, SJ. "Tribal Theology in the North East: Some Suggestions from Sociology," in Vashum, Haokip, and Pereira, *Search for a New Society*, 23–25; Also see Nirmal Minz, "Theology and the Struggle of the Adivasi/Indigenous People of India," in Massey and John, *Rethinking Theology in India*, 406.

81 D.N. Majumdar, "A Study of Tribe-Caste Continuum and the Process of Sanskritization among the Bodo-Speaking Tribes of the Garo Hills," cited in K.S. Singh, ed., *Tribal Situation in India* (Shimla: Indian Institute of Advanced Studies, 1972), 269, in Chhuanawma, "Search for Tribal Identity," 69.

82 Chhuanawma, "Search for Tribal Identity," 73.

83 S.C. Dube, "Inaugural Address," in K.S. Singh, "Tribal Situation in India," 28, in Chhuanawma, "Search for Tribal Identity," 78.

84 To contain the insurgencies, the Government of India has deployed armed forces (military and para-military) with special powers known as the "Armed Forces Special Powers Act 1958" (AFSPA), and by now it has become a serious human rights issue owing to the excesses and brutalities of the security forces (eg.,extra-judicial killings, fake encounters, disappearances, etc.). See Linus Neli, "Vision of a Northeast Community: Based on Peace with Justice," in Vashum, Haokip, and Pereira, *Search for a New Society*, 211.

85 Neli, "Vision of a Northeast Community," 202–203.

to the individualistic and other-worldly tendencies in denominational Christianity in these areas. The basic spirituality of the tribals centres on land, forest, and nature, which are under "community ownership" and not for exploitation by individualistic profit-making enterprises.[86] They traditionally practise indigenous religion, which features worshiping the supreme God (the Great Spirit), minor spirits, and the family deity. Evil spirits are pacified and favours are earned from good spirits. Ancestral spirits form part of the corporate society of the tribal community. Here, Nature-Humans-God/Spirit is a continuum.[87] This religiosity/spirituality has suffered under the imperialistic tendencies in Christianity and homogenising tendencies of *Hindutva* movements (Hindu fundamentalism). In recent times, there have been considerable changes in missions in tribal areas where fewer foreign mission strategies and concepts and more indigenous ones are applied in keeping with tribal customs and traditions. Nirmal Minz reports that "the foreign missions have receded into the background, and indigenous Indian missions have presented themselves as a dynamic movement of the Spirit during the last 25 years in India."[88] The charismatic/pentecostal, evangelistic denominations working in the tribal areas through prayers, preaching, and healing have developed living churches in the region.[89]

In the above section, we have highlighted the struggles and the challenges of the tribals including Christian tribals in central, east, and northeast India. We have noted the discrimination meted out by the government, which the churches must address in order to be in solidarity with the tribals. Particular attention to tribal spirituality that is earth-friendly needs to be given in theology and church practice. The complicated question of conversion, the approaches of the Hindu fundamentalist groups, and the overlapping of boundaries between the old religion and Christianity need to be sensitively addressed by the church. We have seen that in both the Dalit and tribal communities, there is a significant transcending of religio-cultural boundaries. Intermingling and multiple religious belonging are quite common. In terms of this transcending of boundaries, the churches need to develop theologies that cater to these issues of double or multiple religious belonging. There are issues of both adjustment and conflicts in these cases too. These are significant challenges for the church. In the case of both the Dalits and

86 For a discussion on indigenous spirituality, see Longchar, *Returning to Mother Earth*, 19–42.

87 Minz, "Missiology for Twenty First Century," 397.

88 Minz, "Adivasi/Indigenous People," 409.

89 Minz, "Adivasi/Indigenous People," 408–409.

the tribals, the impact of globalisation—land-grabbing by corporate companies and so-called developmental agendas affecting the sustenance of the community—is a critical area to be responded to. Added to this is the need for an ecumenical response to the denominational divisions within churches that continue to threaten the unity of the churches.

Now let us turn to another area of discrimination and marginalisation, i.e., with regard to women in India.

## The marginalisation of women

We will give a general outline on marginalisation of women starting with a brief discussion on the plight of Dalit women who are the worst affected in the Indian context. This will bring out the issues that the churches face regarding the marginalisation of women in India.

### *The plight of Dalit women*

The Dalit women in India are often known as "The Dalit of the Dalit"[90] and find themselves oppressed and violated by various people including their fellow Dalit people. The suffering of Dalit women is due to several factors—namely, caste, patriarchy, globalization, capitalism, and so on.[91] The *International Dalit Solidarity Network* highlights some specific statistics concerning the plight of Dalit women. It notes that a three-year-study of 500 Dalit women across four Indian states has thrown up overwhelming accounts of violence and oppression. It reports that the majority of Dalit women have experienced one or more incidents of "verbal abuse (62.4 percent), physical assault (54.8 percent), sexual harassment and assault (46.8 percent), domestic violence (43 percent), and rape (23.2 per cent)."[92] Further, the "lack of law enforcement" incapacitates women to register their complaint with the police. Even when cases are registered, there can be lack of proper investigation due to caste or gender bias.[93] In addition to Dalit women being oppressed in this way, women in India in general continue to be victims of oppression and discrimination.

---

90 Aruna Gnanadasan, "Dalit Women: The Dalit of the Dalit," in *A Reader in Dalit Theology*, eds. Arvind P. Nirmal and V. Devasahayam (Madras: Gurukul Lutheran Theological College and Research Institute, 1980).

91 Surekha Nelavala, "Liberation Beyond Borders: Dalit Feminist Hermeneutics" (PhD diss., Drew University, New Jersey, 2008), 34.

92 See *International Dalit Solidarity Network* website, accessed October 26, 2019, http://idsn.org/key-issues/dalit-women/dalit-women-in-india/.

93 Ruth Manorama, "Background Information on Dalit Women in India," accessed November 21, 2019, http://www.rightlivelihoodaward.org/fileadmin/Files/PDF/Literature_Recipients/Manorama/Background_Manorama.pdf.

*Rise of violence against women*

Violence against women has been a cause of concern in India. An article in *Asia Times* reveals the report of the *National Crime Records Bureau* (NCRB) that crimes against women have doubled from 1.5 million cases to 3.5 million from the year 2001 to 2014. The capital of Delhi itself has recorded a 566 percent rise in violence against women. Other states include West Bengal, Assam, Bihar, and Orissa.[94] In the northeast, especially in Manipur and in conflict prone areas, women regularly become victims of police brutality. Women's safety, survival, and security depend on the repeal of the AFSPA,[95] which still seems to be a distant dream. National reports suggest that

> all major crimes such as rape, kidnapping and abduction, dowry deaths, and assault with intent to outrage modesty, witnessed increase. Kidnapping and abduction cases showed the highest rise (nearly 300 per cent) from 14,645 in 2001 to 57,311 in 2014.[96]

Domestic violence as defined in India as "cruelty by husband or his relatives" has been on the rise. In 2013, the NCRB reported 118,866 cases.[97] Apart from this increasing violence against women, general attitudes of discrimination continue in the Indian society.

*Status of women in India and the church's responses*

Nirmala Vasanthakumar notes that in India, women's worth is measured by their ability to produce children. They have no share in property. Their roles are expected within their household. The most common societal

---

94 Kadayam Subramanyam, "Rising Violence Against Women in India: Regional Human Development View Needed," November 11, 2015, *Asia Times News & Features, South Asia*, accessed July 22, 2016, http://atimes.com/2015/11/rising-violence-against-women-in-india-need-for-a-regional-human-development-view/. For more details, visit NCRB official website, http://ncrb.gov.in.

95 AFSPA is the Armed Forces Special Powers Act, which is a controversial Act introduced in 1958 for the northeastern states giving powers to the Indian Armed forces to act in "disturbed" areas. This Act is since then criticised from several quarters due to alleged human rights violations. For reports of misuse and human rights abuse in Manipur, see Sandeep Joshi, "Court-appointed Panel Highlights Misuse of AFSPA in Manipur," accessed October 26, 2019, http://www.thehindu.com/news/national/other-states/courtappointed-panel-highlights-misuse-of-afspa-in-manipur/article4921637.ece.

96 Subramanyam, "Rising Violence."

97 See BBC News India, "100 Women 2014: Violence at Home is India's Failing," http://www.bbc.co.uk/news/world-asia-india-29708612. For a detailed picture of crimes against women, visit NCRB official website, accessed October 26, 2019, http://ncrb.gov.in.

image for women is as a "virtuous housewife," as "men's property," or as "sexual objects."[98] Stella Faria, on the other hand, paints a picture of women confronted with "double standards of an androgynous social system," swinging between optimism of new experiences of achievements and facing discrimination in the other.[99] In the church, the plight of women centres on issues of participation in the decision-making processes and in the question of ordination. In CNI churches, however, women's ordination[100] is accepted and the first Indian woman was ordained in 1983. Women continue to be ordained, but there continues to be an imbalance of power between men and women in the different ministries of the church in general.[101] However, the CSI has made a bold step in appointing a woman bishop for the first time in its history in 2013—namely, Bishop Egoni Pushpalalitha.[102] Women are ordained in CSI from the 1960s and to full presbyterate from 1982.[103] In the Baptist churches in northeast India, women do have equal opportunities and many are theologically trained, but at the local level, their roles are "defined and restricted."[104] The Presbyterian churches[105] in the northeast maintain a hierarchical and patriarchal structure. There are theologically trained women, but their ordination is not accepted. In the Catholic church, women are completely excluded from major decision-making bodies of the church. Though they are very active in different ways, ordination is

---

[98] Vasanthakumar quotes Neera Desai and Maithreyi Krishnaraj, *Women and Society in India* (Delhi: Ajanta Publications, 1990), 175; and Anna V. Alexander, "Through the Feminist Looking Glass," in *Emerging Christian Women*, in Nirmala Vasanthakumar, "Role and Identity of Women in the Church," in *Feminist Hermeneutics*, eds. Lalrinawmi Ralte and Evangeline Anderson-Rajkumar (Delhi: IWIT/ISPCK, 2002), 50–51.

[99] Stella Faria, "Keynote Address on Feminist Biblical Hermeneutics," in Ralte and Anderson-Rajkumar, *Feminist Hermeneutics*, 17.

[100] The Church of South India (CSI) consecrated its first woman bishop on September 29, 2013. The Rev. E. Pushpa Lalitha was consecrated bishop in Nandyal in the southern Indian state of Andhra Pradesh. See George Conger, "First Woman Bishop of India Consecrated," October 3, 2013, accessed October 26, 2019, http://www.churchnewspaper.com/35399/archives.

[101] I personally know of some of my recent women colleagues in the Diocese of Calcutta, CNI, who have been ordained into priesthood. Also see Vasanthakumar, "Role and Identity," 55.

[102] "CSI Elects First Woman Bishop," report by ACNS Staff, accessed October 16, 2019, https://tinyurl.com/y6gvluam.

[103] "History of CSI," accessed October 16, 2019, http://www.csimichigan.org/CSIHistory.html.

[104] Vasanthakumar, "Role and Identity," 55.

[105] Mizoram Presbyterian Church, Khasi and Jaintia Presbyterian Church, Manipur Presbyterian Church, and Cachar Hill Tribes Presbyterian Church. See Vasanthakumar, "Role and Identity," 57.

completely denied to them. In Lutheran and Methodist churches, women play active roles as teachers and evangelists and ordination is open to them.[106] In pentecostal churches, women get little participation in the hierarchical church administration. Ordination is not accepted although they actively participate in the rest of the activities of the church.[107] Feminist theologies and feminist hermeneutics have been emerging in response to the marginalisation of women, though feminist concerns have still to take centre-stage in the agenda of the churches.[108]

The preceding discussion has revealed that marginalisation of women in India occurs due to several factors ranging from general socio-cultural-religious norms and patriarchy, to attitudes perpetuated by the caste system. This has been a significant challenge to churches for a long time. Moreover, the increase in violence against women poses a severe challenge to the churches and ecclesiastical responses have become increasingly necessary. With regard to ordination and the issue of participation of women in the decision-making bodies of the church, more needs to be done.

**Marginalisation of the earth: Eco-crisis**

The issue of the environment and eco-crisis in India have not been one of the primary concerns of the government or the church and have been quite neglected so far.

*Ecological crisis—the stark facts*

An article in the *Journal of Applied Ecology* reports that the impacts of climate change and "essential ecosystem services"[109] have found little

---

106 Vasanthakumar, "Role and Identity," 55–56.

107 Vasanthakumar, "Role and Identity," 55–57.

108 However, feminist theologians like Aruna Gnanadasan, Gabriele Dietrich, Evangeline Anderson-Rajkumar, Lalrinawmi Ralte, and others have made significant contributions to feminist theology in India. See Aruna Gnanadasan, *Listen to the Women, Listen to the Earth* (2005), *No Longer a Secret: The Church and Violence Against Women* (1997); Gabriele Dietrich, *Women's Movements in India: Conceptual and Religious Reflections* (1988), *Reflections on the Women's Movement in India: Religion, Ecology, Development* (1992), *Towards Understanding Indian Society* (1998), *A New Thing On Earth: Hopes and Fears Facing Feminist Theology: Theological Ruminations of a Feminist Activist* (2001). Evangeline Anderson-Rajkumar, *Gender and Identity in Envisioning a New Heaven and a New Earth*, eds. Rini Ralte et al. (1999), "New Eyes, New Reading, New Woman...," *Feminist Hermeneutics*, eds. Lalrinawmi Ralte and Evangeline Anderson-Rajkumar (2002), "Women's Movements in Mission: Some Lessons for the Church Today," in *Re-routing Mission: Towards a People's Concept of Mission* (2004), and others.

109 See Navinder J. Singh and Sumanta Bagchi, "Applied Ecology in India: Scope of Science and Policy to Meet Contemporary Environmental and Socio-Ecological

attention among India's ecologists and not much research has been done as there is a lack of interest among Indian scientists in ecology.[110] Yet, India's environmental crisis presents itself in different forms. Generally, there are around six causes of biodiversity loss—the high rate of population growth along with consumption; the narrowing of traded products from agriculture, forestry, and fisheries; economic systems and policies that fail to value the natural environment; inequity in ownership of resources; and deficiencies in knowledge and legal and institutional systems that promote unsustainable living.[111] There are issues of shortage of water, soil degradation and erosion, as well as air and water pollution.[112] Pollution of water is one of the critical ecological problems in India. It is estimated that about 70 percent of all the available water in India is polluted. New Delhi's sewage systems dump more than 200 million litres of untreated waste in the Yamuna river per day.[113] Air pollution and water contamination have led to serious health issues: arsenic poisoning from water has become a serious issue in most of eastern India.[114] For instance, it has been reported that about twelve out of nineteen districts of West Bengal have arsenic in groundwater.[115] Other states in north India have reported the presence of uranium and mercury in groundwater.[116] Huge dams are today one of India's most controversial ecological concerns. The *Narmada Bachao Andolan*, an environmental movement, is well-known for fighting against the displacement of tribals in the area in the Western Ghats.[117] This is true of the rural scene, but it is also seen as a result of an increasingly urbanised population. Several health issues relate to lack of proper waste management.[118] Deforestation is a major problem today. Forests are central to civilisation, culture, and faiths in India.[119] In spite of twenty-one percent of India's land being under forest cover,[120] the country has

Challenges—A Review," *Journal of Applied Ecology* 50 (2013): 10–11. "Essential ecosystem services" relate to clean water and pollination.

110 Singh and Bagchi, "Applied Ecology in India," 50, 10, 11.

111 R.L. Sarkar, *The Bible, Ecology and Environment* (Delhi: ISPCK, 2000), 227–228.

112 Sarkar, *Bible, Ecology and Environment*, 5.

113 George Matthew Nalunnakkal, *Green Liberation: Towards an Integral Ecotheology* (Delhi/Nagpur: ISPCK/NCCI, 2004), 19.

114 Nalunnakkal, *Green Liberation*, 5.

115 See "Our study on groundwater arsenic contamination in West Bengal, India (19 years study)," an independent report by SOES organisation, accessed July 26, 2016, http://www.soesju.org/arsenic/wb.htm.

116 Singh and Bagchi, "Applied Ecology in India," 5.

117 Nalunnakkal, *Green Liberation*, 20.

118 Nalunnakkal, *Green Liberation*, 20.

119 Nalunnakkal, *Green Liberation*, 30, 31.

120 See United Nations FAO *Global Forest Assessment Report* 2010, accessed November 21, 2019, http://www.fao.org/forestry/fra/fra2010/en/.

seen "persistent and chronic deforestation" particularly in the Western Ghats and the Himalayas.[121] Further, regarding soil erosion, recent official reports have suggested that about "130 Mha of land in India has been affected by serious soil erosion."[122] Added to this is the issue of "agricultural intensification," which puts a strain on water resources as India is prone to drought and floods. This has also impacted the aquatic life very seriously and ecosystems in general.[123] Overfishing is a serious ecological concern in India due to using modern fishing techniques threatening survival of the traditional fisherfolks.[124] Related to this is the concern for the loss of habitats for animals and their extinction due to deforestation and illegal wildlife trade.[125] Regarding climate change, studies have suggested that India is the third largest emitter of greenhouse gases, which is about 5.3 percent of global emissions. "Energy, industry, agriculture, and automobiles" are the main emitters of CHGs.[126] Climate changes in India have been known to affect food production, water supply, forestry, and biodiversity. Some estimates project warmer and wetter climates. Several vectorborne diseases are known to occur due to the effects of climate change.[127]

### *Ecological crisis as a justice issue*

The ecological crisis in India is not only a scientific issue, but is very much related to poverty, marginalisation, and deprivation. It is an issue of justice and liberation. K.C. Abraham, a leading Global South theologian from India, insists that:

> It is not a problem created by scientists or by a group of people who fancy growing trees around their houses. It is the problem of the poor.

121 Singh and Bagchi, "Applied Ecology in India," 7.

122 See the Department of Land Resources official website of Government of India, accessed November 21, 2019, https://tinyurl.com/y2b6tf72.

123 Singh and Bagchi, "Applied Ecology in India," 6.

124 Nalunnakkal, *Green Liberation*, 26.

125 Nalunnakkal, *Green Liberation*, 26.

126 Singh and Bagchi, "Applied Ecology in India," 8.

127 Several vectorborne diseases such as malaria, dengue, chikungunya, and elephantiasis are prevalent in India, and climate change is likely to influence their transmission. Estimates suggest about 1.48 million cases of malaria occur annually in India, and 1173 deaths were reported in 2007. See the "National Vector Borne Disease Control Programme 2007," accessed July 26, 2016, http://www.nvbdcp.gov.in/.

It is integral to their struggle for justice and liberation, and basically it is about preserving the integrity of Creation.[128]

Ashish Kothari, the founder of an Indian environmental group *Kalpavriksh*, encapsulates the dilemma of India's environmental concerns as a social justice issue, which he calls "crisis of mis-development."[129] He argues,

> [India's] sordid story of inequality [is]masked by the glitter of the new urban pockets that business and political leaders proudly showcase. Four decades of state-dominated "development" followed by two decades of corporate-dominated economic globalization have led India down the path of unsustainability: it now has the world's third largest ecological footprint. While some forms of poverty have been reduced, others persist. Sixty million people have been forcibly evicted by "development" projects. Roughly three out of four Indians suffer from deprivation of at least one of the following basic needs: adequate and nutritious food, safe drinking water, sanitation, energy, gainful and dignified employment education, health care, and adequate shelter.[130]

Over the years, there have been various social justice movements[131] that have tried to provide resistance to capitalist and corporate endeavour to snatch land, habitats, and forests from the local inhabitants. One

128 See K.C. Abraham, "A Theological Response to the Environmental Crisis," in *Liberative Solidarity: Contemporary Perspectives on Mission* (Thiruvalla: Christava Sahitya Samithi, 1996), accessed July 26, 2016, https://tinyurl.com/yxg3glyf.

129 Ashish Kothari and Aseem Shrivastava, *Churning the Earth: The Making of Global India* (Delhi: Penguin, 2012); Simron Singh et al., "India's Biophysical Economy, 1961–2008: Sustainability in a National and Global Context," *Ecological Economics* 76 (2008): 60 69, accessed October 26, 2019, http://www.sciencedirect.com/science/article/pii/S0921800912000456.

130 Kothari and Shrivastava, *Churning the Earth*; Singh et al., "India's Biophysical Economy," 60–69, accessed July 27, 2016, http://www.sciencedirect.com/science/article/pii/S0921800912000456; Kalpavriksh, *Globalisation in India: Impacts and Alternatives* (Pune: Kalpavriksh, 2013), accessed July 27, 2016, http://www.kalpavriksh.org/images/CLN/Globalisation%20Brochure.pdf, as cited in Ashish Kothari, "Radical Ecological Democracy: A Path Forward for India and Beyond," in *A Great Transition Initiative (GTI) Essay: Towards a Transformative Vision and Praxis*, July 2014, 7–8, accessed July 27, 2016, http://www.greattransition.org/publication/radical-ecological-democracy-a-path-forward-for-india-and-beyond, 10.

131 Movements such as *Narmada Bachao Andolan* (NBA) is a social movement consisting of *adivasis*, farmers, environmentalists, and human rights activists against a number of large dams being built across the Narmada river, which flows through the states of Gujarat, Madhya Pradesh, and Maharashtra. See P.P. Karan, "Environmental Movements in India," *Geographical Review*, American Geographical Society 84, no. 1 (January 1994): 32–41.

such movement is the *Chipko*[132] Movement, which adopted the Gandhian principles of *Satyagraha* (laying hold of truth) and nonviolent resistance to highlight the environmental crisis, especially deforestation in the region of Uttarakhand, an Indian state. This movement saw the participation of huge numbers of people, especially women. On March 26, 1974, women embraced trees in the Reni forest in Uttarakhand to save them from being cut by a government-backed auction in spite of several protests previous to the incident. The women were ultimately able to save the forest.[133] Women have been at the forefront of some of these social movements as environmental crisis has affected women and children the most. A number of women-activist feminists and authors[134] have critically reflected on the impact of the environmental crisis on women and on social justice issues more generally. One of them, Vandana Shiva, well known for her activism, has called attention to the dangers of co-option by environmental metaphors forwarded by governments, the World Bank, and other multinational corporations. Her approach is to focus instead on holistic approach respecting the rights and privileges of all marginalised communities.[135]

### *Response of the churches to the ecological crisis*

To date, there has been a limited response by the churches in India and more needs to be done.[136] The theological community in India, both

132 The word *chipko* means "to stick" or "to embrace."

133 Following the events at Reni, forest auctions were opposed in different parts of Garhwal district. Subsequently, over the next five years, the movement spread to many districts in the region and within a decade, it spread throughout the Uttarakhand and Himalayas. For details of the movement and its aftermath, see Barnali Kalita, "Chipko Movement: A Landmark Effort in Addressing Environmental Crisis in India," *International Journal of Interdisciplinary Research and Innovations* 3, no. 3 (July–September 2015): 17–21. See also, J. Bandopadhyay and Vandana Shiva, *Chipko: India's Civilisational Crisis to the Forest Crisis* (New Delhi: INTACH, 1986); Ramachandra Guha, *The Unquiet Woods: Ecological Change and Peasant Resistance in the Himalaya*, expanded ed. (Berkley, California: University of California Press, 2000).

134 Medha Patkar is a social activist from India and a politician. She is the founder member of Narmada Bachao Andolan and was the National Convener of *National Alliance of People's Movements* (NAPM), an alliance of progressive people's organisations. Another writer activist is Arundhati Roy, best known for her book, *The God of Small Things* (1997) for which she received the Booker Prize.

135 See Vandana Shiva, *Staying Alive: Women, Ecology and Development* (New Delhi: Zed Books, 1989).

136 There have been recognitions of the CSI's commitment to creation care. For example, the United Nations Development Programme in partnership with the Alliance of Religions and Conservation, recognised CSI for "Its Long Term Commitment to Protect the Living Planet" on November 3, 2009 at a ceremony

north[137] and south India, has responded theologically to environmental issues.[138] There are significant publications on ecojustice theologies and concerns of the environment. There are publications linking feminism and ecology, Dalits, tribal concerns, and ecology.[139] Specific commitments about creation care have been made by churches.[140] A particular wing of the CNI known as Synodical Board of Social Services works to empower socially excluded and marginalised communities like Dalits, *adivasis*, women, and children along with issues of climate change.[141] There have been national consultations on climate change organised by the churches to raise awareness and make action plans.[142] The CSI has taken important steps to declare its commitment to ensure green churches through initiatives such as awards, conventions, rallies, rainwater harvesting, etc.[143] Local churches in India have, of course, tried to respond to their environment in small ways, for example, initiatives regarding tree plantation, cleanliness drives, and so on. There has been growing awareness among the churches concerning the environment and climate change, but environmental

---

at Windsor Castle, presided over by Prince Phillip, the Duke of Edinburgh. The awards were presented by Mr. Ban Ki-moon, the UN Secretary-General. See *Ecumenical Water Network*, "Church of South India Recognized for Protecting the Planet," accessed August 25, 2016, http://water.oikoumene.org/en/whatwedo/news-events/church-of-south-india-recognized-for-protecting-the-planet. Also see CSI's seven-year-plan of Green Parishes and Green Dioceses, "1000 Green Schools Plan by Church of South India," accessed August 25, 2016 *ACNS*, http://www.arcworld.org/downloads/Christian-CSI-7YP.pdf, http://www.anglicannews.org/news/2016/06/1000-green-schools-plan-by-church-of-south-india.aspx.

137 For contributions from the northeast India, see the chapter on "Creation-Centred Spirituality and Christian Theology: Some Pointers," by Wati Longchar, *Returning to Mother Earth*, 96–128.

138 See Thomas Samuel and Mathew Koshy Punnackadu, ed., *A Theological Response to Ecological Crisis* (Thiruvalla: Christava Sahithya Samithi, 2009); Nalunnakkal, *Green Liberation*.

139 *Eco-Justice: Implication for Faith and Theology* (Mangalore: Indian Theological Alumni of the Universitat Regensburg and BTESSC, 2011).

140 See the report of Anglican News Service on the CNI pronouncement, "North India Church Urges Determined Commitment to Protecting All of Creation," accessed August 25, 2016, http://www.anglicannews.org/news/2015/07/north-india-church-urges-determined-commitment-to-protecting-all-of-creation.aspx.

141 See "CNI Mission Priorities," http://www.cnisynod.org/mission.aspx. See also, National Council of Churches in India website, accessed August 25, 2016, http://www.nccindia.in/index.php/affiliates-network/member-churches/92-affiliates-network/member-churches/151-cni.html.

142 See the "CNI Consultation on Climate Change and Youth," accessed August 25, 2016, http://www.cnisynod.org/1003/news06.htm.

143 "Church of South India: A Seven Year Plan to Protect the Living Planet." http://www.arcworld.org/downloads/Christian-CSI-7YP.pdf.

concern as a particular and urgent mission for the church has yet to take concrete shape.

Thus, we have described the plural contexts of India along with the plight of the marginalised, the poor, the Dalits, the tribals, women, and dwelt on the ecological crisis. We have pointed out the challenges the church faces in these contexts and thereby, the need for a relook at our ecclesiologies. Now, another challenge that the church faces is that of religious fundamentalism which seems to have gripped the nation in recent times. We now turn to this issue.

## Religious fundamentalism[144] as one of the major threats for Christians and other minorities

India has witnessed onslaughts of fundamentalism from different religions in different forms in different epochs. Religious fundamentalism has been one of the major factors in the religiopolitical conflicts of the nation.[145] Acknowledging that fundamentalisms of different religions including Hinduism, Islam, Christianity, and others have impacted the nation in different ways, the scope here is limited to Hindu fundamentalism.[146]

### The rise of Hindu fundamentalism

India's secular fabric started to be threatened by Hindu fundamentalism in different ways since its rise in the early years of the twentieth century. Hindu fundamentalism has its roots in the Hindu renaissance, which started in the nineteenth century as a reaction to British imperialism and the influence of Western education.[147] Hindu Renaissance, along with na-

---

144 In Christian parlance, the term fundamentalism is derived from a title of a series of booklets, *The Fundamentals*, published in the USA between 1910 and 1915. It referred to central elements of Christian teaching, but fundamentalism's emphasis on biblical inerrancy is always prominent. See Alan Richardson and John Bowden, eds., *A New Dictionary of Christian Theology* (London: SCM Press, 1983), 223. Fundamentalism and fundamentalists are to be found in other religions as well. There are fundamentalist strains in Christianity, Islam, Hinduism, Sikhism, and other religions. India has gone through the effects of these fundamentalist forces and epochs since the pre-Independence times.

145 For a detailed picture of fundamentalism in India, see T.N. Madan, *Modern Myths, Locked Minds, Secularism and Fundamentalism in India*, 2nd ed. (Delhi: Oxford University Press, 2010).

146 I have chosen to focus on Hindu fundamentalism as the issue is a much debated topic in India now.

147 Rodinmawia Ralte, *Hindus and Hindutva, Hindu Tolerance, Hindutva Exclusivism, Emergence of Assertive Hinduism* (Taiwan: PTCA, 2014), 11–12; see also, M.T. Cherian, *Hindutva Agenda and Minority Rights: A Christian Response* (Bangalore: CFCC, 2007), 3.

tionalistic fervours, began in Bengal through the establishment of religious *Samaj* (societies) led by prominent Bengali thinkers like Ram Mohan Roy, Keshab Chandra Sen, and others. Roy established the *Brahmo Samaj* in 1830 along with others, which sought to revive Hinduism against idolatry through Vedantic philosophy and the ethical teachings of Jesus. This was the first attempt of its kind to revive Hinduism from its supposed decline after the colonialism of the West. Later, a more radical organisation known as the *Arya Samaj* was founded by Swami Dayanand Saraswati in 1875, whose main watchword was "Back to the Vedas," and who declared India to be solely the land of the *Aryans* (Hindus). The *Arya Samaj* sowed one of the first seeds of fundamentalism, which was followed up by other well-known leaders of the time. The *Arya Samaj* was also the first to take up the *Shuddhi* movement (purification ceremony for reconversion) to check conversions from Hinduism to other religions.[148] Later, this spirit of Hindu Renaissance, coupled with nationalistic fervours took an extremist turn in the thoughts of prominent Hindu thinkers like Bal Gangadhar Tilak, an ardent nationalist, and V.D. Savarkar, a militant Hindu.

*The concept of Hindutva*

V.D. Savarkar was influential in developing militant concepts, which were later to be followed by the fundamentalist organisations. The term "Hindutva" coined by him, means "Hinduness." For him, a Hindu is a person who recognises the whole Indian subcontinent as one's motherland and fatherland, and a descendant of Hindu parents; and one who accepts Sanskrit to be one's primary language. Savarkar's slogan, "Hinduise politics, Militarise Hindus"[149] went a long way into shaping the nature and motivations of later fundamentalists. His ideas eventually led to the formation of multiple Hindu fundamentalist organisations under the collective name of the *Sangh Parivar.* The main aim of the *Sangh Parivar* is to see India as a country identified as a single nation (Hindu *rashtra*) with one culture (Hindu culture, which is a utopian concept in a multicultural society like India), one religion (Hindu religion, which is again impractical in a multireligious India), and one language (Hindi, inappropriate in the context of twenty-two different official languages of India and the numerous indigenous languages and dialects).

Studies have pointed out that Hindu fundamentalism's narrowness and discriminatory attitude towards other religious minorities is quite different from the traditional Hindu ethos of tolerance and respect as held by the most prominent Hindu philosophers and religious teachers.

[148] Ralte, *Hindus and Hindutva,* 15–18.

[149] Ralte, *Hindus and Hindutva,* 3.

In the earlier periods, Hindu kings gave shelter to Christians, Buddhists, and Muslims on various occasions.[150] However, the arguments of the fundamentalists go the other way. They argue that due to the rule of the Muslims and the domination of the British together for so many years, Hindu culture and religion suffered a major setback and the glory of Hinduism faded away. Therefore, one of the main tasks of these organisations is to bring back the past glory of Hinduism. Added to this is the inculcation of a fear psychosis that the minority population is increasing, which will eventually lead to a decrease in the number of Hindus in India. This accusation is simply not true at least in the case of Christians. Almost 2,000 years of Christian presence in this country has not secured any significant increase in the official numbers of Christians in this country. The Christian population is only around 2.3 percent of the Indian population at present.[151] So, any allegation that Christian missionary activity in India until today has considerably increased the number of Christians in India is untrue.

Here, a brief outline of the *Sangh*'s ideology and agendas would open our eyes to the challenges the Christian community and its institutions and other minorities face at present. One of their first attacks is on the secular fabric of India and minority rights. The *Sangh Parivar* is bent on altering the secular fabric of the nation, which enshrines tolerance and respect for all religions and rights for the minorities. The Indian idea of secularism differs from Western secularism, the latter broadly implying equidistance of the state from religion, which can take the shape of prohibition of religious association in state activities. In India, secularism means neutrality between different religious traditions, not necessarily involving the prohibiting part.[152] For the *Sangh Parivar*, secularism is to be understood in its own brand of Hinduism (or *Hindutva*), and the Indian understanding of secularism has come under attack. They are bent on altering its meaning. Practically, the notion would include "saffronising" (saffron is the colour of *Hindutva*) our educational norms, history, and the Indian Constitution according to their *Hindutva* ideology. M.T. Cherian, who researched *Hindutva* and fundamentalism, notes that in the hands of these fundamentalists,

[150] See Massey and John, *Rethinking Theology in India*, 66.

[151] See "2011 Our Census, Our Future," accessed July 18, 2016, http://www.censusindia.gov.in/2011census/c-01.html.

[152] For a brief discussion on differences of the idea of secularism in India and the West, see Amartya Sen, *The Argumentative Indian: Writings on Indian History, Culture and Identity* (New York: Farrar, Straus & Giroux, 2005), 17–20; also see, Cherian, *Hindutva Agenda*, 49–50.

> The secular education is changed for religious education. Secular historiography is being changed for communal history, and the Constitution which is a guarantee for secularism is under the threat of revision . . .. The minority rights are affected, freedom of religion is curtailed, and provisions guaranteed by the Article 25 of the Constitution of India are curtailed. The members of minority religious communities are alienated by the government headed by the BJP.[153]

The *Sangh Parivar*'s main objection is that the secularist ideals enshrined in the Indian Constitution are pseudo-secularist and Western. This kind of secularism provides special privileges to the minorities (e.g., Articles 25, 30, 44, 370 of the Indian Constitution),[154] which they point out is nothing but appeasement of the minorities for electoral gain. They clamour for equal treatment of the majority Hindu and the other religious minorities by the constitution.[155] Their awkward appeal to all the religious minorities in this country is that they should identify themselves as Hindus. Their justification for such a claim is that Hinduism is basically a way of life. It is a political and geographical identity, to which all who reside in India should subscribe no matter what the individual's religion is. Whoever resides in "*Hindusthan*" (Land of the Hindus—India) are Hindus. People belonging to different religions should accept Hindu culture as their cultural norm.[156] Consequently, Islam and Christianity are considered to be foreign religions. Drawing on the above, the *Sangh Parivar* has a peculiar view of the idea of a minority. To them, those who are born in this country are not minorities as they are supposed to join the mainstream of the majority Hindu community and culture. Their goal of making India a monocultural entity, i.e., Indian-Hindu culture, is behind this strange view of minority. Second, following from such communal agenda and disregard for the minorities, a continuing threat from the *Sangh Parivar* is the persecution of Christians and religious minorities.

---

153 Cherian, *Hindutva Agenda*, 319.

154 Article 25 of the Indian Constitution gives the right to freely practise, propagate, and profess any religion of one's own choice. Article 30 guarantees all the minorities the right to establish and manage their own institutions and the state shall not discriminate against any such institutions in the issue of granting aid. Article 44 allows the laying down of a Uniform Civil Code for all people belonging to different religious groups who have their own religious based civil code. This has not been implemented in view of maintaining the rights and laws of the various minorities regarding public order, marriage, divorce, etc. See Constitution of India, accessed October 27, 2019, https://www.india.gov.in/sites/upload_files/npi/files/coi_part_full.pdf.

155 Cherian, *Hindutva*, 324.

156 Ralte, *Hindus and Hindutva*, 100.

As these organisations represent a militant, fanatical, and extremist side of Hinduism, they have little or no tolerance or respect for other religions.

### The rise of communal violence and persecution of minorities

One of the prominent organisations under the banner of the *Sangh Parivar* is the *Rashtriya Swayamsevak Sangh* (RSS) established in 1925. Its militant and violent exploits are evident from its alleged role in five communal riots in India from 1960 to 1990.[157] The association also includes the *Vishwa Hindu Parishad* (VHP), the religious and social wing; *Bharatiya Janata Party* (BJP), the political wing; and other militant outfits.[158] There were widespread communal riots in Gujarat, a state in western India, and other places in 2002 between Hindus and Muslims. The rise of communal violence has been recorded as having increased to 17 percent in 2015.[159] Incidents such as the lynching of a Muslim man by a Hindu mob for allegedly eating beef were reported on September 28, 2015, in Dadri, Uttar Pradesh, indicating the range of violence that continues.[160]

Several incidents of violence involving destroying churches, mass killings, the rape of nuns, the burning of Christian missionaries, and looting were reported. Added to this was the gruesome incident of the burning of an Australian missionary Graham Steins and his two children, both minors, in 1999. The family was working with people affected with leprosy in a village in Orissa (east India). The incident recorded the alleged assault by members of the *Bajrang Dal*, a violent outfit belonging to the *Sangh Parivar*. However, these persecutions against Christians are often blamed on Christians themselves and their work of conversion. The RSS blames the Christians for converting Hindus to their faith through fraud and allurements. Since the right to profess, propagate, and practise religion is enshrined in the Indian Constitution (Article 25), the *Sangh Parivar* tries to show that all the conversions of the Hindus to Christianity are fraudulent. Further, they allege these conversions to be part of a

---

157 For an account of communal rights in India, see Asghar Ali Engineer, ed., *Communal Riots in Post-Independent India*, 2nd ed. (Hyderabad: Sangam Books, 1997).

158 Cherian, *Hindutva Agenda*, 5.

159 Aman Sharma, "Communal Violence up 17% in 2015," *Economic Times*, February 24, 2016, accessed October 27, 2019, http://economictimes.indiatimes.com/news/politics-and-nation/communal-violence-up-17-in-2015/articleshow/51125252.cms.

160 "Dadri: Outrage after Mob Lynches Man for Allegedly Consuming Beef," *The Indian Express*, December 25, 2015, accessed November 21, 2019, http://indianexpress.com/article/india/india-others/outrage-after-man-lynched-over-rumour-of-storing-beef-in-house/.

conspiracy of the West to turn India into a Christian country. They say that the dress, habits, culture, and religion of the Christians are an import from the West. They try to accuse Christians of being non-patriotic and anti-national. In response to the conversion movements, they promote *Shuddhi* or reconversion to Hinduism. The *Sangh Parivar* has allegedly undergone several "reconversion" movements where Christians and Muslims in some parts of India have been brought back to Hinduism. In 2014, such efforts by one of the *Sangh Parivar* outfits were made.[161] The *Sangh* allegedly continues to visit the tribal population and poor communities of India and indoctrinate them into believing that they are actually Hindus and if they have been converted to Christianity, they must come back through *Shuddhi* (*Ghar Vapsi* or Homecoming). The tribal or indigenous people, whether in northeast India or central India, have their own religion and spirituality. While their religiosity may somewhat resemble some of the features of popular Hindu religion, it is wrong to brand them as Hindus. This kind of assimilation and absorption has been one of the common weapons of the Hindu fundamentalists.

The churches in the tribal majority belt have had to face such threats of "reconversion" and subjugation of the tribal cultures by extremist Hinduism. This also involves multiple socioeconomic and religious factors. Especially in the Dalit and tribal areas, sustained oppression of the lower castes by the upper castes continues. Further complications arise in areas where Christian missionaries and Hindu fundamentalist groups are working simultaneously. Through Christian missionary work, the outcastes of any particular community receive an upward social mobility and dignity through conversion, while on the other hand, the same people are threatened with persecution by the fundamentalists if they do not reconvert to Hinduism. Added to this is the inter-caste, intertribal conflict due to the upward mobility of some of them, which is looked upon with hatred and jealousy by the others. Ultimately, this situation of conflict and instability is cleverly manoeuvred to blame the Christian missionaries and churches working there since they are easy targets. This has been particularly evident in one of the states in east India, Orissa, where in 2007 and 2008, there was considerable communal and ethnic violence, and the people who suffered the most were Christian Dalits and tribals.[162] There

161 See the newspaper report by Venkitesh Ramakrishnan, "The Reconversion Programs of the Dharam Jagaran Samity and Vishwa Hindu Parishad are Part of a Massive Expansion Plan of the Sangh Parivar," *Frontline*, January 9, 2015, accessed October 27, 2019, http://www.frontline.in/the-nation/project-hindutva/article6715464.ece.

162 Chad M. Bauman, "Identity, Conversion and Violence: Dalits, Adivasis and the 2007–08 Riots in Orissa," in Robinson and Kujur, *Margins of Faith*, 263–286.

were reports of widespread destruction of churches, the rape of nuns, and destruction of houses of tribals and *adivasis* where people had to run for shelter in the hills and forests. Communal conflicts and religious persecutions like these have been responsible for strained relationships between Hindus and Muslims, and Hindus and Christians in the long run.

Another related hurdle for the churches is the so-called Freedom of Religion Bills, which is actually a misnomer since these bills, which supposedly give freedom to practice and propagate one's religion are actually attempts to curb religious conversions. In other words, they are actually anti-conversion bills. They are used to check any conversion through force, fraud, or allurement. Eight states—namely, Orissa, Madhya Pradesh, Andhra Pradesh, Gujarat, Chattisgarh, Rajasthan, and Himachal Pradesh—have already passed their own anti-conversion bills. These bills can be easily manipulated by Hindu fundamentalists to harass religious minorities. Any service of uplift by the Christian missionaries or others in the field of education, medicine, etc., can be misrepresented as allurement or inducement. These bills actually violate Article 25 of the Indian Constitution giving freedom to profess, practise, and propagate religion.[163]

So, the above discussion has outlined how Hindu fundamentalism is one of the major threats India faces. We have noted discrimination towards minorities; violence and atrocities against them including Christians, and the passing of anti-conversion bills, which deny freedom of religion. On the whole, Hindu fundamentalism threatens the very fabric of secularism, harmony, and unity in diversity in the nation. In this atmosphere, it becomes difficult for the churches to carry out their ministry and mission. On the one hand, the churches have to be committed to their mission to Christ, serving and uplifting people from all backgrounds possible, and on the other hand, they have to face threats of persecution and fundamentalism which makes their ministry difficult.

## Introducing the Case for a Permeable Ecclesiology and Its Pneumatological Shape

In the previous discussions, there was an attempt to give an overview of India's plural contexts, marginalisation, threats, and challenges both inside and outside the church. In this section, we will introduce the case for a permeable ecclesiology and its pneumatological shape briefly so that it can be taken up in depth in the next chapter. The context of India gives a vivid picture of the immense diversity and complexity of the entire region along with its struggles and challenges for the churches. This has

[163] Ralte, *Hindus and Hindutva*, 119.

multifaceted implications. The ethnolinguistic variety of the people demands that the gospel proclaimed by the churches and their ministries be intelligible and grounded in the very particular ethnic or linguistic setting of the people. Again, the particular religio-cultural setting of each location demands that the ministries of the church be sensitive to the surrounding religious and cultural norms of the people. The sociopolitical environment of each region within India varies. There are both potential for conflicts and of harmonious living, and the churches must consider the challenges and opportunities in both environments. The diversity and plurality of the Indian situation is something that always has to be highlighted against the homogenising and hegemonising attempts of the fundamentalists.

One of the aspects, as we have seen, repeatedly emerging in the Indian situation is the overlapping of boundaries; the fluidity and dual or multiple religio-cultural belonging. This is a significant question regarding the identity of the Christian community in India. A considerable challenge for the church is how to keep its particular Christian identity; yet, be open and engaging with the ethnolinguistic, religio-cultural, and sociopolitical life of the region. Similarly, there is also the challenge regarding the foreignness or Western nature of the church. The foreign missionary movement has sought to establish a church in India that was conceived and "manufactured" in the West, with its own ideas of nature, ministry, and mission. The challenge before the church in India is how to maintain the Christian character of the church, yet redeem itself from the colonial captivity and simultaneously open itself up to the religio-cultural-social environment and ethos of the people. This is crucial because the churches no longer ought to be accused of foreignness, but need to be Indian for all intents and purposes.

Another considerable challenge is the response to the marginalised communities who constitute the majority in the church in India. The churches' solidarity with the marginalised and the oppressed is a much-called-for response, if they seek to be communities of justice and peace. This solidarity inevitably brings with it conflicts with the "powers" and the oppressors. The challenge here is how to pursue "just-peace" between the oppressor and the oppressed within the church and without. Such varied concerns and challenges of the church demands that the church in India ought to be open to diverse understandings of itself in relation to the diverse environment that characterises this region. This possibly indicates that the church has to negotiate its borders, while keeping its distinctiveness and particular identity in the Indian soil. The struggle for the churches is to be both authentically Indian and truly Christian. The struggle to be Indian possibly demands the characteristic of *relationality* in terms of being able to relate to its surrounding situation and challenges, not patronisingly but dialogically. The particular type of relationality required here is Christianity or the Church's relationship to the world in egalitarian terms that would tend to avoid the superior, imperialist, and proselytising tendencies of Christianity. The churches in India have been relational in terms of their philanthropic and spiritual mission, but have not considered the other religions and cultures in India on an equal footing, or as contributing to the kingdom of God. This kind of hierarchical relationality continues to create barriers between Christians and other communities. Thus, egalitarian approach to relationality is argued for.

On the other hand, the struggle to be truly Christian is to be true to the *distinctive* calling and gospel of God as revealed in Jesus Christ, manifested collectively and concretely in the nature, ministry, and mission of the church. The distinctiveness of the Christian community can be maintained through the witness of the living community, the church. It also can be maintained in terms of its response to the world. The Church's relationality with the world does not prevent it from being critical of the world, particularly its assumptions and policies that dehumanise and destroy lives. This envisages a relational community which is distinctive, particular, and has a critical edge. This indicates interplay of the dialectics of what may be called "relational-distinctiveness"[164] in our ecclesiological thinking. Let us term this as permeability. In the following chapter, we will develop this notion of permeability in terms of this relational-distinctive dialectics and arrive at a proposed shape of a permeable church.

The upcoming chapter will argue that the relational-distinctive dialectics regarding the church and its borders can be ensured if ecclesiologcal thinking is based on the joint working of Christ and the Spirit. What it means is that both Spirit and Christ will ensure the relational as well as distinctive aspects. This is not understood in a compartmentalised way as if the Spirit only provides for a relational base while Christ provides for the distinctive basis. But, it will be argued that both of them work dialectically to ensure the relational-distinctive dialectics. The relational part ensures softened borders and permeability to the church, while

[164] The category of "relational-distinctiveness" in Christian theology is not new. S.J. Samartha used it in his book, *One Christ Many Religions* (1991). He uses this term in the sense of Christ being relational with other faiths and, at the same time, Christianity along with other religions ought to have distinctive responses to the mystery of God. See *One Christ Many Religions: Towards a Revised Christology* (Maryknoll, NY: Orbis Books, 1991), 76–77. However, while not denying the above meaning, I have used this as a dialectic favouring an ecclesiological permeability ensured by the joint working of the Spirit and Christ.

the distinctiveness indicates rootedness in Christ, and rootedness in the context and the culture, while also having a critical stance towards the world in terms of marginalisation, injustice, and evils of the world. The relational-distinctive dialectics as will be seen, will work in terms of the unity-diversity, universality-particularity, the spiritual, and the concrete aspects in terms of various issues regarding ecclesiology. All these issues will be dealt with in detail in the following chapters towards ensuring a permeable Spirit ecclesiology.

# CHAPTER TWO

# THE CHURCH AND ITS PNEUMATOLOGICAL SHAPE WITH PERMEABLE BORDERS: EXPLORING WESTERN PARADIGMS

In the previous chapter, we have argued for the importance of a relational-distinctive dialectics or in other words, permeability in ecclesiology working together with the dynamics of the Spirit and Christ. Here, we proceed to explore ecclesiological paradigms in Western theology that might contribute to the understanding of an ecclesiology influenced by pneumatology with its christological dynamics operative. In the following pages we will move forward, determining what constitutes the notion of "permeability" or porous borders in terms of this relational-distinctive dialectics. Following this, various models of ecclesiology will be explored in order to search for a suitable basis for a permeable Spirit ecclesiology. In our discussions of various models, we would look forward to dealing with representative models that are relational and those which are distinctive. Yet, ecclesiological thinking which contains the relational-distinctive dialectics will be emphasised. Both relational and distinctive models of ecclesiology would be evaluated in terms of the basic understanding of permeability that will be established in the following pages.

## The character of permeability

The notion of permeability refers to the phenomenon of the passage of things through porous borders or boundaries. This means that it recognises the presence of a border while determining what type of border it is, i.e., porous. When applied in the context of the church, it would mean that it ought to have borders or boundaries, but those are porous, allowing selective passage of, say, perspectives and people. The recognition of porosity in the church's borders can be broadly conceived through the concept of relationality, while borders can be conceived in terms of providing the character of distinctiveness to the church. However, as porosity and borders cannot be conceived separately, the concept of relationality and distinctiveness cannot operate separately. In other words, borders need porosity to be permeable, while porosity cannot be conceived without borders. This calls for a dialectical understanding of relational-distinctiveness. The permeability of the church would depend on these relational-distinctive dialectics. What this would mean for the church is that relationality of the church cannot be conceived without its counterpart, i.e., distinctiveness, and the distinctiveness of the church cannot be expressed without being relational. Relationality and distinctiveness would work together to complete the cycle of permeability of the church. Relationality would seem to qualify distinctiveness and, in turn, is qualified by the latter.

Relationality, as a counterpart of the relational-distinctive dialectics, will have two characteristics: dialogical mutuality and critical particularity. This is a nuanced understanding of relationality. This is a relationality which can be termed as *distinctively relational*. In this kind of nuanced understanding of relationality, the criterion of dialogical mutuality would require the partners to be in an egalitarian relationship where exchange occurs mutually and not from one side only. This posits that the relationality of the church with other communities or the world would be nonhierarchical or egalitarian, allowing exchange or passage of perspectives and people both ways. While being thus relational, permeability demands that this relationality is also critically particular. What this means is that this relationality is not simply unqualified without a selective or critical edge; nor is it a bland universality without concreteness and particularity. This *distinctively relational* character would be clearer when we discuss it in relation to the particular context of India.

When we refer to the status of the Indian ecclesial relationship with other communities, we do find a form of relationality, but it differs from the one that we are arguing the churches should have. The church in India has always been a relational church in terms of being a missionary church—a church that reaches out to the world, to other communities, seeking to transform and bring people to the saving knowledge of Christ. It has reached out to the poor, the suffering, and the uneducated through spiritual, medical, and educational missions. However, this relationality has not been mutual in the sense that the church has always considered itself as the giver and not the receiver, the teacher and not the learner, the repository of truth and salvation *vis-à-vis* communities that supposedly sat in darkness and ignorance. In other words, the relationality between the church and other communities has been one-sided and not mutual. In addition, the church's link with the colonial powers resulted in a supremacist, imperialist, and patronising tendency in its ministry and mission. It was a hierarchical and not a dialogical relationship. A dialogical relationship would always consider the equal status of partners, however different and diverse; otherwise, it ceases to be a dialogical encounter. The Christian church in India has prided itself on bringing a superior religion and superior culture to a "heathen people" who did not seem to know God and whose culture is devilish at best. It has assumed that the Spirit of God was not at work before Christianity came to India. A seemingly proselytising tendency even lurked behind the church's education and medical missions. We have shown earlier that this created religious, social, and cultural tensions and alienation between Christians and other communities. The attitude of colonial Christianity still remains in these postcolonial times, resulting in continued alienation of the Christian community with respect to others. We have also shown that this alienation has created a false understanding of Christianity as a foreign religion; the religion of the West. People of other faiths often admire and appreciate Jesus and some even seek to follow him, but the foreign nature of the church and Christianity and their claims of supremacy have made it unattractive to Indians. Therefore, it is argued that relationality as explained in terms of dialogical mutuality is an absolute requirement for the churches in India. In the Indian situation, the passage of perspectives and people between the church, other communities, and the world would involve mutual learning, mutual enrichment, mutual conversion, and mutual journeying in search for truth in an egalitarian framework. In this phenomenon of mutual exchange of perspectives and mutual collaboration between peoples, a space is bound to open up for people that will feature heterogeneity and inclusivity. This space might be particularly conducive for people who prefer, or, are in a position of liminality or transcending of religio-cultural-social boundaries. We have already shown that many people in India, especially from the marginalised communities including Christians, live in fluid boundaries or practise dual or multiple religious belonging.[1]

On the other hand, it is argued that the Indian churches need to have the character of critical particularity in their relationships with other communities. What this would mean is that the church's relational engagement with other communities and the world will be that of a critical engagement. In other words, it would include working out of those relationships in concrete and particular contexts while being self-critical

1 I will have occasion to return to this issue of multiple religious belonging at a later stage in the project.

and also critical towards the world, which would be akin to establishing a christological particularity. The effort at ensuring particularity of the churches would be in developing concrete relationships in each ethnolinguistic, religio-cultural, and sociopolitical context. This would rescue the churches from the colonial captivity, on the one hand, by trying to root them in the Indian context, and on the other hand, by avoiding vague universalism. The christocentric paradigm also works prominently in its distinctiveness with other religions. In the church's interfaith relations, therefore, critical engagement would mean engaging with other traditions in mutual dialogue where both commonalities and particularities in terms of christological dynamics are borne in mind. It will not be an effort simply to search for the commonalities, but for the unique contributions that each tradition can offer to the pool of religious resources.

The question that arises here is: How could the churches be permeable in terms of a relationality which demands dialogical mutuality and critical particularity? What theological resources can be drawn in order to make the church relational in this sense? We propose that a pneumatological perspective of the church could be helpful in part for ensuring the kind of relationality that is argued for. We will return to what this pneumatological perspective of the church would mean in the broader project of permeability later in this chapter. In the meantime, let us turn to the other aspect of permeability: the question of borders.

Previously, we have argued that porosity cannot work without borders. The question is, what sort of borders are we looking for? Are the borders hard or soft? We have shown earlier how the dialectics of relational-distinctiveness works through a nuanced relationality, i.e., *distinctively relational*, conceived in terms of dialogical mutuality and critical particularity. The same dialectics is expected to work for the question of borders, but the other way round. If we aim at softening the borders, the dialectics would work particularly well in terms of a nuanced understanding of distinctiveness, which can be termed *relationally distinct*. This nuanced understanding of distinctiveness is required as it can counteract the alienation caused by hard borders. Here, on the one hand, relationality is sought to be qualified by the presence of definite borders; while on the other hand, the borders themselves are qualified by a sort of relationality that makes them softer. The reason relationality has to be qualified or conditioned by borders in the first place is because of the question of identity. Dhirendra K. Sahu argues that "any group forms its identity by marking its boundaries."[2] While mutual intermingling and exchange goes

2 D.K. Sahu, *United & Uniting: A Story of the Church of North India* (Delhi: ISPCK, 2001), xi.

on between various communities on an egalitarian level, as previously argued, an important question arises as to what particularly distinguishes each community. In our bid to be relational, does each community end up compromising its distinctive identity? More precisely: Can the church in its relation to the world and other communities still maintain its identity in such a porous exchange? Is a permeable church conceivable which is relational with the world and other communities, yet holds its distinctive identity? In the Indian context, the question of identity is a crucial issue. The dilemma regarding the identity of the churches in India is: First, struggling to be an Indian Christian church within its continued Western heritage; and second, the struggle to maintain its Christian witness amidst a multicultural, multireligious context, and in the face of hegemonising and homogenising fundamentalist forces. Thus, while the church seeks to be relational, it has to be equally careful about maintaining its identity in the face of the challenges highlighted above and, in the context described earlier.

With regard to the issue of the need for softening of hard borders, it can be said that in the Indian context, the church has always had hard borders. It has well-defined, distinct boundaries as has been shown earlier in two respects: christological-soteriological and an emphasis on being a separated community. In the first respect, the church in India has successfully managed to determine its contours through the affirmation that it has only one Lord Jesus Christ and that salvation is possible through no other. In the second, the church left no stone unturned in claiming that in Christ, Christians are a chosen community, consecrated, called, and separated from the world. This separation wrongly understood has typically resulted in ghettoising the Christian community, often spatially and spiritually, from communities of other faiths. Again, the separation of the church and the world was deepened when other-worldly spirituality pervaded and continues to pervade among Christians in India. Essentially, the hard boundaries in question made the church an insulated community to all intents and purposes. The question arises here as to whether such hard borders, which have made the church an insulated community, are justifiable in a plural society like India. Can the softening of borders be the route to being more *relationally distinct*? Thus, is it possible for the church to be christologically identified and still be open to accommodating the insights and contributions of Indian religio-cultural contexts? Is it possible for the church as a community to continue to be a consecrated witness for Christ and yet overcome the separation and alienation caused by the colonial project? The answer to these questions could well be in softening of the borders. This can be appropriate for the counterpart of a *relationally distinct* dimension of permeability.

While we have suggested that a *distinctively relational* dimension of permeability can be conceived by recourse to a pneumatological perspective of the church, we suggest that a *relationally distinct* dimension of permeability can be conceived through a christological dimension, manifested in and through the ecclesial community in its distinct witness and critical character. The relationally distinct character would engage the church in its distinct mission and ministry while critically responding to issues of injustice and oppression in a particular context. The distinctive witness of the Church in Christ is also relational in the Spirit in terms of its critical engagement with the secular realms, ideologies, and contexts. Hence, the development of a permeable Spirit ecclesiology would depend on applying both the *distinctively relational* and *relationally distinct* counterparts of permeability. In other words, a permeable Spirit ecclesiology would be an ecclesiology with a pneumatological perspective and christological dimension, expressed in relational-distinctive dialectics.

Having now discussed the dynamics involved in the concept of permeability, we will now proceed to engage Western theologians and their theological-ecclesiological thinking to determine what would a permeable border for the church actually mean. We will explore ecclesiologies that are relational and also those which are distinctive and particular and also look for theological contributions which would show relational-distinctive features. We will have Jürgen Moltmann, Stanley Hauerwas, Kathryn Tanner, and Amos Yong for our conversation partners.

## Exploring models for a permeable Spirit ecclesiology

### The relational ecclesiology of Jürgen Moltmann

The ecclesiology of Jürgen Moltmann, the German Reformed theologian, can be said to be basically a "relational ecclesiology,"[3] grounded on Social Trinity with a pneumatological perspective and an eschatological orientation. The reason for taking up an ecclesiology based on the Social Trinity is that this approach has been in vogue for a while with the

3 Moltmann describes his ecclesiology as "relational ecclesiology," alternatively "messianic ecclesiology." See Jürgen Moltmann, *The Church in the Power of the Spirit: A Contribution to Messianic Ecclesiology*, trans. Margaret Kohl (London: SCM, 1977), 20. Also see Richard Bauckham, *The Theology of Jurgen Moltmann* (London: T&T Clark, 1995), 122.

emergence of interest in pneumatology and trinitarian theology.[4] As we proceed towards discussing Moltmann's ecclesiology, it will be evident how his conceptions of the Social Trinity, pneumatology, and eschatology have influenced his understanding of a relational church.

## The basis of the church

Moltmann's ecclesiology is relational on the basis of Social Trinity, his pneumatological perspective, and eschatological orientation. These combine together to bring God, church, and the world into relationship.[5] Moltmann essentially understands the Trinity as "being-in-relationship."[6] The Trinity is in relationship within and with the world. Moltmann's models—namely, monarchical, historical/eschatological, eucharistic, and doxological—all show the three persons of the Trinity taking up their roles in turn in their relationship to the world. The Father sends both the Son and the Spirit into the world, and the Spirit along with other Persons play active roles in the history of the world and in the eschatological consummation of creation, which ultimately results in the eschatological glorification of God.[7]

One of the concepts that Moltmann uses to express the notion of relationality is that of *perichoresis*, a term originating from the Greek Fathers, which essentially means the co-inhering or mutual indwelling or circular movement of the trinitarian persons.[8] He uses this term to safeguard inner-trinitarian relationality and mutuality, but at the same time against modalism and subordination of the Persons of the Trinity.[9] For

4 See Veli-Matti Kärkkäinen, *Pneumatology: The Holy Spirit in Ecumenical, International, and Contextual Perspective* (Grand Rapids, MI: Baker Academic, 2002), 11–20.

5 Richard Bauckham maintains that in Moltmann's trinitarian conceptions of the church, the complementary and competing perspectives of the christological, pneumatological, and eschatological, are at play. See Bauckham, *Theology of Jürgen Moltmann*, 124.

6 Jürgen Moltmann, *The Spirit of Life: A Universal Affirmation*, trans. Margaret Kohl (London: SCM Press, 1992), 289–306.

7 Moltmann, *Spirit of Life*, 289–306.

8 "Perichoresis" was derived from the root verb *perichorein* (*peri*—round about, *chorein*—make room for another) introduced into christological language by Gregory of Nazianzen (ca. 389) and the noun *perichoresis* by Maximus the Confessor (ca. 662). Both were extended into trinitarian language by Pseudo-Cyril (anonymous author, ca. 650) and popularised by John of Damascus (ca. 749). See Michael G. Lawler, "Perichoresis: New Theological Wine in Old Theological Wineskin," *Horizons: The Journal of the College Theological Society* 2, no. 1 (Spring 1995): 49–66.

9 Jürgen Moltmann, *The Trinity and the Kingdom: The Doctrine of God*, trans. Margaret Kohl (London: SCM, 1981), 175.

Moltmann, *perichoresis*, in its relational potential, continues to provide a background to the relationship between immanent and economic trinity. Richard Bauckham suggests that in Moltmann, the "mutual relationships of the three persons of the Trinity as a perichoretic union become the context for the relationships between God and the world."[10] The point of contact between the immanent and the economic Trinity is established christologically and pneumatologically. Christologically, the cross stands at the centre of both the economic and immanent Trinity. In other words, it is the cross of Christ, which gives us an understanding of the inner life of the Trinity.[11] He further argues that if the Trinity is open to history through the cross, then the immanent Trinity is influenced by the external history of God through the cross. He goes to the extent of saying that "the economic Trinity not only reveals the immanent Trinity; it also has a retroactive effect on it."[12] Moltmann insists that "the pain of the cross determines the inner life of the triune God from eternity to eternity."[13] In other words, the suffering of the Son on the cross pains even the Father, so the "Father suffers this disaster inwardly in himself."[14] The love of God only becomes meaningful when communicated like this. Moltmann is thus of the view that "*opera trinitatis ad extra* corresponds to the *passiones trinitatis ad intra*."[15] However, Moltmann is quick to point out that the Father neither suffers as the Son nor dies like him, but the Father and the Son are in a kenotic relationship.[16] Pneumatologically, both God and human beings are perichoretically transcendent and immanent in each other. Moltmann contends, "The possibility of perceiving God in all things, and all things in God, is grounded theologically on an understanding of the Spirit of God as the power of creation and the well-spring of life."[17]

---

10 Richard Bauckham, "Jurgen Moltmann," in *The Modern Theologians: An Introduction to Christian Theology since 1918*, eds. David F. Ford and Rachel Muers, 3rd ed. (Blackwell: Oxford, 2005), 149.

11 See Randall Otto, "Moltmann and the Anti-Monotheist Movement," *International Journal of Systematic Theology* 3, no. 3 (2003): 294, 306–7, cited in Stephen Holmes, *The Holy Trinity: Understanding God's Life* (Milton Keynes, England: Paternoster Press, 2012), 21.

12 Moltmann, *Trinity and the Kingdom*, 161.

13 Moltmann, *Trinity and the Kingdom*, 161.

14 Moltmann, *Trinity and the Kingdom*, 160.

15 Moltmann, *Trinity and the Kingdom*, 160.

16 Jürgen Moltmann, *The Crucified God: The Cross of Christ as the Foundation and Criticism of Christian Theology*, trans. R.A. Wilson and John Bowden (London: SCM, 1974), 271, 207, 204.

17 Moltmann, *Spirit of Life*, 7, 35.

Related to this is the idea of the Jewish concept of *Shekinah*,[18] which Moltmann uses. *Shekinah* is the "descent and indwelling of God in space and time, at a particular place and a particular era of earthly beings in their history."[19] For him, *Shekinah* means: First, affirming the personhood and agency of the Holy Spirit in God's indwelling; and second, *kenosis* of the Spirit where God is able to suffer and identify with the suffering creation through the Spirit. Christologically, *Shekinah* would mean that "in Christ the fullness of the Godhead dwells bodily."[20] Thus, *Shekinah* can incorporate the incarnation of God in Jesus Christ, through which the infinite God is able to dwell in his finite creation.[21] Pneumatologically, *Shekinah* is the continued presence of God even in wayward humanity, however estranged, so that it can bring humanity back to God once again.[22]

Thus, while perichoretic relationality allows the church to participate in the inner life of the Trinity, the *Shekinah* or the indwelling of God in Christ through the Spirit in the world allows God to continue to relate to human beings and creation. It is evident that Moltmann draws a close relationship between the sufferings of God in Christ with the sufferings of humanity as found in the world. He seems to suggest a close relationality between God and the world on the basis of common suffering between God in Christ and the world. This happens because of his proposal of the centrality of the cross in both immanent and economic Trinity. The close relationship between the immanent and the economic Trinity, which is a central assumption of the social Trinity, allows the church to be involved in the trinitarian involvement of God in the world. Moltmann writes that "the church is called to participate in such a trinitarian history of God. It participates in the trinitarian history of 'gathering, uniting, and glorifying of the world in God and of God in the world.'"[23]

Having outlined the basis of the Social Trinity for the church in terms of perichoretic relationships between the God and the world, we will now show what this basis implies for understanding the character of a Spirit ecclesiology in terms of the nature, ministry, and mission of the church.

18 Moltmann draws from the Jewish theology of Franz Rosenzweig and Gershom Scholem. See Moltmann, *Crucified God*, xi.

19 Moltmann, *Spirit of Life*, 47.

20 Moltman, *Experiences in Theology*, 323.

21 Moltmann, *Experiences in Theology*, 323.

22 Moltmann, *Spirit of Life*, 50.

23 Moltmann, *Church in the Power of the Spirit*, 60.

## Shape of the church

### *The nature of Spirit ecclesiology*

We have shown that Social Trinity allows the church to participate in the trinitarian involvement of God in the world. For Moltmann, this trinitarian involvement also draws in the implications of the church in terms of the eschatological future of God. In other words, as the church is caught up in trinitarian relationship, it is also caught up with God's eschatological future in relation to the world. Along with its social trinitarian basis, the eschatological orientation allows the church to be open, dynamic, and forward looking. Therefore, Moltmann holds that the church's nature or the particular question of "what is the church?" cannot be determined universally. He argues instead that we at least know "where the church happens" or is present. It is "present wherever the manifestation of the Spirit (1 Cor 12:7) takes place."[24] This accounts for the dynamic character of the church. For Moltmann, this eschatological church in its dynamism constitutes an "exodus community," which finds itself in the movement of the kingdom of God, but not greater than the latter.[25] This also carries with it a sort of provisionality in understanding the church. Moltmann argues that the church of the kingdom of God should realise itself in tension between the "already" and "not yet" character of the kingdom. In this sense, it must realise its provisional nature in history and the anticipation of the future new creation.[26] Moltmann writes, "In provisional finality and in final provisionality, the church, christendom, and Christianity witness to the kingdom of God as the goal of history in the midst of history. In this sense, the church of Jesus Christ is *the people of the kingdom of God.*"[27] Richard Bauckham argues that the pneumatological perspective of the church in Moltmann's ecclesiology facilitates such a conception of the church as he notes that it is the pneumatological dimension that allows an emphasis on the "eschatological fulfilment of the history of Christ; it is the Holy Spirit who mediates eschatology and history and the church."[28] Thus in Moltmann's ecclesiology, the shape of the church is determined by Social Trinity as the foundation along with a pneumatological perspective and an eschatological orientation.

Moltmann articulates this shape in terms of his understanding of the four marks of the church: One, Holy, Catholic, and Apostolic. In these

24 Moltmann, *Church in the Power of the Spirit*, 65.

25 Moltmann, *Church in the Power of the Spirit*, 83, 84.

26 Moltmann, *Church in the Power of the Spirit*, 189–195.

27 Moltmann, *Church in the Power of the Spirit*, 196.

28 Bauckham, *Theology of Jurgen Moltmann*, 123–124.

four marks, the close relationship between God, church, and the world in its eschatological orientation is evident. A dynamic character is also evident in such an understanding. The suffering of God and humanity occupies a central place in God-world relationship, as previously shown, and Moltmann seeks to address this relationship through a liberationist understanding. He argues that the unity or oneness of the church derives from the unity of Christ and this unity is in "freedom and diversity of the gathered congregation in proclamation, calling, and sacraments."[29] The church is said to be holy in the sense that it understands itself as in continual forgiveness, sanctification, and reformation, whose holiness is derived from the holiness of God and looks forward to its full sanctification in the *eschaton*. This holiness does not put the church onto a higher or separate pedestal, but in relationship of fellowship with others, especially the poor and the suffering.[30] The church is catholic in the sense that it corresponds to its inner wholeness and spatial wholeness in its relation to the world and eschatologically with God's coming kingdom. The church is also catholic in the sense that it seeks to restore the lost, rejected, and the oppressed.[31] The church is apostolic in the sense that its "gospel and doctrine is founded on the testimony of the first apostles . . . and it exists in carrying out of the apostolic proclamation, the missionary charge."[32] So, it "denotes both the church's foundation and its commission" and is strongly determined eschatologically by the risen Christ and "suffering and sacrifice in the discipleship of Christ."[33] Thus, the shape of the church in terms of the four marks brings together aspects of fellowship with the world, suffering in solidarity with the oppressed, and universality in terms of the eschatological goal of the kingdom of God.

### *Ministry of a Spirit ecclesiology*

The ministry of such a Spirit ecclesiology based on Social Trinity, with a pneumatological perspective and eschatological orientation has an egalitarian shape. In this church, the powers and gifts of the Spirit are for all and not for a select few.[34] This egalitarian character is manifested through the proclamation of the Word, worship, and sacraments. For Moltmann, proclamation is a broad category not exclusively limited to preaching of the Word in the church, but includes the whole witness of a believer of the

---

29 Moltmann, *Church in the Power of the Spirit*, 337–347.
30 Moltmann, *Church in the Power of the Spirit*, 352–357.
31 Moltmann, *Church in the Power of the Spirit*, 352.
32 Moltmann, *Church in the Power of the Spirit*, 358.
33 Moltmann, *Church in the Power of the Spirit*, 358–361.
34 Moltmann, *Church in the Power of the Spirit*, 198.

truth of Jesus Christ in the varied relationships of life.[35] It is a church of the community, a participatory congregation where there is no hierarchy between the clergy and the laity; a church that links generations, genders, and diverse groups together.[36] The scope of the "charismata of the Spirit," Moltmann contends, is not limited to specific groups of people or only to office-bearers, but to all people. Though there are functional differences, the gifts of the Spirit make for an egalitarian community. Moltmann writes, "The widow who exercises mercy is acting just as charismatically as a bishop."[37] Moltmann also draws from eschatological pouring out of the Spirit on all flesh (Joel 2) and the Pentecost event (Acts 2), the principles of nonhierarchy and egalitarianism. Moltmann's reflection on the "pouring out of the Spirit on all flesh" leads towards an understanding of a community based on justice for women, young people, the old, and the outcast.[38] The sacraments of baptism and the Lord's Supper also reflect an egalitarian and liberationist character. Baptism sets us in the triune history of God. It is a public witness and a "liberating event" in Christ's fellowship, taking us into a life in the Spirit with believers in Christ towards a new creation. Baptism is a call through the proclamation of the gospel to the rule of God in personal and communal life.[39] The Lord's Supper is understood as a "repeatable *sign of hope*" and a "*sign of being on the way*."[40] It is the open invitation of Christ that reaches beyond denominations and even beyond the church to the weak, the sinners, and the nations in the kingdom of God (Isa 25:6–8).[41] In sum, the ministries of the church in the Spirit based on a social trinitarian model reflect the egalitarian, inclusive, and liberationist character.

### *Mission of a Spirit ecclesiology*

The mission of the church based on Social Trinity is eschatologically expansive in the Spirit and includes interfaith and cosmic perspectives. Moltmann argues that the church has a "messianic mission" that draws from the messianic mission of Jesus through his death and resurrection. Through participation in the death and resurrection, the church becomes the church of the kingdom and human liberation.[42] Moltmann reminds us

---

[35] Moltmann, *Church in the Power of the Spirit*, 206, 225.

[36] Moltmann, *Spirit of Life*, 235–245.

[37] Moltmann, *Church in the Power of the Spirit*, 298.

[38] Moltmann, *Spirit of Life*, 57.

[39] Moltmann, *Church in the Power of the Spirit*, 226. See Moltmann's discussion on Baptism, 226–242.

[40] Moltmann, *Church in the Power of the Spirit*, 243.

[41] Moltmann, *Church in the Power of the Spirit*, 246, 248–249, 259.

[42] Moltmann, *Church in the Power of the Spirit*, 85.

that "it is not the church [that] has a mission [but] it is the mission of the Son and the Spirit through the Father that includes the church, creating a church as it goes on its way."[43]

The church's mission importantly includes the church's or Christianity's relationship with other world religions. Moltmann suggests a dialogical approach that would recognise other religions as being on par with Christianity and appreciates the richness of other religions by becoming a part of "the wider framework of liberation of the whole creation for the coming of the kingdom."[44] The mission of the church goes beyond to include the earth and the cosmos. Using the pentecostal pouring out of the Spirit on all flesh as a perspective, Moltmann highlights its universal, eschatological, and cosmic appeal which includes the whole creation. The charismatic power through the Spirit's outpouring is the power of the world to come, which renews all of the present creation in eschatological anticipation of the future. This leads to a cosmic eschatology that conceives the redemption *of* the body and the world in contrast to the gnostic doctrine of redemption *from* the world or the body.[45] In this sense, Moltmann essentially understands the redemption of human beings to include the redemption of creation. He writes that "it is impossible to conceive of any salvation for men and women without the 'new heaven and a new earth.'"[46]

In the preceding section, we have described the shape of a Spirit ecclesiology based on Social Trinity with a pneumatological perspective and eschatological orientation. This Spirit ecclesiology has some strong points keeping in mind the need for the relational dynamics in a permeable Spirit ecclesiology. There are obvious gains in terms of relationality, openness, and inclusivity in this ecclesiology. Moltmann's open church has the potentiality in the Spirit to include diverse groups of people. Its dynamic nature stands as a critique of institutionalism and the static nature of the church. The ministry of the church is egalitarian and through the Spirit allows access to participation for various groups of people. The Spirit's ecclesiological mission includes other religions and expands its horizon to the new creation. Moltmann shows some inclination to a liberationist perspective while remaining largely superficial, without concreteness and specificity. Some of these features can contribute to the permeable Spirit ecclesiological model that we are seeking to construct. Setting aside these strong points, the very basis of Social Trinity unfortunately creates a

43 Moltmann, *Church in the Power of the Spirit*, 65.
44 Moltmann, *Church in the Power of the Spirit*, 163.
45 Moltmann, *Coming of God*, 259.
46 Moltmann, *Coming of God*, 260.

problematic paradigm for understanding human relations in the church. In the following, we will show the drawbacks of conceptualising the church on the basis of a social trinitarian model.

*Drawbacks of a social trinitarian model for the church*

The primary problem with the model of the Social Trinity is in its handling of God-church-world relationship. The Social Trinity model essentially conflates God's inner trinitarian relationship and God's relationship with the world, and fails to maintain the distinctiveness necessary for the relational-distinctive dialectics of a permeable ecclesiology to work. Gary Badcock contends that for Moltmann, there seems to be no essential distinction between who "God is in himself" and who "God is for us."[47] The question is, whether God's indwelling in his inner life and God's dwelling in us are the same. In other words, is the nature of God's perichoretic unity or indwelling in Trinity the same as the relationship through which God is related to us? Trevor Hart argues that it is not. Hart maintains that there ought to be a distinction between how God relates within the Trinity and how God relates to human beings, the world, and the entirety of creation. Hart notes that this happens at two levels, between "that in God which is participable by humans and that which is not . . . between *Koinonia* and *perichoresis*."[48] Hart maintains that *perichoresis* is different from *koinonia*, and this differentiation is intended to be safeguarded by the word *homoousion*.[49] Stephen R. Holmes notes that in terms of the relationship between immanent and economic Trinity, Moltmann takes Rahner's axiom of "The immanent Trinity is the economic Trinity and vice-versa"[50] to the extreme. The standard complaint is that this surrenders God's aseity and freedom where God becomes caused by the world.[51] Others suggest that this reduces God's inner life into God's activity in history and divine transcendence is therefore put in question.[52] Karen Kilby points out the problematic method of "projection" which social trinitarianism seems to

47 Gary D. Badcock, *Light of Truth and Fire of Love: A Theology of the Holy Spirit* (Grand Rapids, MI: William B. Eerdmans, 1997), 206–207; See Holmes, *Holy Trinity*, 151–152.

48 Trevor Hart, *Regarding Karl Barth* (Carlisle, England: Paternoster Press, 1999), 114.

49 Hart, *Regarding Karl Barth*, 114.

50 Karl Rahner, *The Trinity*, trans. Joseph Donceel (New York: Crossroad, 1977, original 1970), 22.

51 Holmes, *Holy Trinity*, 21.

52 See Mann Park, "Jurgen Moltmann's Theology of the Trinity and Its Significance for Contemporary Social Questions: A Dialogical Approach," 126. Accessed July 2019, https://tspace.library.utoronto.ca/bitstream/1807/10516/1/NQ54052.pdf. See also, Holmes, *Holy Trinity*, 22.

employ in projecting notions of the human community onto relationships of the Trinity and questions the surety of our knowledge about the inner life of the Trinity.[53]

The particular use of the notion of *perichoresis* as used by Moltmann is also questionable. For example, Moltmann's use of the idea varies from that of the Greek Fathers (Gregory of Nazianzus, Maximus the Confessor, and John of Damascus) from whom the concept originated.[54] In fact, the idea of *perichoresis* found in the Greek Fathers accommodates both asymmetry and symmetry in God's relation to the world.[55] The Greek Fathers' idea of *perichoresis* and the relationship between God and the world accommodates both the transcendence and immanence of God with no hint of God's life being contingent on the world; there is both discontinuity and continuity in God's relationship to the world. The discontinuity is in terms of God's transcendence, initiative, and freedom. The continuity is in terms of affirming that the Trinity is an open and outgoing relationship in and through the indwelling of God's Spirit (*Shekinah*) in the world.[56] Kilby suggests that, often, the concept of *perichoresisis* is rather filled out with qualities and virtues about human relationships.[57]

On the other hand, questions regarding the hierarchical or egalitarian nature of the church can be dealt with from another angle. It can be shown that even the hierarchical, institutional structure, and ministries of the church are derivatively and functionally the work of the Spirit and Christ. Roger Haight, in an article entitled *The Structures of the Church*, argues from a sociohistorical perspective that even hierarchical institutions may be measured on their functionality in terms of their abilities to mediate ministry. From a theological angle, the offices of the church like bishops, priests, and deacons can be said to be "divinely instituted"

53 See Karen Kilby, "Perichoresis and Projection: Problems with Social Doctrines of the Trinity," *New Blackfriars* 81, no. 957 (November 2000): 432–445, accessed November 2015. *Wiley Online Library*. doi: 10.1111/j.1741-2005.2000.tb06456.x.

54 Jürgen Moltmann, *Experiences in Theology: Ways and Forms of Christian Theology*, trans. Margaret Kohl (Minneapolis, MN: Fortress Press, 200), 316.

55 Pseudo-Cyril of Alexandria (ca. 650) in his *De Sacrosanta Trinitate* discusses *perichoresis* in terms of the incarnation of the divine and the deification of humans. But, he brings the idea of a certain kind of asymmetry in that this union is taken to be achieved or initiated by the divine and not the human. In this case, incarnational *perichoresis* is fully not mutual. The asymmetry as in John of Damascus maintains God's transcendence and initiative in the relationship between God and the world, while the symmetry lies as far as the paradox of the divine incarnation in humans is involved. See Verna Harrison, "Perichoresis in the Greek Fathers," *St. Vladimir's Theological Quarterly* 35, no. 1 (1991): 62.

56 Harrison, "Perichoresis in the Greek Fathers," 62.

57 See Kilby, "Perichoresis and Projection," 432–445.

in terms of being derivatively inspired through the gifts of the Spirit and therefore valid.[58] On the other hand, Joseph Fitzmyer, reflecting on the structured ministry of the church from the Pastoral Epistles, notes the importance of the hierarchical ministries of the church. He notes that "although the Pastorals contain counsels that promote the respect for fellow Christians and for unity, the idea of the church as *koinonia* is wholly absent from them."[59] Thus the question is, can the principles of egalitarianism and hierarchy go together? Is church as an institution compatible with the church constituted of the Spirit and Christ?

Miroslav Volf argues that it is commonplace in Protestant circles to pit the Spirit of God against church institutions. Institutions are most often thought of as "mechanisms of repression,"[60] but he argues that the essential sociality of the church requires institutions and the question is not "*whether* the church is an institution, but rather *what* kind of institution it is."[61] Volf contends that "the church needs the vivifying presence of the Spirit, and without this presence, even a church with a decentralized participative structure and culture will become sterile, and perhaps more sterile even than a hierarchical church."[62] Haight argues that the idea of divine institutions does not mean that they are not changeable or cannot be diverse. This focuses on the dynamic character of the institutions whose functional validity depends on the ministry that is needed according to the changing times.[63] Thus, a hierarchical structure of the church with egalitarian principles, which is dynamic and open to change, seems to hold more promise.

Moltmann's proposals regarding open invitation to the Lord's Supper implied on trinitarian and eschatological grounds are open to controversy. It is not clear whether this openness is implied with respect to other Christian denominations or other religious communities. Do the same criteria hold for both Christians and people of other faiths? He does not explain whether different liturgies are needed for the unchurched or the unbaptised. Further consideration regarding the church traditions of the past two centuries is perhaps needed. Is there a way of having an open Eucharist, without neglecting the tradition that stresses "Christian

58 Roger Haight, "The Structures of the Church," *Journal of Ecumenical Studies* 30, no. 3–4 (Summer–Fall 1993): 403.

59 Joseph A. Fitzmyer, "The Structured Ministries of the Church in the Pastoral Epistles," *The Catholic Biblical Quarterly* I, no. 66 (2004): 584.

60 Miroslav Volf, *After Our Likeness: The Church as the Image of the Trinity* (Grand Rapids, MI: William B. Eerdmans, 1998), 234.

61 Volf, *After Our Likeness*,235.

62 Volf, *After Our Likeness*, 257.

63 Haight, "Structures of the Church," 413.

formation" and "catechumenal processes"?[64] We will later return to Moltmann when we arrive at a comparable analysis of this model. But for now, let us now look at the ecclesiological model from Stanley Hauerwas which is representative of a distinctive ecclesiology.

## A distinctive (ecclesiocentric) model from Stanley Hauerwas

Stanley Hauerwas's ecclesiology occupies the central place in his entire project. He aims to integrate ethics and theology, and respond to contemporary concrete issues of the world from the particular vantage point of ecclesiology.[65] Stanley Hauerwas's project, with his background from the Yale school, is a critical response to post-Enlightenment liberalism with its privatisation of religion, its co-option of religion as an instrument of the state, and its devaluation of the church as a community. His ecclesiological project aims to secure a distinct place for the church as an "alternative community" in contrast to the world. Not only that, Hauerwas seeks to highlight the fact that the church has something distinct to say to the world, a different and unique story to tell. Hauerwas maintains that the church's task is to be the church and show the world what it is, and that the world cannot set agendas for the church. Hauerwas places a strong emphasis on the embodied character of Christianity, particularly in the church and its practices. Also being a theologian with a strong ethical emphasis, Hauerwas highlights the importance of these two disciplines working together.[66] We will now highlight Hauerwas's ecclesiology in terms of its nature, ministry, and mission.

### Nature and ministry of the church

Hauerwas's idea of the church as an alternative community arises, as we have noted earlier, in reaction to modernity's project of liberalism and thereby strives for an alternative politics. Thus, Hauerwas strongly argues for a distinctive politics to counteract this force of liberalism and the

---

64 See Melissa Marie Hartley, "The 1979 Book of Common Prayer and the Practice of the Open Table in the Episcopal Church" (PhD diss., Drew University, New Jersey, 2012); Rowena J. Ropelt, "Ecclesiology of the Open Table: Intercommunion in the Church of England, A Historical and Theological Analyses" (PhD diss., Catholic University of America, Washington D.C., 2003).

65 See Nicholas M. Healy, *Hauerwas: A (Very) Critical Introduction. Interventions* (Grand Rapids, MI: William B. Eerdmans, 2014), 17–38.

66 See Stanley Hauerwas, *A Community of Character: Toward a Constructive Christian Social Ethic* (Notre Dame, IN: University of Notre Dame Press, 1981), 1; Stanley Hauerwas, *Truthfulness and Tragedy: Further Investigations in Christian Ethics* (Notre Dame, IN: University of Notre Dame Press, 1977), 8.

instrument best suited to do this is no other than the church. Hauerwas writes, "Christianity is mostly a matter of politics—politics as defined by the gospel. The call to be part of the gospel is a joyful call to be adopted by an alien people, to join a countercultural phenomenon, a new *polis* called church."[67] The distinct nature of the church is brought about in contrast to so-called "Constantinianism."[68] Constantinianism is the decisive shift in the nature and understanding of the church that took place when the church turned from a minority sect to the majority religion of the state after the reign of Constantine. Hauerwas notes that the problem with Constantinianism is its liberal universalism with its power to forge a set of principles which is taken for granted by the church.[69] Hauerwas suggests that the church must develop a distinctive politics in contrast to such Constantinianism. This distinctive politics presupposes that the church is distinct or different from the world. He claims that "the world cannot be the church, for the world, while still God's good creation, is a realm that knows not God and is thus characterised by the fears that constantly fuel the fires of violence."[70]

Where does the distinctiveness of the church lie? Hauerwas claims that the church's distinctiveness from the world lies in the "virtue of the distinctive narrative that forms their community."[71] While admitting that every community has its own narrative or story that shapes it,[72] the church becomes distinctive by the particular nature of the overarching narrative.[73] The church's distinctive narrative is the narrative of God's dealings with Israel, with a christocentric perspective in which the death and resurrection of Jesus becomes central.[74] Hauerwas writes that "Jesus is the story that forms the church."[75]

In a recent monograph entitled *The Holy Spirit* (2015), Hauerwas also shows that the Holy Spirit, who rests on Christ's body, ensures the embodiedness of the church, by helping believers to live out the story. Moreover, he shows that it is only by the power of the Holy Spirit that believers can

67 Stanley Hauerwas, *Resident Aliens: Life in the Christian Colony* (Nashville, TN: Abingdon Press, 1998), 30.

68 Hauerwas borrows this term from John Howard Yoder. See Healy, *Hauerwas*, 35.

69 Stanley Hauerwas, *After Christendom? How the Church is to Behave if Freedom, Justice, and a Christian Nation Are Bad Ideas* (Nashville, TN: Abingdon Press, 1991), 18–19.

70 Hauerwas, *Community of Character*, 109.

71 Stanley Hauerwas, *Peaceable Kingdom* (Notre Dame, IN: University of Notre Dame Press, 1983), 60.

72 Hauerwas, *Community of Character*, 121.

73 Hauerwas, *Community of Character*, 4.

74 Hauerwas, *Peaceable Kingdom*, 24–29.

75 Hauerwas, *Community of Character*, 50.

witness to Christ. The Holy Spirit calls the church into existence, and through it the church avoids the polarity of the docetic[76] and the ebionite[77] understandings.[78]

The story that makes the church distinct also enables the church to be living witnesses to the truth of the narrative through its practices. Hauerwas, therefore, holds that salvation is integrally related to the church because he believes that truth or falsity of Christian convictions cannot be addressed with doctrines and dogmas, but through the practices of the church as an embodied political community.[79] In this sense, he writes, "For Christians, without the church there is no possibility of salvation and even less of morality and politics."[80] The statement "outside the church there is no salvation" is actually about the nature of salvation that proclaims the Lordship of Christ to all creation.[81] Hauerwas further maintains that for this truth or story to be told and lived, liturgy is more important than doctrine or creeds;[82] therefore, his understanding of the marks of the church centres on preaching of the Word, sacraments, and the life of the congregation. Baptism, for him, is the rite of initiation through which we become part of the story of Jesus's death and resurrection. Eucharist, on the other hand, is an eschatological meal, which makes possible "a people of peace."[83]

Hauerwas insists that the church's distinctiveness also lies in the use of a different language, which can only be learnt through participation in the church. It is only by learning the language of the church that one can notice how that is different from the "language of the state."[84] This is also what discipleship is, which is learning different practices of a different community rather than merely a matter of "new or changed self-understanding."[85] In other words, Hauerwas endorses a strong community character to discipleship. For him, it seems that one cannot be a true follower

76 The understanding of the church as a purely spiritual institution.

77 The church as purely a human institution.

78 See Stanley Hauerwas and William H. Willimon, *The Holy Spirit* (Nashville: Abingdon Press, 2015).

79 Hauerwas, *After Christendom?*, 18.

80 Hauerwas, *After Christendom?*, 18.

81 Hauerwas, *After Christendom?*, 37.

82 Hauerwas, *Community of Character*, 240.

83 Stanley Hauerwas, "The Servant Community: Christian Social Ethics," in *The Hauerwas Reader*, eds. John Berkmann and Michael Cartwright (Durham and London: Duke University Press, 2001), 383.

84 Stanley Hauerwas, "Why the Sectarian Temptation Is a Misrepresentation: A Response to James Gustafson (1988)," in Berkmann and Cartwright, *Hauerwas Reader*, 102.

85 Hauerwas, *After Christendom?*, 107.

of Jesus without the church. Hauerwas cites the example of the disciples, called by Jesus, who were called to leave all that they had. This was a call to a "radical break with security and possessions, with the customs and habits of everyday life."[86] Understood in terms of a radical break, a line is therefore drawn between the church and the world depending on those who confess Jesus as Lord and those who do not.[87]

Hauerwas proposes that the church is a social ethic, but challenges the notion that in being so, the church should rally around others on the basis of common moral commitment and action. Instead, the church's distinctive role is to show the world what it ought to be as God's creation and he emphasises that it is only the church that can do this and nobody else.[88] The church does not have a social ethic, it is a social ethic.[89]

Hauerwas's understanding of the church as a distinct and alternative community brought for him the charge of "sectarianism."[90] He responds to it by negating that he ever suggested Christians should withdraw from the world, but that more positively Christians should "recover the church as the locus of habits of speech to sustain . . . lives in service to the world."[91] In this regard, Hauerwas proposes that the church be a tactic, not a strategy.[92] The church as a tactic does not withdraw from the world in terms of carving out a separate place for itself. The church remains within the space of the other and operates within the law of the space. It does not have the power to form a general strategy, but operates on its own as opportunity arises.[93] Nevertheless, Hauerwas admits that the church is imperfect and has been unfaithful, but he maintains that "holiness exists even in our unfaithfulness."[94] He contends that the church's unfaithfulness is no disqualification for it to be a witness to God's kingdom.[95]

86 Stanley Hauerwas, "Jesus and the Social Embodiment of the Peaceable Kingdom (1983)," in Berkmann and Cartwright, *Hauerwas Reader*, 133.

87 Hauerwas, "Servant Community," 375.

88 Hauerwas, "Servant Community," 375.

89 Hauerwas, *Resident Aliens*, 43; Hauerwas, *Peaceable Kingdom*, 99.

90 See discussions in Healy, *Hauerwas*; John B. Thomson, *The Ecclesiology of Stanley Hauerwas: A Christian Theology of Liberation* (Aldershot: Ashgate New Critical Thinking in Religion, Theology & Biblical Studies, 2003).

91 Hauerwas, *After Christendom?*, 6–7.

92 This concept of the distinction between tactic and strategy is drawn by Hauerwas from Michel de Certeau. See Michel de Certeau, *The Practice of Everyday Life*, trans. Stephen Rendall (Berkeley: University of California Press, 1988), 35–36.

93 Hauerwas, *After Christendom?*, 18.

94 Stanley Hauerwas, *Sanctify Them in Truth: Holiness Exemplified* (Nashville, TN: Abingdon Press, 1998), 10.

95 Hauerwas, "Servant Community," 373.

## Mission of the church

For Hauerwas, the mission of the church follows from the above distinct nature of the church. On the one hand, it nurtures a distinctive people of peace as opposed to the world's ways of coercion and violence, and on the other, it opens up the way for the care for strangers and the earth. The church's mission is essentially an eschatological task towards building the kingdom of God. Hauerwas's call for the integrity of the church does not mean that the church should withdraw from the economic, social, legal, and political life of our societies but the difference is in the nature of participation. He writes, "The most important political service the church does for any society is to be a community capable of developing people of virtue."[96] In this way, the church provides the skills and interpretative space to "help us recognize the possibilities and limits of our society."[97]

Hauerwas is against abstract rights or theories of justice. In his opinion, issues of justice should spring from our distinct witness for God, which allows us to approach the issue of justice from a different angle than from where post-Enlightenment would stand.[98] In other words, the church's relation to the wider society is that of critical engagement, not simply taking society's norms and principles for granted. For the Christian, the distinctive story of Christ provides the "means for recognizing and critically appropriating other stories that claim our lives."[99] For example, the church is expected to especially withhold cooperation with the forces (of the state) that resort to violence.[100] In an essay published in 1985, entitled "Peacemaking: The Virtue of the Church," Hauerwas writes about how a church as a community of forgiveness can approach peace amidst the church and peace with the world by confronting the "false peace" that the world has.[101]

Hauerwas sees the kingdom of God as an eschatological reality and as a wider context of the church's mission. He agrees with the dynamic and eschatological character of the church. He writes, "The church . . . can never be limited to the present moment but reaches back into history and forward into the future, as both directions provide an indication of

96 Stanley Hauerwas, *Christian Existence Today* (Grand Rapids, MI: Brazos Press, 2001), 13.

97 Hauerwas, *Community of Character*, 74.

98 Hauerwas, *After Christendom?*, 45–68.

99 Hauerwas, *Community of Character*, 96.

100 Berkmann and Cartwright, *Hauerwas Reader*, 104–105.

101 Hauerwas, "Peacemaking: The Virtue of the Church," in Berkmann and Cartwright, *Hauerwas Reader*, 325.

what we ought to be."[102] In the church's relation with the kingdom of God eschatologically, we can argue, Hauerwas could silence his critics regarding the charge of sectarianism. Hauerwas recognises that the kingdom of God is broader than the church.[103] He maintains that Jesus's eschatological kingdom is a kingdom of peace, forgiveness, and reconciliation, and as members of this kingdom we are called to "extend God's peace through the care and protection of his creation."[104] The openness of the church through the kingdom of God is further brought out when he writes, "For the Church does not possess Christ, his presence is not confined to the church. Rather, it is in the church that we learn to recognise Christ's presence outside the church."[105] The church, on the other hand, has "no right to determine the boundaries of God's kingdom,"[106] and so it is our "happy task [as Christians] to acknowledge God's power to make his kingdom present in most surprising places and ways."[107]

An interfaith engagement is implicit in this affirmation, but unfortunately, Hauerwas does not proceed towards such an engagement. Instead, he reacts against religious freedom or freedom of religion in the modern world, arguing that it dilutes the particular witness of particular religions and makes religious convictions a matter of private confession rather than a community affair.[108] Hauerwas's church is open to the outsider and the stranger as he argues that Jesus was himself a "stranger."[109] He believes that the particularity of Jesus's story breaks down false boundaries and enables regard for the other and makes the church truly universal. He writes, "The universality of the church is based on the particularity of Jesus's story and on the fact that this story trains us to see one another as God's people."[110] Furthermore, he suggests that there is no reason to believe that the church is superior to other communities. He writes that the church's narrative does not "underwrite the assumptions of superiority or Christian dominance," but serves "to remind the Christians of the radicalness of the gospel."[111]

---

102 Hauerwas, *Community of Character*, 109.

103 Stanley Hauerwas, "Why the Sectarian Temptation Is a Misrepresentation: A Response to James Gustafson (1988)," 108.

104 Hauerwas, "Jesus and The Social Embodiment," 134.

105 Hauerwas, "Servant Community," 372.

106 Hauerwas, "Servant Community," 377.

107 Hauerwas, *Peaceable Kingdom*, 101.

108 Hauerwas, *After Christendom?*, 69–92.

109 Hauerwas, "Servant Community," 385.

110 Hauerwas, *Community of Character*, 51.

111 Hauerwas, *Peaceable Kingdom*, 60.

Hauerwas's ecclesiology outlined above shows a clear ecclesiocentric model with a distinctive feature. His ecclesiocentric model secures for the church a distinct identity and ensures an alternative community in contrast to the world. An ecclesiocentric model clearly has its benefits in terms of ensuring a distinct witness for Christ in its proclamation of the unique narrative of Christ's death and resurrection. It shows the importance of a concrete community living out such a witness through worship, liturgy, and practices of the church. His stress on discipleship and witness of the community for Christ, for that matter, is very relevant for any church. It also has a critical edge with respect to responding to the assumptions of the world. While all these benefits can be reaped from Hauerwas's ecclesiology which speaks of distinctiveness, there are drawbacks especially when this ecclesiocentric model is situated in the Indian context and particularly when seeking to develop a permeable Spirit ecclesiology with a relational-distinctive dialectics.

### Drawbacks of Stanley Hauerwas's ecclesiocentric model

Hauerwas's ecclesiological project seeks to emphasise the church as a contrastive and distinct community with ideals and affirmations different from that of the world and the state. He seeks to secure a distinct witness for the church as a separate community. Although we have noted its values and strengths, Hauerwas's concept when uncritically applied in the Indian context could lead to problematic results. The church in India has different concerns compared to that of the West, as we have noted in the previous chapter. The churches in India are not troubled by the challenges of Enlightenment liberalism, the modernist project of rationalism or individualism, nor nonreligious secularism, philosophies, or cultural ideologies and traditions of the West. Instead, one of the struggles of the church in India is its foreign nature which has resulted in the alienation and separation of Christian communities from their Indian culture, tradition, and the wider community. This alienation has continued for centuries and while such separation and distinction has successfully made the church a distinct community, it has failed miserably in its witness. No wonder, the church in India continues to be a miniscule minority after two millennia of Christian presence. It is clear from the above context that while Indians admired Jesus, they were extremely critical of the foreign, colonial, and alien nature of the church on Indian soil. In other words, there needs to be recognition more of continuity than discontinuity between the Indian church and wider society.

Hauerwas's project affirms that it is only through the faithful witness of the church as an embodied community and through its practices that the unique story of the death and resurrection of Jesus can be proclaimed. This solely ecclesiocentric witness of the gospel is also problematic when viewed in relation to the Indian context. The question has to be asked as to what kind of witness for the gospel the church, in its nexus with colonialism, has given through two centuries of subjugation, domination, and exploitation of the Indian people. According to Hauerwas's argument, it would follow that if the church fails to witness faithfully to the gospel, the gospel itself is discredited as the church is the primary locus for such a witness. In the Indian scene, it is clear that the church has failed its witness, as the gospel mediated by the church was discarded by the people. However, Hauerwas is only partly right because the gospel seems to have travelled different routes, through unofficial channels, through missionaries' sacrificial efforts and labours of love, through education and medical missions,[112] and created communities who believed in Christ, but who were not willing to be part of the imperial and colonial church. This again shows that there could be ways and practices that are not bound to the church's institutional practices, which can be an effective witness to the gospel too. Moreover, Hauerwas's contrastive ecclesiology seems to have handicapped him in his relations with the wider society. The only relation that the church seems to have is a critical relation to the world without any space for amicable engagements. His theology on behalf of strangers and others seems to be peripheral at best and simply an add-on to his ecclesiology. In the Indian context, with the history of alienation and separation between different communities, the church needs to build bridges with other religions and cultures to develop integral relationships with them so that the damage that was done during the colonial times is rectified.

Again, Hauerwas's ecclesiology seems to be inadequate for a permeable Spirit ecclesiology since his ecclesiology does not show the potential for a dialectical engagement with other communities and the world, which is required for our project. Nor does it emphasise the perspective of the Spirit adequately in order to develop a Spirit ecclesiology. His ecclesiology seems to be lopsided in terms of the distinctiveness based on the christological basis of the church while neglecting that the Spirit of God is at work even beyond the church. In his ecclesiology, God is somehow bound within the church.

In the preceding discussion, we dealt with Moltmann's relational ecclesiology and Hauerwas's distinctive ecclesiology and have critically reflected on them. In the following, we will proceed to discuss a

---

112 See the chapter on mass movements and medical and technical missions in India in C.B. Firth, *Introduction to Indian Church History*, 197–214.

christo-theocentric model with Kathryn Tanner to further our discussions about viable ecclesiological models.

## A christo-theocentric model with Kathryn Tanner

Kathryn Tanner has not explicitly discussed the church in her writings.[113] However, in most of her works clear models for the human community are recognisable. In the "Introduction" to a recent book entitled *The Gift of Theology: The Contribution of Kathryn Tanner* (2015), she is classed as a "constructive theologian," among those who deal with the question of whether theology has anything important to say to the world and our way of life.[114] In her own words, Tanner's theology concerns "How might a contemporary Christian theology promote (or not) a more adequate understanding of the world and a more just way of living?"[115] Tanner's model for the human community can be described as christo-theocentric since it is based on the transcendence of God and the emphasis on the link between God and humanity, the incarnation of Christ. This forms an important basis for nearly all her theology. In the following, our focus will be to draw out this christo-theocentric model for the human community from her writings and point out the ecclesiology inherent in them. Tanner's approach will be shown here as a critique for both Moltmann's social trinitarian model and Hauerwas's ecclesiocentric postliberal approach.

### Tanner's christo-theocentric model as critique of social trinitarianism

Tanner's christo-theocentric model will be dealt with first as a critique of the social trinitarian model, as in Moltmann's ecclesiology. In her work, *Christ the Key*, she highlights several problems about Social Trinity. First, she argues that the claim that trinitarianism is better than monotheism for sociopolitical purposes is faulty. This is because trinitarianism has not always been an egalitarian construct, as Tanner shows that it rose in "tandem with Christian support for an increasingly centralised Roman

113 See Brad East, "An Undefensive Presence: The Mission and Identity of the Church in Kathryn Tanner and John Howard Yoder," *Scottish Journal of Theology* 68, no. 3 (2015): 328–329.

114 Rosemary P. Carbine and Hilda P. Koster, "Introduction: The Gift of Kathryn Tanner's Imagination," in *The Gift of Theology: The Contribution of Kathryn Tanner*, ed. Rosemary P. Carbine and Hilda P. Koster (Minneapolis, MN: Fortress Press, 2015), xxvi.

115 Kathryn Tanner, "How My Mind Has Changed: Christian Claims," *Christian Century* 127, no. 4 (2010): 40, cited in Carbine and Koster, *Gift of Theology*, xxvi.

emperor"[116] after Constantine. Instead, monotheism could well suggest rightly that no one, no earthly Lord, shares, or stands in as God's representative.[117] Second, she fears that, without some sort of Tritheism, it is not possible to translate relationships among the Trinity to distinct and separable relationships among human individuals.[118] Third, following on from the above, a mistaken notion emerges that divine persons, constitutive of their relations and acts, could easily square with fostering an egalitarian community. In fact, the divine persons themselves seem to have a hierarchical relationship. Tanner notes, "Order among the divine persons is thereby ripe for justification of hierarchy. It easily supports claims of fixed social roles, and the idea that people are equal despite the disparity of their assignment to such roles is faulty."[119] Fourth, even if divine genders are not understood strictly or even if one completely does away with them, there remains the problem of "unassigned genders"[120] leading to "heterosexism"[121] and the consequent inappropriateness of such models for the human community.[122] Thus, Tanner shows that trinitarianism could be as dangerous as monotheism. Further, she points out that this rules out the "progressive political" potentials of monotheistic religions like Judaism and Islam and thus drives an unrealistic wedge between monotheism and Christian trinitarianism;[123] only a particular type of trinitarianism could be viable, if at all. For this, she refers to the "politically progressive theologians'"[124] proposal of a perichoretic relationship among the Trinity as a viable model. While acknowledging that it has social and political implications, she asks how this perichoretic relationality could be compatible especially with the Father-Son hierarchical relationship in the economy.[125]

Further, the increasing modification of this perichoretic relationship by theologians in terms of redefining the persons and relations ultimately shows that trinitarianism can be modified in accordance with one's own inclinations, thereby risking the loss of the Trinity's unique characteristics. Ultimately, it gets to the stage where we know no more about the Trinity than we do about human relationships and Trinitarianism as a concept

116 Kathryn Tanner, *Christ the Key* (Cambridge: Cambridge University Press, 2010), 208–209.

117 Tanner, *Christ the Key*, 208–209.

118 Tanner, *Christ the Key*, 210–211.

119 Tanner, *Christ the Key*, 211.

120 Tanner, *Christ the Key*, 216.

121 Tanner, *Christ the Key*, 216.

122 Tanner, *Christ the Key*, 216.

123 Tanner, *Christ the Key*, 217.

124 She takes Moltmann as an example.

125 Tanner, *Christ the Key*, 217–219.

then ceases to contribute anything new.[126] A significant problem, Tanner highlights, as pointed out earlier is that we are not absolutely sure what we mean by our affirmations of the Trinity, especially in terms of persons, or relations, or the *perichoretic* nature of it. This is due to our finitude, sin, and suffering existence that is different from the life of God. This is also because the perichoretic co-inherence of divine persons cannot be taken for granted for human relations.[127]

Thus, Tanner suggests an alternative model to Social Trinity for the church or human community. It will be seen that in this christo-theocentric model, the transcendence of God, our limitation as sinful human beings, and our hope of being taken up into the Trinity by grace through Christ's incarnation, provide a basis for the human community or the church in two different ways. It provides a paradigm for the believing community to be in relationship with its Creator through reverence, worship, and adoration while simultaneously providing a model in Jesus to be followed.

Tanner argues that Christology drawn from the relationships of the Second Person of the Trinity is a better, simpler, and more direct way of expressing the God-church-world relationship.[128] To counteract the problems mentioned so far, Tanner suggests that the Trinity in the economy, the Second Person of the Trinity should be our model. The essential premise of this model is the difference or contrast between God, "the wholly other," and ourselves. Tanner argues that in this scheme, there is no effort to close the gap between the Trinity and human beings. Rather, it opens up an avenue to look at what the Trinity has done for us in Christ. She writes,

> The trinity does not do so, however, in the way the previous strategy (Social Trinity) suggested—by showing us a form of itself that we can hope to approach and thereby providing us with an external model to which we might more easily conform. The Trinity in the economy does not close the gap by making trinitarian relations something like human ones, but by actually incorporating the human into its very own life through the incarnation. We are therefore not called to imitate the Trinity by way of the incarnation but brought to participate in it.[129]

Tanner actually points out with Richard Bauckham that there is no biblical basis that suggests human relationships ought to reflect trinitarian relationships and argues that the New Testament theme about the image

126 Tanner, *Christ the Key*, 220–221.
127 Tanner, *Christ the Key*, 222–224.
128 Tanner, *Christ the Key*, 207–208.
129 Tanner, *Christ the Key*, 234.

of God is not to be used in this way.[130] Here, the differences between the Trinity and us fuel the hope of us being taken up into the Trinity's life through the Second Person. The fact of our finitude and sinfulness does not stop us being united with God through Christ. Here, the Trinity does not have to stoop to become like us, but we are called to become like Christ.[131] She writes, "The Second Person of the Trinity takes the humanity united to it into its own relations with Father and Spirit; and we are to enjoy those same relations through him by the power of the Spirit."[132] The gap between the trinitarian relations and the human relations are not closed up by assuming that both those relations are similar but by joining the two different human and divine relations together into one in Christ in his incarnation.[133] Tanner argues that this avoids two problems in the earlier model of Social Trinity. One, it avoids the problem of superfluity and redundancy in the scheme of social Trinity, which ultimately comes to the point where trinitarian relations resemble human relationships so adequately that there is nothing new to know from the former. Second, it avoids the presumptive hope that trinitarian relations are close enough to be imitated by human relations.[134] How this entire scheme works out is that human beings while remaining fully human are made into the image of God not by their nature, but by being participants in the trinitarian life through Christ.[135]

Tanner, however, contends that modelling our relationships on the Second Person of the Trinity has to be further qualified. Are we to look at the Son's relationship with the Father for our human relationships or the Son's relationship in the flesh with human beings? Tanner argues that, in the first place, the Son's relationship with the Father and the Spirit cannot be assumed to be similar to Jesus's relationship with other human beings. She suggests that Jesus's relationship with the Father can only be imitated in terms of "relations of worshipful dedication to the Father's mission, empowered by the Spirit,"[136] but Jesus's relationship with other human beings can be actually a model for our relationships. Tanner writes,

> Jesus's life in short, exhibits not just the sort of relations that humans, in the image of the Son, are to have with the Father and the Spirit—relations of worshipful dedication to the Father's mission, empowered by

[130] See Richard Bauckham, "Moltmann's Trinity and the Kingdom of God," 160, cited in Tanner, *Christ the Key*, 234.

[131] Tanner, *Christ the Key*, 235–236.

[132] Tanner, *Christ the Key*, 235.

[133] Tanner, *Christ the Key*, 235.

[134] Tanner, *Christ the Key*, 235.

[135] Tanner, *Christ the Key*, 236.

[136] Tanner, *Christ the Key*, 236.

> the Spirit—but, in his relations with other people, Jesus also shows how those relations with the Father and the Spirit are to work themselves out in community with other people. If one wants to know how a Trinitarian life impacts one's relations with other people, this second part of the story is very obviously the place to look: Jesus's relations with other people constitute the sort of human relations that the economy of the Trinity itself specifies. Jesus's way of life toward other people as we share in it is the Trinitarian form of human social life.[137]

Tanner moves further to suggest that through Christ and the work of grace, Christians as a body are taken up into the trinitarian dynamic of oneness and diversity and move together, rather than the trinitarian relationship itself becoming a model for the human community's unity and diversity.[138]

Tanner further argues that the incarnation can be a better analogy for the kingdom of God than the Trinity. The Trinity suggests that the kingdom of God ought to be a life-affirming, Spirit-filled community for the utmost flourishing of all. It suggests a community of mutual fulfilment for one and all. Tanner contends that incarnation does this and more in a different manner. Tanner argues that it "sets up kinship, in this case between humanity and divinity, a community of now mutual fulfilment in that the human is to benefit from what the divine already enjoys."[139] She maintains that through Christ, we are brought into an "unnatural" community where diverse people once divided are brought together and made one in Christ in the same way as the humanity and divinity of Christ.[140] Thus, modelling the human community or the church on the Second Person's relationship with the Father and the Son brings us closer to evaluating the goals of a particular community. The evaluation can be in the nature of:

> Are those communities dedicated to anything like what Jesus was dedicated to in his relations with other people? Are they dedicated to policies ensuring the comprehensive well-being of all their members, especially the disempowered, following Jesus's own concern for the physical and spiritual well-being of the poor and suffering?[141]

In the above discussion, we have shown how Tanner's christo-theocentric model bases the human community on the relationships of the Second Person of the Trinity. We showed that it is premised on the transcendence of God which removes a lot of problems in the social trinitarian

---

137 Tanner, *Christ the Key*, 236.
138 Tanner, *Christ the Key*, 238.
139 Tanner, *Christ the Key*, 241.
140 Tanner, *Christ the Key*, 241.
141 Tanner, *Christ the Key*, 243.

model and allows an easier avenue for us to model the human community or the church on. We will further show that the same christo-theocentric model in terms of God's transcendence and our status as God's creatures and Christ forms the basis for Tanner's arguments for a human community or church with elements of self-critique, social justice, and a relational community of diversity and particularity. It will be seen that this form of human community with postmodern leanings is in contrast with the postliberal assumptions found in Hauerwas.

### Tanner's christo-theocentric model as building a community of socioeconomic justice

In Tanner's christo-theocentric model, the concept of the transcendence of God serves as the basis for conceiving of a human community or church that is concerned with "cosmos-wide transformation of the broadest possible socioeconomic and political sort."[142] God's transcendence and God's grace correspond in Tanner's model to provide alternative socioeconomic structures. This is encapsulated in the notion of God as the giver of all good gifts.[143] Tanner stresses that God's gifts to humanity and the world are unconditional and they ought to elicit Christian social responsibility towards others.[144] Particularly, she explores the contradictions of God's gifts and God's grace in the inequalities and competitive culture created by global capitalism. God's gracious gifts of grace imply that gifts are for all and to be equally shared in contrast to capitalistic assumptions of selfish ownership.[145]

The notion of divine transcendence is also used in a different sense by Tanner. This transcendence also recognises the finite nature of human ideas, proposals and norms, their historical and social conditioning, and their fallible character.[146] It stands as a protest against all absolute and unconditional claims. God's transcendence and therefore the illogicality of absolutising any particular social or political agenda or movement provide resources for Tanner for a progressive social agenda with radical and revolutionary effects.[147] Using the notion of divine transcendence, Tanner makes a case for Christian opposition to fixed hierarchies of superiors and

[142] Kathryn Tanner, "The Church and Action for the World: A Response to Amy Pauw," *Scottish Journal of Theology* 57, no. 2 (2004): 228.

[143] Kathryn Tanner, *The Politics of God: Christian Theologies and Social Justice* (Minneapolis, MN: Fortress Press, 1992), 155.

[144] Kathryn Tanner, *The Economy of Grace* (Minneapolis, MN: Augsburg Fortress, 2005). See Carbine and Koster, "Introduction," xxx.

[145] This is the central argument in Tanner's book, *Economy of Grace*.

[146] Tanner, *Politics of God*, 56–57, 66–69.

[147] Tanner, *Politics of God*, 251.

subordinates, and to oppressive relations of dominance and oppression and intolerance towards others.[148]

Tanner's christo-theocentric model of divine transcendence and the corresponding respect due as God's creatures, along with a postmodern perspective helps her to conceive of a community featuring diversity and particularity, while critiquing the postliberal assumptions of the Christian community. This also shows that Tanner leans towards a permeable character of the Christian community. Tanner argues that all God's creatures due to their relationship with God are to be respected. This means that a decent life is a question of right for all God's creatures. This includes a critical self-reflection of the society or particular community so that the rights of healthcare, housing, and a decent wage, etc., can be met.[149] Tanner correlates respect for others as God's creatures with the respect for particularity. She writes,

> The claim that human beings are given due respect as creatures of God is a standard for respect for all but it is not a standard that requires anyone to renounce her or his particularity by conforming to it . . .. My standard for respect points away from itself, therefore, to distribute a worthiness for respect to the distinctive particularities of others.[150]

The basic notion of the otherness of God and the respect due as God's creatures fuel Tanner's motivations towards justice. She writes that the "fundamental implication of the simple claim of living lives under God, a concern for justice should be part of all those ends to which human beings are called."[151] The respect owed as creatures of God blocks motivations for assimilating others to oneself. As God is the other, one's relation with God is the relation of difference or plurality in which the other is recognised as the other. In this scheme, others are allowed to be others without coercion or which is the foundation of respectful relations with others.[152]

## Tanner's christo-theocentric model as critique of Hauerwas's postliberalism

Drawing on God's transcendence, Tanner's critique of postliberal assumptions is basically against discontinuity between the Christian community and the world, or the wider society, or culture. Postliberalism conceives of culturally defined social groups, and particularly Christian communities as distinct units whose identity is built out of discontinuity with the

148 Tanner, *Politics of God*, 130–132.
149 Tanner, *Politics of God*, 179–180.
150 Tanner, *Politics of God*, 208.
151 Tanner, *Politics of God*, 225.
152 Tanner, *Politics of God*, 193–224.

wider society or culture. Tanner notes that this form of identity building is unreal as the church is also part of the society or culture in which it belongs. Contrary to postliberal assumptions, she maintains that "Christian identity itself is relational" and that it cannot be secured by sharp boundaries. Essentially, from a postmodern perspective, Tanner maintains that sharp cultural boundaries do not establish a distinctive way of life as the postliberals affirm. "Boundaries are determined . . . by how a Christian way of life is situated within a whole field of alternatives."[153] She shows that drawing sharp boundaries does not settle anything because, essentially, there are elements in religious society that are borrowed from the wider culture. She contends that "Christian social practices form a voluntary association within a wider society, rather than a separate society in and of themselves."[154] Tanner is in favour of a church that is

> analogous to a new social movement, an association with a social agenda (but not exclusively so), that takes people in in order to change their ways (say, by consciousness-raising) but that also intends to shake up the social practices of those outside, and not just by bringing them into the fold.[155]

In this way, she prefers to think of the Christian community as essentially relational. She argues that ""A Christian way of life is . . . essentially parasitic; it has to establish relations with other ways of life, it has to take from them, in order to be one itself."[156] Tanner argues that the church's identity is essentially hybrid and is determined at its boundary. She opines that

> the boundary . . . allows Christian identity to be essentially impure and mixed, the identity of a hybrid that always shares cultural forms with its wider host culture and other religions.[157] ". . . the distinctiveness of a Christian way of life is not much formed *by* the boundary as *at it*."[158]

Tanner's conceptions of the church thus move away from an ecclesiocentrism found in Hauerwas. The church, for her, is where God continues to be central and Christ's work in the Spirit is highlighted. She manifests her christo-theocentricity when she defends her theological stance putting emphasis on Christ's work through the Spirit in and beyond the church. She explains:

---

153 Kathryn Tanner, *Theories of Culture: A New Agenda for Theology*, Guides to Theological Enquiry (Minneapolis, MN: Fortress Press, 1997), 111.

154 Tanner, *Theories of Culture,* 103.

155 Tanner, *Theories of Culture,* 103.

156 Tanner, *Theories of Culture,* 113.

157 Tanner, *Theories of Culture,* 114.

158 Tanner, *Theories of Culture,* 115.

> I have therefore tried my best to stress the difference between humans and Christ, and to give the privilege to him (not the church) as our means of access to the fount of goodness he calls Father by the power of the Spirit—Christ's powers are never transferred to Christians as their own property. I have also strongly stressed the universal reach of Christ's work in ways that would not limit Christ's influence to that of the church; there is every reason to think that, on my account, the Holy Spirit works to bind human life to that of Christ beyond the reach of explicitly Christian worship and witness.[159]

Brad East captures Tanner's ecclesiology succinctly. He maintains that

> Kathryn Tanner's ecclesiology is marked by a theocentric universalism of radical gift-giving, epitomised in the free grace of the Word incarnate and manifested in a human community as messy as any other, but which for just that reason remains resistant to all attempts to arrest or subdue God's freedom. Turned towards the world in unanxious mission, the church becomes "a community of mutual fulfillment"; in the gracious cycle of baptism, Eucharist, commission and in turn, human persons are caught up into the life of the triune God, blessing as they have been blessed, performing (out of) the indiscriminate economy of grace.[160]

In other words, Tanner's ecclesiology talks about a human community where God's grace and the Word are active and manifest in the life of the community. Yet, such divine manifestation does not take away God's freedom and otherness. On the other hand, through participation in the ministry and mission of the church, believers are caught up into the triune life of God by grace.

As we sum up Tanner's position for our purposes, her christo-theocentric model therefore provides the church, on the one hand, with an easier structure in the Second Person of the Trinity as a route to conceiving human relations in contrast to the problematic model of social trinitarianism. Tanner's model based on the transcendence of God and dignity of God's creatures provides avenues for a self-critical stance and a sociopolitical critique of the society towards human social justice. It also upholds the dignity of the particular and the "other" in human relations. It rescues the Christian community from the exclusivity and rigid boundaries and provides a relational character to the same. It presents a solution to several of the problems encountered in the social trinitarian model (as in Moltmann) and adequately resolves the non-relationality of Hauerwas's ecclesiocentric model.

159 Tanner, *Theories of Culture*, 230.

160 East, "Undefensive Presence," 332.

## Drawbacks of Tanner's model

The above discussion brings out the significance and strengths of Tanner's model for the human community or the church. Now the question is, is Tanner's model fully adequate to develop a permeable Spirit ecclesiology? I have shown that her model leans towards a permeable ecclesiology in terms of negotiable borders between the Christian community and other communities with regard to intercultural exchange. It also holds out a theology of particularity and the other and seeks to find a basis of socio-economic justice in the human community. However, Tanner's model is not fully adequate for a permeable Spirit ecclesiology for the following reasons: First, Tanner does not fully flesh out what her model would mean for developing a full-grown ecclesiology. In other words, Tanner does not have a full-fledged ecclesiology which could be delineated in terms of nature, ministry, and mission of the church. Second, her model, as we mentioned, can be described as christo-theocentric and places little emphasis on the work of the Spirit. She develops, of course, the mutuality of the Father, Son, and the Spirit in her understanding of the trinitarian relations,[161] but this dynamic fails to be explicit in the economy of God's relationship with the world concretely. In a Spirit ecclesiology, the Spirit's role will be important to consider along with the Son. In her model, the Spirit's presence and work in the world are not equally emphasised. Third, although Tanner tries to develop a theology of diversity and particularity, what is missing is a dialectical emphasis integrating universality-particularity and unity and diversity. A permeable Spirit ecclesiology would essentially need to integrate the above dialectics into its scheme. Fourth, her concern for socioeconomic justice and critique of society based on the otherness of God is commendable, but there is a lacuna concerning the Spirit's role as liberator or Christ's death and resurrection as reinforcing people's freedom from unjust structures. Fifth, she does not have an explicit theology of religions or interfaith relations in her theology which is important for the relationality aspect in the Indian context.

For these drawbacks, we will examine another model which will hope to fulfil the criteria for a permeable Spirit ecclesiology and provide the dynamics that are lacking in the above models. The following discussion focuses on determining the particular shape of a permeable Spirit ecclesiology with the Spirit ecclesiology of Amos Yong.

---

161 See Tanner, *Christ the Key*, 140–206.

## The shape of a permeable Spirit ecclesiology with Amos Yong

### Exploring Irenaeus's metaphor as a model for a permeable Spirit ecclesiology

We have previously argued that for permeability of the church, the relational-distinctive dialectics are needed and that can be understood to happen through the joint working of the Spirit and Christ. The working of these dialectics could be more nuanced than simply assuming that the Spirit's role is the relational dimension while the role of the Word or Logos is the particular and the distinct. To express these dialectics, the Irenaean metaphor can be helpful.[162] The Irenaean metaphor is well-known. Irenaeus follows the thought of Hellenistic Judaism in identifying the divine wisdom of Proverbs 8 with the Spirit. The Father has the Son who is the Word and the Spirit is wisdom which are two hands by which he created all things.[163] Taking a clue from this metaphor, our project proposes that the Spirit and the Word *each* supply both relational and distinctive dimensions. In other words, as the Spirit ensures the universal and the particular dimensions, so is the Logos or the Word both particular and universal. This is needed to ground the complex *distinctively relational* and *relationally distinct* dialectics that we have been arguing for, which are necessary to develop a permeable church in India. It will be found that Amos Yong's efforts have been similar in terms of exploring the Irenaean metaphor to highlight the distinct, yet relational economies of both the Spirit and the Word in the world.

Originally, Amos Yong's concern was to acknowledge the particular role of the Spirit in God's economy so that it is not subordinated to that of the Word. His effort is to emphasise the distinct economies of both the Spirit and the Word, in addition to their reciprocity and conjunction; the latter always being highlighted in the Western Christian tradition.[164] Moltmann also seeks to maintain both distinction and mutuality in his

---

[162] Irenaeus, *Adversus Haeresus* IV. xx. 3, IV. xx.1. New Advent, accessed October 28, 2019, https://archive.org/details/SaintIrenaeusAgainstHeresiesComplete/page/n10.

[163] Alasdair I.C. Heron, *The Holy Spirit: The Holy Spirit in the Bible, the History of Christian Thought, and Recent Theology* (Philadelphia: Westminster Press, 1983), 65. For a detailed study of the theology of the Holy Spirit by Irenaeus, refer to Anthony Briggman, *Irenaeus of Lyons and the Theology of the Holy Spirit*, Oxford Early Christian Studies (Oxford: Oxford University Press, 2012).

[164] The Western tradition has always highlighted the fact that the external works of God are undivided (Latin, *opera ad extra trinitatis indivisa sunt*). The question of trinitarian unity has largely overshadowed its diversity in the Western tradition.

trinitarian understanding of the immanent Trinity, but as we have seen, he fails to maintain their distinctiveness in the economic Trinity. Yong's apprehension is that, an emphasis on reciprocity over distinct economies subordinates the economy of the Spirit to that of the Son. To correct such an overemphasis and to bring a balance between the economies of the Spirit and the Son, he turns to Irenaeus's metaphor of the "two hands of the Father."[165] Of course, Yong admits that Irenaeus originally used this metaphor to argue for the distinction between the soul and the flesh against his gnostic critics. Nevertheless, as Yong suggests, this was done to carve out a distinct mission for the Son, to be incarnate; and the Spirit's mission was to apply the implications of the incarnation to the world.[166] Yong suggests that the Irenaean metaphor allows us to recognise the economies of the Word and the Spirit as "overlapping dimensionally."[167] He explains:

> This allows for the interrelationship as well as distinction between both economies to be further defined as we gain theological, ontological, and historical precision. At the same time, non-Christian faiths can be understood as belonging to both economies, but in different respects. For starters, then, it allows that they be conceived in pneumatological terms, related but not subordinated to or redefined by the Word.[168]

Yong contends that the failure to differentiate between the economies leads to a definition of soteriology in ecclesiological terms, while acknowledging the distinction enables a "robust trinitarian and cosmological understanding of soteriology to emerge in the long run."[169] Yong thereby attempts to maintain both the relational and distinct components in the working of the Word and Spirit in the world by developing a "trinitarian

165 The original text is as follows: "Now God shall be glorified in His handiwork, fitting it so as to be conformable to, and modelled after, His own Son. *For by the hands of the* Father, *that is, by the Son and the* Holy Spirit [italics mine], man, and not [merely] a part of man, was made in the likeness of God. Now, the soul and the spirit are certainly a *part* of the man, but certainly not *the* man; for the perfect man consists in the commingling and the union of the soul receiving the spirit of the Father, and the admixture of that fleshly nature which was moulded after the image of God." Irenaeus, *Against Heresies*, Book V, Chapter VI, New Advent, accessed September 28, 2016, http://www.newadvent.org/fathers/0103506.htm. For a detailed discussion on the thoughts of Irenaeus, see Robert M. Grant, *Irenaeus of Lyons* (London: Routledge, 1997).

166 Amos Yong, *Discerning the Spirit(s): A Pentecostal-Charismatic Contribution to Christian Theology of Religions* (England: Sheffield Academic Press, 2000), 61–62.

167 Yong, *Discerning the Spirit(s),* 62. Yong's choice of the notion of dimension here is to avoid spatialisation of hierarchisation of reality in the recognition of unity above conflicts.

168 Yong, *Discerning the Spirit(s),* 62.

169 Yong, *Discerning the Spirit(s),* 64.

metaphysics of creation."[170] The reason for Yong's interest in developing such metaphysics is that it can prove to have potential for highlighting the relationship between one and the many, the unity in relationship to plurality. Moltmann and Tanner of course talk about unity and diversity, but not in terms of a dialectic and in their theologies, there is a basic lack of a foundational theory for upholding the dialectic. Yong shows why turning to such a trinitarian metaphysics of creation is suitable for his project of emphasising relational, but distinct economies of the Spirit and the Word. He writes,

> Most pertinent for our purposes is the perennial connection made between the Spirit and universality in the history of Christian thought . . . the Christian encounter with the non-Christian religions in the twentieth century has led many to align the domain of the Spirit with that of the cosmos or creation at large even as that of Christ's has been more strictly delimited to the incarnation and the church. What we have in common with everything and everyone else, regardless of nationality, ethnicity, or gender, is our createdness—our dependence on something other than ourselves.[171]

To develop such metaphysics, Yong turns to Robert Neville, a philosophical theologian in the American pragmatist tradition. Yong draws from him his theory of creation, *ex nihilo*, in particularly addressing the problem of the relationship between the one and the many. Neville begins by exploring what the pluralities of the world are and that they are held together. Yong notes Neville's suggestion that "the manyness of the world is held together in relative unity rather than being simply a welter of chaotic pluralities."[172] Yong agrees with Neville that "a thing is what it is only by virtue of its being determinate relative to other things, and what relates any two things is itself a third."[173] Neville posits that God is the indeterminate, who holds together the pluralities of this universe. Yong argues that in this sense God is the indeterminate, the transcendent creator of all things, *ex nihilo*. Creation is distinct from God in terms of being determinate by its relationship to other things, but Yong argues with Neville that the creative act of God is trinitarian in character. Yong agrees with Neville that "an analysis of the creative act itself reveals creator, created, and the power of creating that mediates between the two."[174] Conceived from another angle, this trinitarian character unveils a harmonious configuration of pluralities bound together by norms of determinateness. These

170 Yong, *Discerning the Spirit(s)*, 104.
171 Yong, *Discerning the Spirit(s)*, 105.
172 Yong, *Discerning the Spirit(s)*, 105.
173 Yong, *Discerning the Spirit(s)*, 105.
174 Yong, *Discerning the Spirit(s)*, 108.

normativities in themselves are entirely transcendent and indeterminate since they are prior to all harmonies that exist. Yong explains what this implies when expressed in terms of the Logos/Word and the Spirit trajectory. He writes: "What we have then is God as the aboriginal source, the Logos as the norm, and the Spirit as the power of the eternal creative act, each relative to the created order."[175] Yong contends that in this way, it is possible to avoid the difficult conjectures of the immanent Trinity while, at the same time, understanding the trinitarian act of God in creation clearly expressed through the joint working of the Spirit and the Word.[176]

Moving on further, Yong adopts and modifies the metaphysics of the American pragmatic philosopher, Charles Sanders Peirce, which categorises reality in terms of *firstness*, the quality of a thing in itself; *secondness*, the factuality of things in relation to others; and *thirdness*, the norms and generalities that mediate between the above two.[177] Yong further explains thirdness thus: On an ontological level, *thirdness* is relationality and process; on a metaphysical level, it is rationality and legality that points to the Spirit as the divine wisdom or mind; on the logical level, it is generality and vagueness. Yong elaborates the last as:

> suggestive of reality and of the relationship between the one and the many, the universal and particular. This is the Spirit as the universal-particular and particular-universal, the perennial hidden member of the divine trinity, always pointing away from the Spirit to the Father and the Son.[178]

Further, elaborating on such metaphysics, Yong shows that the Spirit can be understood as "divine law that endowed reality with continuity and as the divine interpretant that is God's experiencing, cognizing, evaluating, and responding to the world."[179] Thus, applying trinitarian relations to Peircean metaphysics, Yong maintains that the Father is the "qualitative source of creative efficacy" and the Son is "the decisive sign or image of the Father through whom the Godhead is embodied and efficaciously interacts with the world," and the Spirit is "the interpretant of the divine relationality both ad intra and ad extra."[180] Thus, the firstness with its attendant abstraction is correlated with the Father, the secondness with the concreteness of the Son, and the thirdness with the dynamism of the Spirit. William Oliverio notes that against Hegelian dialectics or dualism,

---

175 Yong, *Discerning the Spirit(s)*, 108.

176 Yong, *Discerning the Spirit(s)*, 108–109.

177 Yong, *Discerning the Spirit(s)*, 112.

178 Yong, *Discerning the Spirit(s)*, 112.

179 Yong, *Discerning the Spirit(s)*, 111.

180 Amos Yong, *Spirit-Word-Community: Theological Hermeneutics in Trinitarian Perspective* (Eugene, OR: Wipf & Stock, 2002), 95.

Yong's dependence on Pierce's metaphysics leads him to claim that a relational pneumatology "mediates the poles of abstract and concrete as an essential third force."[181]

Yong claims that the Spirit helps us to know reality by interpreting the symbolic in creation for us. "Every determination of being therefore reveals the divine through the Word and by the Spirit, at least partially. The more intense the concentrations of the form of the Logos in any field of the Spirit, the more harmonious the determination of being."[182] Yong is convinced that pneumatological relationality[183] is crucial in order to understand the relationship of one and many, universality and particularity, God's relationship to the world, and vice-versa.[184] He notes that "Pneumatological relationality, however, is a distinctively complex form of interrelationality which includes duality, transcends and yet preserves the distinctiveness of the transcended dyad even while such transcendence posits the third precisely as imminent in the dyad."[185] Yong quotes James Loder to further clarify the aspect of relationality of the Spirit.

> That God is Spirit (John 4) and that the Spirit is also one member of the Trinity (John 17, Eph 2:18, 4:4–6) is not a contradiction. The potential confusion is resolved if it is recognized that it is inherent in the nature of

---

181 L.W. Oliverio Jr., "An Interpretive Review Essay on Amos Yong's Spirit-Word-Community: Theological Hermeneutics in Trinitarian Perspective," *Journal of Pentecostal Theology* 18 (2009): 306.

182 Yong, *Discerning the Spirit(s)*, 118.

183 To highlight pneumatological relationality, Yong also takes recourse to Augustinian mutual love model. He takes clues from David Coffey and Thomas Weinandy to highlight the Spirit's relationality to the Trinity. For David Coffey, see *Grace: The Gift of the Holy Spirit* (Milwaukee, WI: Marquette University Press, 2011) and *Deus Trinitas: The Doctrine of the Triune God* (New York: Oxford University Press, 1999). For Weinandy, see *The Father's Spirit of Sonship: Reconceiving the Trinity* (Edinburgh: T&T Clark, 1995). Yong draws three implications from the mutual love model for pneumatology and the Trinity. First, as the mutual love of the Father and the Son, the Holy Spirit brings the triune life to fullness. Second, both the Irenaean and Augustinian models preserve the Spirit's unique mission in both the immanent and economic Trinity, without subordinating it to the Son and Father's roles. Third, the relationality of the Spirit plays a vital role in the doctrine of trinitarian co-inherence. As the Father and Son's mutual love, the Holy Spirit completes the triune identity of God; the Spirit emerges as a distinct person and as the one who fulfils the Father and Son's communion. See Yong, *Spirit-Word-Community*, 73–75, cited and discussed in Steven M. Studebaker, "Towards a Pneumatological Trinitarian Theology: Amos Yong, the Spirit and Trinity," in Vondey and Mittelstadt, *Theology of Amos Yong*, 87.

184 Yong, *Spirit-Word-Community*, 59.

185 Yong, *Spirit-Word-Community*, 75.

> the Spirit to be relational and at the same time to relate to itself. That is, both God is Spirit and has Spirit.[186]

Yong claims that a pneumatological theology holds dialectics in tension. He writes,

> While pneumatology in abstraction gives rise precisely to the theological and philosophical wrong turns of speculative or absolute idealism (Hegel), a robust pneumatological theology brings vagueness and generality together with the distinctiveness, particularity, and individuality of concrete actualities. Here, the subject-object distinction or difference is not only preserved but insisted upon, yet not in the Cartesian sense of re-asserting a metaphysical dualism between the knower and the known.[187]

While highlighting how a pneumatological theology brings together the universality and the particularity, Yong argues that the historical particularity of the incarnation of the Logos goes hand in hand with the cosmic universality of the Spirit. But, on the other hand, there is also a universal dimension to Logos as the particular dimension of the Spirit.[188] In order to elaborate on the above functionally, Yong describes the dimension of the Word as "the thisness and whatness of things . . .; that of the Spirit is the howness and relatedness of things—their continuity and significance."[189] Yong explains that "the Logos as concretely manifest in Jesus is revealed to us by the Spirit. . . .. Apart from the Logos, the Spirit is impotent and empty . . . whereas Logos-Christology accounts for the what of incarnation, the Spirit-Christology answers the question of how."[190] In other words, Yong claims that the determination of beings in creation is a joint action of the Word and the Spirit. He writes that both Word and Spirit are "universally present and active because they are at the heart of every particular determination of being, albeit in different ways."[191] This correspondence between Word and the Spirit is supremely shown in Jesus's incarnation. Yong writes,

> Every determination of being exhibits the presence and activity of the divine being: Father creating something through the Logos by the Spirit.

186 James Loder, *The Logic of Spirit: Human Development in Theological Perspective* (San Francisco: Jossey-Bass Publishers, 1989), 195, cited in Yong, *Spirit-Word-Community*, 57.

187 Yong, *Spirit-Word-Community*, 104.

188 Yong, *Discerning the Spirit(s)*, 116. Yong refers to Colin Gunton's work here. See Colin Gunton, *The One, the Three and the Many: God, Creation and the Culture of Modernity* (Cambridge: Cambridge University Press, 1993), 180–209.

189 Yong, *Discerning the Spirit(s)*, 116.

190 Yong, *Discerning the Spirit(s)*, 119.

191 Yong, *Discerning the Spirit(s)*, 116.

> The person of Jesus is simply the most complete instance of this. It should therefore be clear that even as pneumatology needs Christology, so is the reverse true. Apart from the Spirit, the Word remains indeterminate.[192]

In other words, every living being is determined by God's presence in Word and Spirit, but it is only in Jesus that this mutuality is revealed perfectly. In terms of Logos Christology, following Neville, Yong argues that to say Jesus was the incarnation of the Logos is to say that the character of God is epitomised in Jesus in the "form, components, actuality, and value" of God in some perfect way.[193] In terms of Spirit Christology, Yong contends that the Holy Spirit is "the measure of divine activity, the guarantee of continuity in the divine plan of salvation, the legal guardian of the divine intentions, the mediator of the Logos to the world, and the presentational reality of God to the human inferential perception, illuminating especially to those who have faith."[194] What this means is that the presence and activity of the Logos in Jesus and derivatively in creation is set within the movement of the force fields of the Spirit: "The Logos is the concrete form or pattern of each thing even as the Spirit is the power of its actualization and instantiation."[195]

Setting this dialectic in the context of the church, Yong explains that the church continues to be influenced by the life of Jesus, which releases a powerful force field, through the resurrection power of the Spirit. Yong suggests that the church has both continuity and discontinuity between itself and the incarnation through the Spirit. The continuity is in terms of the norms, ideals, and values most completely revealed in the person of Jesus. We get a heightened sense of the Spirit's presence through our participation in Christ's body. The discontinuity is in the imperfection of the church in following such norms. However, Yong claims that in the incarnation of Jesus and the Church, the actualisation of the Logos occurs by the working of the Spirit.[196] Oliverio admits that in this way, the dialectics of the abstract and the concrete, the unity and plurality, the universality and the particularity, work in Yong's theology. He writes,

> Yong's understanding of the dynamism of reality . . . [exists] alongside concreteness and abstraction. Such a dynamic and relational metaphysics entails both unity and continuation in truth and plurality, difference,

[192] Yong, *Discerning the Spirit(s)*, 120.

[193] Yong, *Discerning the Spirit(s)*, 116–17; cf. Robert Cummings Neville, *A Theology Primer* (Albany, NY: State University New York Press, 1991), 45.

[194] Yong, *Discerning the Spirit(s)*, 117. Yong shows this drawing on the charismatic Jesuit theologian Donald Gelpi's pneumatological appropriation of C.S. Pierce's categories as mentioned earlier.

[195] Yong, *Discerning the Spirit(s)*, 118.

[196] Yong, *Discerning the Spirit(s)*, 123.

and change. Yong's metaphysics gives account of *both* the oneness *and* plurality of things.[197]

In the preceding discussion, we have explored the potential of the Irenaean metaphor[198] as the ground for a permeable Spirit ecclesiology and showed its usefulness in maintaining the dialectics of relational-distinctiveness in terms of the one and the many, the universal and particular, the spiritual and concrete, and unity and diversity. Now let us see how this dialectic plays out in the conception of the nature, ministry, and mission of the church in Yong's model.

## Permeable Spirit ecclesiology in Yong's model

### *The nature of Spirit ecclesiology*

One of Yong's central theses on Spirit ecclesiology is found in his book, *The Spirit Poured Out on All Flesh*,[199] which states that "the church is an organic, dynamic, and eschatological people of God called after the name of Jesus and constituted in the fellowship of the Holy Spirit."[200]

In terms of conceiving the nature of the church, one of the ways Yong maintains the dialectics we have previously mentioned is by holding together varied and even contrasting traditions of understanding the church. Yong tries to hold the classical, Reformation, and contemporary

197 L. William Oliverio Jr., "The One and the Many," in Vondey and Mittelstadt, *Theology of Amos*, 57.

198 Yong has been criticised for his use of Irenaeus's model. Steven Studebaker points out that Yong's use of the Irenaean metaphor of the two hands of the Father to highlight two distinct economies of the Son and the Spirit and an emphasis on the latter is controversial. At times, it seems that the Spirit's role, for example, in a theology of religions could proceed without a functional dependence on Christology. Though Yong emphasizes on the mutuality of the two economies, generally, it seems that Christology comes after pneumatology instead of being simultaneous. But, Veli Mati Kärkäinnen observes that Yong essentially broadens the framework especially of his theology of religions through pneumatology, but does not separate Christology from pneumatology. Yong has been commended for his efforts, however, to show that a pneumatological theology "grants God's redemptive and empowering presence through Christ implicitly greater breadth," and for highlighting the Spirit's witness to Jesus outside the boundaries of the church. But, on the other hand, pentecostal theologian Simon Chan observes that Yong does not represent the deepest pentecostal instinct as he seems to surrender the particularity of Christ to the expansiveness of the Spirit. There are others who disagree. Ritchie notes that Yong might be representing the inclusive genre of the Pentecostals while Chan represents the exclusivist. For the above critiques of Amos Yong's theology, see Vondey and Mittelstadt, *Theology of Amos Yong*.

199 Amos Yong, *The Spirit Poured Out on All Flesh: Pentecostalism and the Possibility of Global Theology* (Grand Rapids, MI: Baker Academic, 2005).

200 Yong, *Spirit Poured Out*, 22.

understandings of the church in tension and contends that all these concerns should be taken into account when developing a contemporary ecclesiology. He begins by classifying ecclesiology historically and theologically into four types: "classical," "free churches," "spiritual body" and "postliberal ecclesiology."[201] The classical type holds that there is an integral link between baptism and salvation, and the church's prerogative for baptism as initiation into the Christian community successfully accommodated the notion of *extra ecclesiam nulla salus*.[202] The free-church ecclesiologies, following from the Reformation and through the idea of the priesthood of all believers, emerged more as a congregationalist and democratic institution, and through their pietistic influence emphasised an individualistic understanding of salvation of Christ instead of salvation mediated exclusively through the church.[203] On the other hand, those who understand the church as a spiritual body, in Yong's terms, "soteriological inclusivists,"[204] share a notion of the church not as a visible, hierarchical, and institutional body, but a church that is a spiritual reality.

This mystical-spiritual body of Christ, the church, therefore, would include those who explicitly confess the name of Christ and even those who are not aware of the name of Christ, yet are spiritually united to him by the power of the Spirit.[205] The postliberal ecclesiologies stress that the church should not be defined by outside forces, neither Constantinian (church as controlled by the secular state) or post-Enlightenment dictates of reason and liberalism. Rather, Christians and the church should be an alternative community, distinct with their own ethical principles, narratives, and virtues that help to distinguish the church and also make the world aware of what it is.[206] This parallels Hauerwas's ecclesiology as discussed earlier. Yong thinks that all of the above ecclesiological perspectives make valid contributions, which should not be brushed aside. Thus, for Yong, conceiving the nature of the church includes a critical appropriation and holding of all these traditions in tension. Yong claims that

> the classical ecclesiologies can no longer be simply dismissed in our ecumenical age, just as free-church ecclesiologies cannot be uncritically repeated. Further, the pentecostal disposition toward spiritualizing the nature of the church demands that the promise and challenges of

201 Yong, *Spirit Poured Out*, 128.

202 *extra ecclesiam nulla salus* means "outside the church, no salvation." Yong, *Spirit Poured Out*, 128.

203 Yong, *Spirit Poured Out*, 128–129.

204 Yong, *Spirit Poured Out*, 130.

205 Yong, *Spirit Poured Out*, 130.

206 Yong, *Spirit Poured Out*, 130–131. Yong in fact refers to Stanley Hauerwas and George Lindbeck while explaining this category.

> soteriological inclusivism be confronted. Finally, the embodied and communal vision of postliberal ecclesiologies is attractive for various reasons today.[207]

In other words, Yong seeks to open interactive spaces for conversation between different ecclesiologies. Various ecclesiologies have their contribution to make if one wants to build a contemporary ecclesiology. The classical ecclesiologies cannot be dismissed, simply because they are time-worn. On the other hand, the free-church ecclesiologies can be critically appropriated. The pentecostal ecclesiologies with their inclination towards spiritualising ought also to be soteriologically inclusive. Moreover, the postliberal ecclesiologies can be relevant due to their particular stress on embodiedness.

From the perspective of a permeable ecclesiology with porous and softened borders, the above consideration—holding different traditions of understanding the church in tension—holds promises for softening of the borders of the churches between them. A possibility is opened here for more ecumenical dialogue and cooperation between the churches as they are led to consider and respect the positions and perspectives of others while holding on to their own. This opens the way for enriching each other's traditions through mutual dialogue and sharing of perspectives. Here, it will be interesting to consider whether Yong's ecclesiological framework can accommodate or hold in tension Moltmann's social trinitarian model, Hauerwas's ecclesiocentric model, and Tanner's christo-theocentric models. Situating their models in the Irenaean paradigm would mean that Moltmann's relational character of ecclesiology in the Spirit would be complemented by the embodied contrastive character of Hauerwas's church; further qualified by the christo-theocentric nature of the human community dependent on God and modelled on Jesus's life.

Yong moves on to deal with the four marks of the church: One, Holy, Catholic, and Apostolic, in terms of the dialectical features of universality-particularity, the spiritual and the concrete, unity-diversity, and the static and the dynamic. Yong discusses the four marks drawing from Yves Congar's pneumatological ecclesiology, but goes beyond it.[208] Yong's concept of oneness and unity recognises the essential diversity in the church and the world while affirming unity in the Spirit. Yong's concern is rather that unity should not be centred on a particular church and that both the spiritual and embodied realities of the church are upheld. In this endeavour, Yong uses and goes beyond Yves Congar's proposals of

[207] Yong, *Spirit Poured Out*, 131.

[208] See Yves Congar, *I Believe in the Holy Spirit*, trans. David Smith, 3 vols. (New York: Geoffrey Chapman, 1983) in Yong, *Spirit Poured Out*, 133.

pneumatological ecclesiology, emphasising unity in terms of the centrality of the Spirit and Christ in contrast to the particular Roman Catholic self-understanding of unity only under the Roman Catholic Church.[209] In the Roman Catholic conception, the church is essentially understood to be united in the Petrine office, which Yong points out as a "scandal of particularity in the ecumenical church's self-understanding."[210] Instead, Yong contends that a pneumatological/pentecostal ecclesiology would deny that the unity of the church is solely based on any one episcopate. Unity is both spiritual and concrete in Yong: he explains that unity is to be concretely manifested through the recognition of diversity among different forms of the church.[211] Here, the unity of the Spirit in the church links itself to the concreteness of the manifested Word incarnated in the church through its embodiedness.

Yong further notes that this unity is not the abstract unity of the so-called "universal" or "invisible" church. It remains spiritual, but that does not negate the church's eschatological, particularistic, and sacramental aspects. Yong holds that there is an aspect of "Pentecostal sacramentality,"[212] not in the sense of salvation mediated through priesthood or sacraments, but through the presence of the Spirit as in Jesus, in terms of an "incarnational logic"[213] palpably, through "the materiality of personal embodiment and congregational life."[214] While concreteness and particularity is thus evidenced, the Spirit poured out eschatologically, the "Word made flesh and the Spirit breathing and making the Word real"[215] in and through the church constitutes the one work of the triune God. Here, ecclesial unity is envisaged as both spiritual and embodied and exemplifies the notion of unity in diversity.[216] However, this unity is not static as it is eschatological in the recognition of our status as being united, but also in a process of continued efforts at unity until its perfection is reached at the eschaton. Yong proposes that "the church is one only even while she is being made one"[217] and at present, we have only a foretaste of this communion through the Holy Spirit in the church. [218]

---

209 Yong, *Spirit Poured Out*, 135.
210 Yong, *Spirit Poured Out*, 135.
211 Yong, *Spirit Poured Out*, 135.
212 Yong, *Spirit Poured Out*, 136
213 Yong, *Spirit Poured Out*, 136.
214 Yong, *Spirit Poured Out*, 136.
215 Yong, *Spirit Poured Out*, 136–137
216 Yong, *Spirit Poured Out*, 136–137.
217 Yong, *Spirit Poured Out*, 139.
218 Yong, *Spirit Poured Out*, 139.

A further dimension to unity of the churches and beyond is brought about by Yong's linking of unity with the idea of hospitality of God. He states that "the Christian practice of hospitality is the means through which Christians encounter the *poiesis*[219] of the Spirit not only in and through other Christian movements (the ecumenical context), but also through those outside the church."[220] Yong explains ecumenical unity occurs through the pouring out of the Spirit ensuring that "the many tongues and many gifts of the Spirit are particular expressions of the church universal, each with its own role in the wider church and indispensable regardless of how small or insignificant such may appear."[221] Yong proposes a pneumatological solution to the challenges of ecumenism. He states that

> if the challenges posed by ecumenical division do not seem capable of being resolved either through structural-institutional organization or through doctrinal-theological agreement, perhaps the many tongues of Pentecost is suggestive of a new model of ecumenical relationship which features unity precisely through diversity.[222]

Yong's suggestion of the unity of the church centred on the Spirit and Christ following from the Irenaean metaphor ensures, on the one hand, that the church's institution and constitution are grounded on God. On the other hand, it rescues the church from ecclesiocentrism that prioritises one church over the other, which is a barrier to ecumenism. His holding in tension of the spiritual-concrete and the universal-particular dialectics of the nature of the church gives room for negotiating and softening of the borders among the churches that hold either of the poles. Actually, Yong's concept of unity and ecumenism somewhat resembles Moltmann's dependence on the unity in the Spirit brought about by the pouring out of the Spirit at Pentecost. However, Moltmann does not use the concept of hospitality to conceptualise unity as Yong does.

Further, dialectics are brought in with regard to Yong's understanding of the holiness of the church. This holds in tension the static and the dynamic characters, the individual and the corporate, and an idea of sanctification that features a separated community while still engaging as a distinctively prophetic one. Yong agrees with Congar that a

---

219 *Poiesis* means "creativity."

220 Amos Yong, *Hospitality and the Other: Pentecost, Christian Practices, and the Neighbor* (Maryknoll, NY: Orbis Books, 2008), 62.

221 Amos Yong, *In the Days of Caesar: Pentecostalism and Political Theology—The Cadbury Lectures 2009* (Grand Rapids, MI: William B. Eerdmans, 2010), 94.

222 Yong, *Spirit Poured Out*, 22. See Jakob D. Dodson, "Divine Hospitality and Human Diversity," in Vondey and Mittelstadt, *Theology of Amos Yong*, 133.

pneumatological/pentecostal[223] ecclesiology would hold the Spirit to be both the principle and sanctifying agent of the church, but reminds us that holiness is brought about as a dynamic eschatological gift.[224] Sanctification is understood here as the setting apart of members of the body of Christ from the world by the Spirit for the work of the kingdom. The Spirit empowers believers with "power from on high" (Luke 24:49; Acts 1:8) in order for them to be witnesses for the kingdom.[225] In this aspect, holiness becomes a dynamic reality while considered within the wider ambit of the kingdom of God. This view of holiness also mediates between individual holiness—as in free-church traditions—and corporate ones, through participation in the practices of the church as in postliberal ecclesiologies.[226] Yong's concept of holiness in the Spirit is concretised through the building up of an egalitarian community but with a distinguishing mark. Yong suggests that the pouring out of the Spirit has an eschatological dimension (Joel 2) that levels out "socioeconomic, ethnic, and gender differences even while these . . . identify, mark, and guide the people of God."[227] The distinguishing marks of the community here are the witness of Christ through the *kerygma*, but also the prophetic engagement, and socioethically, its care for the least and the vulnerable.[228] This understanding of dynamic holiness has the potential to bring the churches together, appreciating each other's journey towards the goal of the kingdom, while avoiding complacency and a sense of superiority in interchurch relations. While on the journey of holiness, the church in the Spirit develops a critical and prophetic edge in its relation to the world. Yong thus comes fairly close to Moltmann in his view of holiness as dynamic, and he also shares with Moltmann the sense that the building of an egalitarian community is dynamic.

Regarding the catholicity of the church, Yong once more brings forward the dialectics of the static and dynamic features; particular (locality or concreteness) and universal. Yong's emphasis on catholicity is based on the eschatological universality of the kingdom of God. These concepts are similar to Moltmann's understanding of catholicity. In this sense, a pneumatological/pentecostal ecclesiology would affirm that the catholicity of the church cannot be separated from the universality of the kingdom which will be fully manifested in the end (Rev 21:22–26). Yong holds that

223 In his corpus, Yong uses pneumatological and pentecostal ecclesiology interchangeably.

224 Yong, *Spirit Poured Out*, 139.

225 Yong, *Spirit Poured Out*, 140.

226 Yong, *Spirit Poured Out*, 141.

227 Yong, *Spirit Poured Out*, 141.

228 Yong, *Spirit Poured Out*, 140.

this catholicity is both static and dynamic as "the church is catholic and being made catholic."[229] This catholicity is universal as the church extends the mission of Jesus in the Spirit to various peoples, tribes, and nations, signifying the "whole faith" as belonging to "the whole body of Christ for the whole world."[230] This universality is also particular as the church situates itself in diverse cultural/national contexts bound together by "the experiences of Jesus in the power of the Spirit."[231] In this sense, the church's catholicity is integrally connected to missiological efforts that situate the gospel in a particular culture, language, and context. Here, the basic assumption is that the gospel belongs to all peoples and particular peoples and that its reception should be in one's own indigenous terms.[232] This cultural mutuality on the other hand, argues Yong, provides "theological rationale for embracing cultural diversity" that is "embodied and environmentally rooted."[233] Yong holds that "catholicity neither excludes nor minimises particularity; rather, each particular is caught up into the church catholic by the Spirit poured out on all flesh. In this way, the church's catholicity is informed concretely by her historicity and locality."[234]

In terms of apostolicity, Yong understands it as following on from the apostles, and the proclamation by the members of the church of the apostolic message of the death and resurrection of Christ. Yong agrees with Congar that the Spirit empowers this missionary charge and the Spirit enables the correct faith to be preserved from error. Yong contends that "the Spirit is . . . given to the Church as its transcendent principle of faithfulness."[235] Yong's effort of holding divergent views in tension is evident again as he addresses the controversial question of the apostolic succession of the papal office of Peter from a pneumatological perspective and seeks to build a bridge between the Roman Catholic and Protestant denominations. Yong claims, through a re-reading of the Jerusalem Council account (Acts 15:1–29, especially 15:28) that it was ultimately the charismatic illumination of the Spirit that sanctioned the apostolic authority to reach a final decision on the dispute and not the other way round.[236] He hopes that in so far as the "magisterium is led by the Spirit,"

---

229 Yong, *Spirit Poured Out*, 144.
230 Yong, *Spirit Poured Out*, 143.
231 Yong, *Spirit Poured Out*, 145.
232 Yong, *Spirit Poured Out*, 145.
233 Amos Yong, "Poured Out on All Flesh: The Spirit, World Pentecostalism, and the Renewal of Theology and Praxis in the 21st Century," *Penteco Studies* 6, no. 1 (2007): 33–34.
234 Yong, *Spirit Poured Out*, 146.
235 Yong, *Spirit Poured Out*, 146.
236 Yong, *Spirit Poured Out*, 150.

there should not be a hindrance among other Christians to recognising the "provisional authority of the Pope (or episcopate) as a symbolic representation of the apostolic faith"[237] and in eschatological anticipation of its full realisation in the "*pleroma* of Christ" (Eph 4:11–13).[238] Yong claims that there is potential in the pneumatological perspective to build a bridge between different confessions that are divided on dichotomies in theology and practice. He argues,

> it is perhaps only from a pneumatological perspective that the dichotomies between apostolic succession and restoration, between Episcopal and congregational structures, between tradition as past and as presently instantiated, between councils/creeds and kerygmatic proclamation, and so forth, might be overcome.[239]

In the preceding discussion of the nature of the church, it is clearly evident that the relational-distinctive dialectics are played out in terms of universal and particular, spiritual-concrete, unity-diversity, static-dynamic features, and a bringing together of different traditions and perspectives of the church. This enables the church to be relational in the Spirit with other churches and traditions, yet brings a distinct and particular character regarding its own traditions. On the other hand, it enables the church to be particular and distinct regarding the witness of Christ while being relational in terms of its particular context. Here, the distinctively relational and relationally distinct dialectics come into play leading to a permeable church in the Spirit.

### *The ministries of the church in the Spirit*

In the ministries of the church, a clear joint working of the Spirit and Christ manifests itself through the church's liturgy and the sacraments. Here, the ministries of the Spirit lead the believer into a deeper relationship with Christ. Yong understands the church to be a sacrament with the Spirit operative in and through worship, liturgy, baptism, and the Lord's Supper. It is the presence and action of the Spirit that makes the whole church sacramental in its "structures, institutions, practices, congregations, and individuals, all inspired by the Spirit of God for the purposes of establishing the kingdom of God."[240] Sacraments are not here limited to baptism and the Lord's Supper, as in the Protestant thought.[241] The acts

237 Yong, *Spirit Poured Out*, 150.
238 Yong, *Spirit Poured Out*, 150.
239 Yong, *Spirit Poured Out*, 151.
240 Yong, *Spirit Poured Out*, 156.
241 The Roman Catholic Church recognises seven sacraments: Baptism, Eucharist, Penance, Confirmation, Marriage, Holy Orders, and Anointing of the Sick.

of the Spirit in the church become all comprehensive as the entire liturgy or worship becomes a "sacrament of the Spirit."[242] This notion of *church as sacrament* is not new. This type of ecclesiology began with Cyprian and Augustine, and was followed up by Aquinas among others.[243] Avery Dulles argues that this model is especially useful to bring together an institutional and mystical (spiritual) model of the church and serves to solve the problem of the relationship between a visible community and a "communion of grace."[244] In Yong's model, the church as a sacrament becomes both spiritual and concrete through the joint action of the Spirit and the Word. In this sense, through the Holy Spirit, the eschatological resurrection power of Christ is made present in the worshipping community that is transformed progressively into the image of Christ.[245]

The presence and action of the Spirit enables "testimony, confessional praise, manifestation of charisms, of word of wisdom, word of knowledge, and tongues and their interpretations."[246] Therefore, in and through the liturgy and the word of Christ, in the power of the Spirit, the church "accomplishes transformation, grants forgiveness, provides release, reconciles the estranged" and "exorcises the demonic" in our daily lives,[247] emphasising both the spiritual and material (bodily) aspects. Thus, a pneumatological theology of liturgy emphasises the "centrality of the Spirit's presence and activity" in the worship of God even as the word of Christ quickens through the Spirit to give life to people not only in worship, but also in daily life.[248] Here, liturgy and worship, though spiritual, become embodied and concrete in the real lives of the people.

Yong's understanding of the sacraments of baptism and the Lord's Supper also holds in tension the action of the Spirit and the Word. In terms of baptism, he holds the significance of both water and Spirit baptism together. Yong upholds the role of the Spirit in both, along with its christological implications. Following on from the document of *Baptism, Eucharist, and Ministry* (BEM),[249] Yong explains baptism. Baptism as a

242 Yong draws this phrase from the Theological-Historical Commission for the Great Jubilee of the Year 2000, *The Holy Spirit, Lord and Giver of Life*, trans. Agostino Bono (New York: Crossroad, 1998), 92, and Walter Hollenweger, *Pentecostalism: Origins and Developments Worldwide* (Peabody, MA: Hendrickson, 1997).

243 See Avery Cardinal Dulles SJ, *Models of the Church*, exp. ed. (New York: Doubleday, 2002), 55.

244 Dulles, *Models of the Church*, 65.

245 Yong, *Spirit Poured Out*, 161.

246 Yong, *Spirit Poured Out*, 162.

247 Yong, *Spirit Poured Out*, 162.

248 Yong, *Spirit Poured Out*, 161.

249 World Council of Churches, *Baptism, Eucharist and Ministry*, Faith and Order Paper 111 (Geneva: WCC, 1982).

Christian rite includes the invocation of the Holy Spirit, the gifts and the fruit of the Spirit and their reception, and our participation in the death and resurrection of Christ.[250] It includes the corresponding transforming act of God's grace on the community of faith in the "entire process of initiation, confirmation, discipleship, and ongoing . . . conversion."[251] Yong particularly stresses Spirit baptism along with this. He affirms that Spirit baptism is an open invitation by Jesus to all (John 16:7–8); including repentance and baptism for the forgiveness of sins (Acts 2:38); being justified, sanctified, and made righteous through the Spirit's raising of Jesus from the dead (Rom 4:25). It also unites and empowers believers in the resurrected power of Christ in the Spirit and is the down payment for the eschatological redemption of God (Eph 1:13–14; 2 Cor 1:21–22), which also implies redemption through *theosis* (deification) and consequent participation in the divine nature.[252] What is evident in separately outlining the implications of water and Spirit baptism in the above is that, while water baptism ensures participation in the death and resurrection of Christ and the community of new creation, the church, Spirit baptism actually enables repentance and transformation, and empowers this participation and sanctification of the baptised in Christ. Here, one cannot occur without the other as both contribute to salvation.

Regarding the Lord's Supper, Yong understands it as creating an alternative community, providing prophetic direction and counter-discourse. He writes that the Lord's Supper "celebrates its constitution through the transgression of all legal, class, gender, sexual, ethnic, and national boundaries."[253] This is the relational aspect of the Lord's Supper that creates an egalitarian community brought about by the action of the Spirit. This has parallels to the egalitarian community envisaged in Moltmann's Spirit ecclesiology. This same community with its prophetic Word introduces an alternative way of life and a counter discourse in contrast to the world.[254] The Spirit also works simultaneously to make the community prophetic and to liberate individuals and communities in Christ "to enact the kingdom of the future in the present."[255]

250 Yong, *Spirit Poured Out*, 158–159.
251 Yong, *Spirit Poured Out*, 160.
252 Yong, *Spirit Poured Out*, 102.
253 Yong, *Spirit Poured Out*, 165.
254 Yong, *Spirit Poured Out*, 165.
255 Yong, *Spirit Poured Out*, 165.

## *Mission of the church in the Spirit*

Yong's concept of the mission of the church involves the broad spectrum from interfaith engagement to creation and cosmos. Here too, it will be evident that Yong continues to maintain the dialectics of relational-distinctiveness in the church's mission to other religions as well as to creation and the earth. Yong's interreligious engagement is built on the joint working of the Spirit and Christ in a trinitarian framework. Here, the relational aspect with other religions can be said to have been expressed in his development of the concept of "foundational pneumatology" and a common human experience, which he terms "pneumatological imagination." Again, it is evident that the universality found in this enterprise also includes concreteness and particularity. On the other hand, the distinctive and critical aspect of Christianity's relationship with other religions is its continuing struggle to search for the criterion of discernment, which occupies a crucial position in his theology of religions.

Yong seeks to engage with other religions on the basis of his concept of foundational pneumatology.[256] He deals with the particular nature of such foundational pneumatology in *Beyond the Impasse*,[257] drawing on Donald Gelpi's foundational pneumatology,[258] but with a difference. Foundational pneumatology, for Gelpi, meant "a fundamental category of reality, including God, as descriptive of human experience, and as both prescriptive and normative for the ways in which Christians (and others) have and should experience God."[259] Gelpi took Christian conversion experience as normative, which Yong rejects as narrow and proposes instead a "pneumatological imagination" as human experience.[260] The proposal of a common experience in terms of pneumatological imagination shows a holding in tension of several aspects of the dialectics of human experience. He writes that it is

256 Yong claims to have arrived at a Christ-centred and Spirit-driven theology and ecclesiology inspired by the work of the Roman Catholic theologian Adam Mohler to start with. But, he goes beyond Mohler into what he calls "shifting foundationalism" in a foundational pneumatology in the direction of assigning particular agency to the Spirit in a trinitarian framework, which Mohler could not ultimately arrive at, as Yong argues.

257 Amos Yong, *Beyond the Impasse: A Pneumatological Theology of Religions* (Eugene, OR: Wipf & Stock Publishers, 2003).

258 See Donald L. Gelpi, S.J., *The Divine Mother: A Trinitarian Theology of the Holy Spirit* (Lanham, MD: University Press of America, 1984).

259 Amos Yong, *Beyond the Impasse: Toward a Pneumatological Theology of Religions* (Eugene, OR: Wipf & Stock, 2003), 59–60.

260 Yong, *Beyond the Impasse*, 60– 64.

> a way of seeing God, self, and the world that is inspired by the . . . experience of the Spirit (and includes the dialectics of) Scripture and experience, of thought and practice, of theology and doxology, of reason and narrative, of object and subject, of a priori rationality and posterior empiricism, of the self and its sociohistoric location, in community, in all knowledge.[261]

The claim here seems to be that there is a general experience of God in humans through the presence and action of the Spirit, in its universality and particularity that can be a source of relationships and engagement between different communities, and especially between the church and other communities beyond the church. What this kind of foundational pneumatology essentially does, according to Yong, is that it highlights the "common themes of human religious quest"[262] and experiences, and encourages correspondence and contrasts with common human epistemological categories and natural sciences, thereby moving from a notion of "truth as coherence to truth as correspondence."[263] The aspect of searching for truth as correspondence opens the way for dialectical and dialogical relationships between religious communities. This aspect of foundational pneumatology seems to bring together people of different communities into a journey of searching and sharing of truth in collaboration with one another. While this suggests a sort of universalism, Yong claims that this approach is also particular as it tries to be applicable to particular contexts and traditions. He writes that such an approach of foundational pneumatology "in its aspiration to be globally accountable and applicable . . . makes itself contextually particular to each religious-cultural-linguistic tradition."[264] The concreteness of the common experiences of the Spirit is mediated through traditions, religions, and the sciences, in fact through our entire lives. In proposing a foundational pneumatology, Yong actually highlights one of the important bases of interreligious engagement, which is the universal presence and activity of the Holy Spirit. He argues that the awareness of the universal presence of the Holy Spirit, particularly in a plural setting, can lead us to the truth wherever it may be found beyond Western categorisations. Yong claims,

> The universal presence and activity of the Holy Spirit speaks of the universality of truth. Christian theology that claims to be true and universally applicable cannot continue operating according to the parochial categories of a Western, institutionalised Christendom.. . . In a multi-religio-cultural world, a Christian theology aware of the universal and

261 Yong, *Beyond the Impasse*, 64–65.

262 Yong, *Beyond the Impasse*, 68–71.

263 Yong, *Beyond the Impasse*, 68–71.

264 Yong, *Beyond the Impasse*, 71.

> prevenient presence and activity of the Spirit cannot but be open to the truths of the Spirit wherever they may be found.[265]

Yet, Yong does not stop at this initial attempt of foundational pneumatology as the basis for interfaith engagement. Yong goes further and proposes a pneumatological theology of religions. His tentative propositions for such a theology of religions show the dependence on the joint working of the Spirit and the Word/Christ and holding dualities in tension: Yong contends that understanding this effort in the above framework enables the churches to recognise religions as created by God through Word and Spirit. This framework would enable us to hold general human experience and the experience of salvation, in particular, in tension. Yong claims that "Non-Christian faiths can be regarded as salvific in the Christian sense when the Spirit's presence and activity in and through them are evident."[266] This theology of religions would acknowledge the complexity of religions as both consisting of the spiritual forces of the divine and the demonic, and should be able to discern between the two. Such a theology of religions would be able to learn from other religions, seek interreligious dialogue and participation while continuing to proclaim the Christian gospel of Christ in the eschatological horizon of the Spirit.[267]

The distinctive and critical edge to this pneumatological theology of religions is provided by taking seriously the question of discernment in terms of Christian relationship with people of other faiths and even in situations that suggest divine absence and plural spirits at work.[268] Here, he also acknowledges the working of both the Spirit and the Word/Christ. For Yong, the criteria for discernment are both christologically and pneumatologically conditioned. He affirms that

> all things and events can and should be evaluated both pneumatologically and christologically. In fact, a more thorough understanding of anything or event cannot be attained apart from the acknowledgement and assessment of the contributions of both hands of the Father.. . . All pneumatological criteria, however, have their corresponding christological dimension.[269]

Yong correlates such a pneumatological theology of religions to the concept of the hospitality of God in Jesus. Through the concept of

---

265 Yong, *Discerning the Spirit(s)*, 318.

266 Yong, *Discerning the Spirit(s)*, 312.

267 Yong, *Discerning the Spirit(s)*, 311–313.

268 Yong deals with this topic of discernment in Yong, *Discerning the Spirit(s)*, 243–255, and in his later book, Yong, *Beyond the Impasse*, 129–162, where he seeks to develop a pneumatological theology of discernment.

269 Yong, *Discerning the Spirit(s)*, 315.

hospitality, he seeks to widen the engagement to include diverse people seeking unity in the Spirit. This shows the emphasis of unity in diversity in his interreligious engagement. He claims that,

> only a pneumatological approach to the religions enables us to hold in tension the distinctive confessional claims of Christian faith alongside the actual claims of the religions themselves, because the Spirit's being poured out upon all flesh does not cancel out but instead preserves the diversity of human voices.[270]

In the *Hospitality and the Other*, Yong explores this further through his theology of "hospitality." He shows that through the radical hospitality of Jesus and the early church practices, participation in the hospitality of God involves the reconciliation of aliens and strangers to God.[271] Yong suggests here a "stranger-centred" rather than a "church-centred theology."[272] There is a particular emphasis on inclusiveness and diversity here. According to him, a reading of Acts 2 could be that the early church was beginning to understand itself as the new people of God, no longer limited to the Jews, but incorporates the gentiles also. Herein, the borders of the church were extended from Jerusalem, Judea, to the rest of the world.[273] Referring to episodes from the Old Testament, Yong holds that the Spirit's anointing power is not limited to any particular people as the Spirit came upon Balaam, the Macedonian soothsayer (Num 24:2), and Cyrus, a Chaldean ruler (Isa 45:1).[274] This breaks the assumption regarding who is thought to be "in" or who is "out" of the kingdom of God. Yong writes, "Christian mission is not only about bringing Christ to our neighbours of other faiths, but may also serve the important purpose of our meeting Christ in them."[275] In this sense, he points out the possibility of conversion without a change of religion, thus signifying dual or multiple religious belonging and views the religious other as equal, though he does not elaborate on it further.[276]

In terms of the cosmic mission of the church, Yong shows that cosmic and eschatological salvation are both spiritual and material or bodily,

---

270 Yong, *Spirit Poured Out*, 236.

271 Yong, *Hospitality and the Other*, 131, citing John Navone, "Divine and Human Hospitality," *New Blackfriars* 85 (2004): 329–40.

272 Yong, *Hospitality and the Other*, 132, citing Charles Maahs, "Hospitality, Power, and Mission: A Review of the Writings and Leadership of Roger W. Fjeld," in *Currents in Theology and Mission* 30, no. 3 (2003): 168–72.

273 Amos Yong, "Poured Out on All Flesh," 17.

274 Yong, *Spirit-Word-Community*, 47–48.

275 Yong, *Hospitality and the Other*, 152.

276 Yong, *Hospitality and the Other*, 82–83.

both universal and particular, united in diversity.[277] Yong also sees the resurrection of the body as a critique of the present world order and an inauguration of the eschatological kingdom of God.[278] Again, the nature of the eschatological universal salvation cannot bypass the particular salvation of a particular community whether it is Israel or the Church. Yong suggests that the eschatological outpouring of the Spirit is for both Jews and Gentiles, where the universal salvation does not "revoke the distinctiveness of Israel's role and place in God's providential history."[279] Yong maintains, therefore, that the Lukan narrative of the Pentecost brings unity in diversity as "the Spirit's outpouring on Jews (with multiple identities and many tongues) and proselytes in the last days preserves the multiplicity of diasporic Jewish identity, with each difference enriching the whole."[280] Thus, in this case, Yong contends that "no particular nation can displace the role of the church, and any exaltation of a nation as more elect than others in the contemporary political landscape is in danger of idolizing a state rather than acknowledging the supremacy and lordship of Christ and YHWH."[281] Yong argues that the Spirit brings solidarity among various groups of people. But, this solidarity has an eschatological future in that we come together and be transformed not only for the present, but for the divine future that awaits us. He claims that the

> solidarity across peoples, tribes, and nations, brings about the harmony of many otherwise opposing voices for the glory of God. The result is not the end but the redemption of history; not an escape from the world's (coming) tribulations but an empowered perseverance in view of its eschatological transformation; not a temporary human accomplishment in the present but the opportunity to participate in the apocalyptic (revelatory) in-breaking of the Spirit from the (heretofore hidden) divine future.[282]

Thus, we have shown that even in his conceptions of the mission of the church, Yong holds on to the dialectics of relational-distinctiveness based on the model of the Spirit and the Word/Christ working together in terms of unity in diversity, and universality and particularity in its interfaith and cosmic-eschatological engagement.

---

277 Yong, *Spirit Poured Out*, 95–96.
278 Yong, *Spirit Poured Out*, 96–97.
279 Yong, *In the Days of Caesar*, 333.
280 Yong, *In the Days of Caesar*, 334.
281 Yong, *In the Days of Caesar*, 337.
282 Yong, *In the Days of Caesar*, 342–343.

## Conclusion and Looking Further

Thus, through the preceding arguments of the entire chapter, we have been able to make a case for a permeable Spirit ecclesiology and have arrived at a shape for a permeable Spirit ecclesiology in terms of nature, ministry, and mission of the church. This shape is characterised by the relational-distinctive dialectics where the borders of the church are softened and made porous or permeable. The dialectics play out in terms of unity and diversity, universal and particular, spiritual and concrete, static and dynamic, and one and many. The church's engagement at its borders and with the world is thus empowered by the Spirit and defined by the Word in both relational and distinctive aspects.

In a nutshell, in the above arguments, we have explored the relational Spirit ecclesiology of Moltmann with its pneumatological emphasis and eschatological orientation based on Social Trinity. It was found that Moltmann's Spirit ecclesiology has several merits. His formulations of an open and dynamic church in the Spirit would be helpful as a counter to the rigidly institutionalised churches of India. His proposition of an egalitarian ministry also challenges the prioritisation of the offices of the church over lay ministry. The mission of the church also extends from interreligious dialogue to ecological and cosmic redemption along with human beings. All these positive strengths have been articulated with a pneumatological emphasis and eschatological orientation on the basis of Social Trinity. We have also shown that in many respects, Moltmann's model parallels Yong's model. However, it was argued that the Social Trinity model itself is a highly problematic model for the church or human relationships. Social Trinity provides relationality, but essentially fails to provide any distinctiveness, particularity, and concreteness to conceiving God-church-world relationship.

An ecclesiocentric model was also explored through the distinctive and contrastive model of Stanley Hauerwas. Several aspects of this model are valuable as regards the Indian context. Especially commendable is his view of the church as a community of virtue, the embodied character, the need for witness and discipleship, the critical attitude to the world, and the distinctive element of the narrative of the gospel of the death and resurrection of Jesus Christ. While these strengths are particularly helpful for witness to Christ in a diverse and pluralistic setting, they can also lead to the negative features of alienation, separation, and triumphalistic attitude of one community over another. The last thing that the Indian community needs is alienation of different groups of people on the basis of religion or caste. Moreover, an ecclesiocentric model puts the church at the centre instead of God or the kingdom of God within the mission of the Son and the Spirit which is narrow and exclusive.

Tanner's christo-theocentric model was also explored and its strengths found in avoiding many of the problems of the social trinitarian model and in critique of an ecclesiocentric model. The strengths of Tanner's model can be particularly helpful for Indian situations where christological particularity needs to be explored in terms of witness, mission, and an ethical model for the community. In a diverse religio-cultural environment, in situations of ambiguity and dilemma, Jesus's life becomes the model to be followed by the individual Christian and the church. Tanner's model reminds us that in Christ, the church is identified and its essence is constituted. On the other hand, her model emphasises on particularity and the other and yet facilitates a socioeconomic critique of the human community and self-critique of the church leading to a community of justice. Tanner's model also leans towards permeability in terms of the negotiable borders of a Christian community. In spite of these strengths, Tanner's model does not hold out a developed ecclesiology and the question of permeable borders of the Christian community is not worked out further in developing a theology of religions or theology of dialogue. There is a significant lack as is mentioned earlier of the dialectic of Spirit and the Word working together in the economy which would have facilitated the relational-distinctive dialectics.

Comparably, it was evident that Yong's Spirit ecclesiology has a truly permeable character in its nature, ministry, and mission and complements the lack of the previous approaches. Building up his ecclesiology on the basis of the Spirit and the Word/Christ, he has managed to uphold the complex relational-distinctive dialectics required for a permeable ecclesiology. His pneumatological emphasis has shown relational potential as well as offering a basis for particularity and concreteness. For Yong, the presence and work of the Spirit in the church and the world open up the church to engage with other communities. This is the porosity that contributes to permeability. On the other hand, the christological dimension has provided the distinctive and particular character of the church along with a prophetic and critical edge. Yet, these borders determined by the christological dimension are softened in terms of the recognition of the work of the Logos in human beings and creation. The borders are further softened by the encompassing hospitality of God in Jesus. All throughout, the Spirit becomes the driving force behind the church's engagement with the world in Christ. A pneumatological turn to his ecclesiology has avoided ecclesiocentrism or christomonism in his approach. On the other hand, any pneumatomonism in his ecclesiology is counteracted by correspondingly turning to the christological dimension. In this sense, the Spirit and Christ being the foundation of the church together, it offers a justified model for ecclesiology. Broadly speaking, Yong's approach brings the distinctiveness that Moltmann lacks, the relationality that Hauerwas lacks, and the emphasis on the dialectics of the Spirit and the Word/Christ which Tanner lacks. Yong's model quite efficiently upholds the dialectics of the church where the borders of the church ensure relationality and distinctiveness with the dialectical features of universality and particularity, static and the dynamic, spiritual and the material or bodily, and unity and diversity. The church with borders incorporating the above dialectics can truly become permeable in its relationship to the world.

Thus, we have arrived, at the conclusion to this chapter, at a particular shape of ecclesiology: a permeable Spirit ecclesiology based on Yong's theology. However, it remains to be seen whether such an ecclesiology is fully adequate for the Indian context and Indian theological perceptions. At this stage, this question is crucial because an effort to develop an Indian ecclesiology cannot bypass the contributions and thoughts of Indian theologians on this topic. It is obvious that the views of Indian theologians will contribute significantly towards revitalising the permeable Spirit ecclesiological model in focus. To this crucial task we now turn in the following chapter considering select Indian Christian theologians.

# CHAPTER THREE

# THE SHAPE OF THE CHURCH: OVERVIEW OF INDIAN ECCLESIOLOGICAL CONVERSATIONS

The Indian church or, more appropriately, the churches in India, have their own unique history and development. The peculiar thing about the churches in India is that most of the churches have been established by foreign missionary agencies. This happened in part due to India's colonial history while Christianity spread, although Christian history in India is 2,000 years old. However, the churches seem to continue with their colonial heritage. The European colonial history of India and the Christianity that was brought on the sails of imperialism have not left a wholly positive picture of the religion in the nation. In particular, the colonial efforts towards religious conversion were not only to alter people's religion, but also to transform their culture, habits, and entire lifestyle in favour of a "superior" European culture, alien to Indians. Mohandas Karamchand Gandhi's comments bring home the point very clearly. He wrote,

> About the same, I heard of a well-known Hindu having been converted to Christianity. It was the talk of the town that, when he was baptized, he had to eat beef and drink liquor, that he also had to change his clothes, and that henceforth he began to go about in European costume including a hat.. . . I also heard that the new convert had already begun abusing the religions of his ancestors, their customs, and their country. All these things created in me a dislike for Christianity.[1]

The colonial project not only subjugated a people politically, but religiously, economically, culturally, and socially which often led to an

1 M.K. Gandhi, *The Story of My Experiments with Truth: An Autobiography* (Ahmedabad: Navajivan Publishing House, 1984), 17–18, accessed November 23, 2019, http://www.arvindguptatoys.com/arvindgupta/gandhiexperiments.pdf.

unfavourable witness for Christ in India. The first prime minister of independent India, Jawaharlal Nehru wrote,

> With the coming of the British power, a new type of missionary came to India. He was attached to officials, and the British army of occupation, and represented the British imperialism far more than the spirit of Christ.[2]

The church and the missionary movement found itself under scathing criticism for its alliance with imperialism and because of its status as a "foreign" religio-cultural institution. The church, in all practical purposes, remained a foreign entity, with its architecture, vestments, liturgy, worship, and institutions with foreign funds and foreign mission-body regulations.[3] Christianity, for all its positive contributions towards education, health, and elevation of life by well-meaning missionaries, had also managed to completely alienate the Indian Christians from their counterparts in other religions and cultures. Further, Indian Christians faced a serious dilemma whether they should extend support to the national movement for Indian independence or stay away from it. The arrival of Christianity in its nexus with imperial European cultural domination, therefore, began to produce different reactions in India. On the one hand, prominent Hindu thinkers in the nineteenth century, partly influenced by European Enlightenment thinking, pushed for reforms in Hinduism; leading to the creation of communities like *Brahma Samaj*, focussing on intellectual, religious reform, and *Arya Samaj*, a militant reform movement against the British cultural and religious hegemony. Implicit in this endeavour was the new surge of the spirit of nationalism in the minds of the people. On the other hand, there were genuine efforts by Hindu converts to Christianity to reinterpret their new-found religion in light of this struggle for religio-cultural-political identity.

The basic struggle for Christians at this time was how to still be Indian (Hindu) in culture and, yet, be a Christian in religion. There were efforts and experiments both in terms of new "ecclesial" movements and theological-intellectual engagement with Hinduism to realise this. According to David Barrett, from 1858 to 1975, India had more than

---

2 Jawaharlal Nehru, *The Unity of India: Collected Writings 1937–1940* (New York: The John Day Company, 1942), 50–51, accessed November 19, 2019, https://ia802707.us.archive.org/13/items/unityofindiacoll006382mbp/unityofindiacoll006382mbp.pdf.

3 Michael Amaladoss, *Beyond Inculturation: Can the Many Be One?* (Delhi: ISPCK/Vidyajyoti, 2005), 2.

"150 Hindu-Christian"[4] movements or churches as well as "neo-Hindu groups of devotees of Jesus" who explicitly acknowledged Jesus.[5] Efforts were made to start indigenous churches that broke away from "missionary" churches leading to churches like the *Hindu Church of the Lord Jesus Christ* in 1857 in Tamilnadu, *The National Church of India* in 1886 in Madras (Chennai), *The Calcutta Christo Samaj* (1887), and *The Church of the New Dispensation* in Calcutta (Kolkata).[6] These churches or movements, however, were short-lived, but they represented genuine and pioneering efforts by Indians to root the church and Christianity on Indian soil. Intellectually and theologically, there were also prominent thinkers who tried to bridge the gap or develop a positive dialogue between Hinduism and Christianity. Personalities like Brahmabandhav Upadhyaya (1861–1907), Vengal Chakkarai (1880–1958), Pandipeddi Chenchiah (1886–1959), Aiyadurai Jesudasen Appasamy (1891–1975), and others were prominent in this sense.[7] Although these movements, both ecclesial and intellectual, revealed genuine efforts to reclaim an Indian identity for the church and theology, they were later criticised as elitist and intellectual, failing to raise the concerns of outcastes and the marginalised.[8] These efforts, however, continue even today along with the emergence of theologies with liberation perspectives in India.

The "colonial captivity"[9] of the church seems to be an appropriate nomenclature for the phenomenon that describes the foundation and nature

4 David Barrett, *World Christianity Encyclopaedia* (Nairobi: Oxford University Press, 1982), 374.

5 Barrett, *Encyclopaedia*, 374.

6 See Roger E. Hedlund, *Christianity Is Indian, The Emergence of an Indigenous Community* (Delhi: ISPCK, 2004), 47. Also see Kaj Baago, *Pioneers of Indigenous Christianity* (Madras: Christian Literature Society, 1969). See a description of these different types of indigenous churches in Vijaya Joji Babu Valle, "Becoming Indian: Towards an Indian Contextual Ecclesiology" (PhD diss., Katholieke Universiteit Leuven, Faculty of Theology, 2010), 26–38, accessed November 21, 2019, https://lirias.kuleuven.be/bitstream/123456789/287832/1/Valle+Thesis.pdf.

7 See discussions on all these theologians in Robin H. Boyd, *An Introduction to Indian Christian Theology* (Delhi: ISPCK, 2000).

8 These theologies have been countered by subaltern theologies like that of Dalit theology that sees itself as a counter theology to Brahmanic theologies of the nineteenth century. See Sathianathan Clarke, "Dalit Theology, Introduction, Interrogation and Imagination," in *Dalit Theology in the Twenty First Century: Discordant Voices, Discerning Pathways,* eds. Sathianathan Clarke, Deenabandhu Manchala, and Philip Vinod Peacock (Delhi: Oxford University Press, 2010), 23–27.

9 The term is not new and was previously used by Somen Das in the Indian context in his book, *The Church and the World: Towards a Biblical-Ethical Understanding* (Delhi: ISPCK, 2006), 99. The term *captivity* is also used regarding Indian theology and the church by Robin Boyd in his recent book entitled *Beyond*

of the Indian churches. Since the advent of the British in India, till the present times, the churches of different denominations have been very slow in gaining an Indian identity. Christianity's link with colonialism and its resultant alienating attitude towards Indian religions and cultures have been a significant factor for such misunderstanding to prevail in Indian society. The church in India is a community with little meaningful and dialogical relationship with the wider society, except through works of educational and medical missions. This situation prevents the churches from becoming more open and permissive in their nature and ministry. This has resulted in several challenges and issues, four of which can be identified as relevant for our purposes: First, the identity of the Indian Christians; second, institutionalism and identity of the Indian church; third, divisive denominationalism; and fourth, an exclusive and other-worldly theological-missiological emphasis.

## The identity of the Indian Christians

The question of identity is an important issue here since the foreignness of the Indian church is a reality as mentioned earlier. This foreign identity is both cherished and treated as a burden by Indian Christians. Let us take the example of CNI, which brings together six denominations with people of different caste, class, tribe, and language groups, forming both homogenous and heterogeneous congregations. These congregations are scattered over north India across a plural society. In terms of defining their identity, the challenges for the CNI church members are threefold. First, to be true to God's calling among diverse religious convictions. Second, maintaining inherited meaningful Western traditions. And third, to continue to be critically engaged with the diverse socioreligious character of Indian society. The task of the congregations therefore is to integrate such convictions and realities, and to identify themselves as both Indian and Christian.[10] Here is where congregations find themselves in a dilemma. It is a complex and difficult task to uphold all the above realities together in a healthy balance. This is far more challenging for the majority of Indian Christians who are Dalits and tribals or *adivasis* who have to reckon with discrimination and alienation religio-culturally, economically, and socially. As we have shown, they seem to live in two worlds, struggling to reconcile their newfound identity as Christians on the one hand, and their sociocultural identity as Dalits or tribals on the other hand. They seem to be torn between privilege and discrimination, self-determination and an

---

*Captivity: Explorations in Indian Christian History and Theology* (Bangalore: CFCC, 2014), xvii–xviii.

10 Sahu, *United and Uniting*, xv.

identity crisis. There have been few efforts at easing the situation through indigenisation, inculturation, or contextualisation, but since there is no definite consensus about these efforts, ordinary Indian Christians often find themselves in a dilemma.

## The institutionalism and identity of the Indian churches

The churches in India have succumbed to institutionalism rather than being living communities of religio-cultural vitality. Western colonisers brought their structures of churches, administration, hierarchy, bureaucracy, and architectural styles, which were quite alien to the Indian situation. Further, considerable time and effort are spent in maintaining and upholding the bureaucratic and institutional structures rather than developing a living spirituality. Funds are often used up in maintaining huge church structures and properties. The legacy of the church's association with colonial power, money, and tradition has led to its alienation from its neighbours. Church institutions are often seen serving people of power and influence, but of little service to the minorities and the marginalised. Therefore, ordinary Indian people are unable to find spiritual vitality in the church, which shares so much power with the world.[11] Such institutionalism has served to maintain the status quo and the organisational life of the churches, but has contributed little towards church growth and the spiritual development of the people. Rigid institutionalism has also resulted in the church restricting itself to pastoral care and wellbeing only within the Christian community. Thus, cultural and social alienation have become an inevitable consequence of this rigid institutionalism.[12] Kurien Kunnumpuram, a Jesuit theologian, comments that a "Christian in India is a person who prefers to occupy the rear-seat in a church and listens to the word of the minister while remaining unmindful of the Christian's role and responsibilities."[13] Institutionalism is also seen in the structure and administration of most of the churches. Their ministry is still patriarchal and hierarchical with little space open for the inclusion of power and authority of women and the weak.[14] Due to institutionalisation and bureaucracy, the church has become exclusive and this has become its identity. This often prevents the church from venturing into new

11 Wilfred, *Banks of Ganges*, 219–220.

12 Kurien Kunnumpuram et al., *The Church in India in Search of a New Identity* (Bangalore: NBCLC, 1997), 184–186.

13 Kunnumpuram, *Church in India*, 389–390.

14 Roshan Jambhale, "Ecumenism in India Today: Church Perspective," in *Ecumenism in India Today: A Search for a Relevant Ecclesiology and Churches and Theological Education in India*, ed. James Massey (Bangalore: BTESSC & SATHRI, 2008), 107–109.

structural adjustments, new alliances, and subsequently, it fails to express itself in plural forms.

Another moot issue is that of identity of the Indian church. In other words, Christians have continued to struggle regarding the question of "What does it mean to be an Indian church?" or, "Is the church in India truly Indian?" Paul Puthanangady observes that the church in India has become largely an institutional one which inevitably leads to sociocultural alienation. Identity is based on one's own congregation or denomination which creates barriers between congregations and the larger society. Alienation of the church from the human reality in India is a stark fact.[15] Questions have been raised early on regarding the nature of institution that the church is in India: what its goals are and if an institutional church is a threat to India?[16] With this comes the inevitable question as to what kind of structures the Indian church should have, notes Mathai Zachariah.[17] D.A. Thangasamy contends that it is important that the church should have some kind of structure so that it can assist in the mission of the church. He argues that the structures of the church in India need to be renewed according to the context of the particular congregation based on their needs.[18] O.V. Jathana also notes that Indian ecclesiology must take seriously what it means to be an Indian Christian church. Jathana points out the strands in Indian ecclesiology which favour a deliberate giving-up of our communal identity as a Christian community and to identify with the larger society, their aspirations and concerns. This was evident in theologians like Raimon Panikkar, a pluralist Indian theologian, and others.[19] Panikkar wrote that the church in India has undergone the "unnatural experience of inheriting an organisation, accepting an institution, and from there striving to convert itself into an organism."[20]

---

15 Fr. Paul Puthanangady, "Christian Community as a Multi-Cultural Reality," in Kunnumpuram et al., *Church in India*, 184–191.

16 R.D. Joshi, "The Church in India and Its Institutions," in *Indian Church: Identity and Fulfilment*, ed. Mathai Zachariah (Chennai/Delhi/Lucknow: CLS/ISPCK. LPH, 1971), 64–73.

17 Mathai Zachariah, "Introduction" in Zachariah, *Indian Church*, v–ix.

18 D.A. Thangasamy, "Relevant Patterns of Church Structures," in Zachariah, *Indian Church*, 53–58.

19 O.V. Jathana, "Ecclesiology in Context: Reflections from an Indian Perspective in the Light of Current Ecumenical Deliberations," in *Ekklesia: Indian Conversations—A Study of the Church*, eds. Dr. Samuel George, H. Joseph Lalfakmawia, and Ajungla Jamir (Vishakapatnam/New Delhi: CWI & MCT, 2015), 298, 300.

20 Raimon Panikkar, "The Dream of an Indian Ecclesiology," in *Searching for an Indian Ecclesiology*, ed. Gerwin van Leeuwen (Bangalore: ATC, 1984), 36.

### Divisive denominationalism

Indian Christianity comprises diverse denominations, as noted earlier. Such denominational diversity is rendered more complex as different churches continue to follow different administrative and mission strategies of their own mission founding bodies. They have simply become replicas of Western church mission organisations without much grounding in the socioreligious climate of the people in India.[21] As T.V. Philip argues, the "Indian churches were burdened with Western ecclesiasticism and the church unity movement was preoccupied with Western denominational problems."[22] The historical reasons behind schisms in the West are of little relevance for many Indians.[23] The sacrament of the "Eucharist was successfully converted into a weapon of exclusion by the denominational churches."[24] Partly, to counteract such schisms there have been efforts at church union. The church union movements of CSI and CNI are prominent examples. O.V. Jathana holds that the church union movement has been instrumental in evolving an Indian ecclesiology. He points to some significant publications from the National Christian Council of India and others which led the way towards ecclesiological thinking in the present decades.[25] One of the first proposals for formulating a basis for church unity in India in the nineteenth century was by Rev. Lal Behari Day (1824–1894), a Bengali missionary of the Presbyterian Church of Scotland. He proposed that the foundation for a national church in India could be on the basis of the Apostle's Creed, inclusive of the Roman Catholics, and free from foreign control. He proposed this while addressing some European missionaries in Kolkata.[26] M.M. Thomas notes that for Day, the saving doctrines of Christianity constituted the essence of the Christian church. Day was one of the first persons in India to see the divisions in the Indian church as against the form the church should take in our country. Thomas pointed out that Day was envisioning the Apostle's Creed as the basis because it was broad enough to include even the Roman Catholics and has the authority of tradition and Scripture. Day thought that if the churches take the Apostle's Creed as their basis, then all the churches in christendom can find a common basis, even the Greek

21 Mathai Zachariah, *Inside the Indian Church* (New Delhi: ISPCK, 1994), 2, 21.

22 T.V. Philip, *Ecumenism in Asia* (New Delhi: ISPCK & CSS, 1994), 6.

23 Aram Keshishian, *Conciliar Fellowship: A Common Goal* (Geneva: WCC Publications, 1992), 55.

24 Moses P. Manohar, "Emerging Ecclesia: Societal View," in Massey, *Ecumenism in India Today*, 97.

25 Jathana, "Ecclesiology in Context," 294.

26 M.M. Thomas and P.T. Thomas, *Towards an Indian Christian Theology: Life and Thought of Some Pioneers* (Thiruvala: CSS, 1998), 32.

and the Latin included. Thomas notes that Day's proposal did not take any practical shape at that time, but continues to be food for thought for latter days to come.[27] The church union movement has its own worth as it brought together diverse denominations and still continues to witness through it, but Limatula Longkumer, an Indian theologian, argues that the ecumenical movement in India is a "top down model," which included the mainline denominations, but ignored the Pentecostals, Evangelicals, and other independent churches. It also neglected the marginalised groups like the Dalits, tribals and *adivasis*, and their concerns.[28] The true unity of the church in India ought to be manifested at a "local level across national, ethnic, and cultural boundaries" notes Aram Keshishian,[29] but in reality, this is not the case. There is little cooperation and solidarity among the older and younger churches even if they choose to work in the same areas. The common people of other faiths have little understanding of the diverse and divisive Christian denominationalism and cannot understand how this whole situation fits into the little they know about Jesus Christ and Christianity.

Again, the picture of northeast India, mostly in states with a Christian majority, shows more rigidity and divisiveness regarding denominationalism. Here, the denominational pattern of missionary work has led to the establishment of a Christian community divided into several church bodies. Factors such as language, tribe, and culture have put strains to ecumenical unity among the churches in this area or region.[30] The churches are identified as Ao church, Mizo church, Khasi church according to different tribes. Church identity is based on tribal identity and it is very difficult for people here to come out of narrow tribalism. Ecclesial differences are stronger than any efforts at unity. In fact, the word *ecumenism* has almost a wrong connotation in northeast India, and it is understood as anti-Christian or liberal. Efforts at ecumenical unity among the northeast churches resulted in the formation of The North East India Christian Council (NEICC), but due to differences in culture, ecclesiastical structures, deep-rooted denominationalism, and conservative theology, it is not very effective. The churches in the northeast are mission-oriented, but the understanding of mission is dominated by church planting, conversion, and aggressive evangelism. This way of doing mission creates more

---

27 Thomas and Thomas, *Towards an Indian Christian Theology*, 35.

28 Limatula Longkumer, "Wider Ecumenism and Ecclesiology," in Massey, *Ecumenism in India Today*, 45.

29 Keshishian, *Conciliar Fellowship*, 55.

30 Vanlal Chhuanawma, "Ecumenical Realities in Indian Context Today," in Massey, *Ecumenism in India Today*, 40.

denominationalism than unity in the churches, says Longkumer.[31] In a multicultural and pluralistic context, divisive and narrow denominationalism is a threat to unity and witness.[32]

*Colonial theology and missiology*

Somen Das, a Bengali theologian, noted that "historically and empirically, the modern church in India is postcolonial, but psychologically, ethically, and theologically, it continues to operate within the colonial framework. Colonial captivity of the church is not over."[33] Jacob S. Dharmaraj explains what colonial theology means.

> Colonial theology was conditioned by European political thought and shaped by its cultural elements. The intellectual path that the mission historians and the missionaries often followed in India was drawn from the scientific and colonial theories . . . of the nineteenth century.[34] [It] attempted to transplant one particular form of spiritual expression to people of another culture.[35]

Dharmaraj further points out that this kind of theology failed to take into account the struggles of the common people and their aspirations for freedom. It also failed to acknowledge India's rich cultural heritage, language systems, and philosophical thoughts, and sought to replace them with abstract religious formulations.[36] So, what resulted was an emphasis in the churches of otherworldly theology which is still perpetuated. The churches continue to have an idea of ecclesiology and mission similar to the mission-theology of the mission bodies that established them.[37]

James Massey notes that the average Christian in India has a "pietistic outlook" towards life, featuring holiness in personal lives, and other-worldly thinking,[38] which encourages a type of individualistic and selfish spirituality unconcerned with the world. In the beginning, the aim of the Protestant movement in India was not to develop an indigenous church, but to "save souls."[39] Indian Christians learned therefore that the

31 Longkumer, "Wider Ecumenism," 47.

32 Longkumer, "Wider Ecumenism," 52.

33 Das, *Church and the World*, 99.

34 Jacob S. Dharmaraj, *Colonialism and Christian Mission: Postcolonial Reflections* (Delhi: ISPCK, 1999), 118.

35 Dharmaraj, *Colonialism and Christian Mission*, 117.

36 Dharmaraj, *Colonialism and Christian Mission*, 121, 121.

37 Valle, "Becoming Indian," 17.

38 James Massey, "Christianity to Be Renewed? Rethinking Theology," in Massey and John, *Rethinking Theology in India*, 65.

39 T.V. Philip, "Ecclesiological Discussions in India during the Last Twenty-Five years," accessed November 19, 2019, https://tinyurl.com/y24nmj6s.

church's ultimate goal is to win souls. Somen Das observes that while the missionary era is over, the "missionary mentality, mission-compound syndrome," arrogant, aggressive attitude, and superiority complex still prevails.[40] This understanding of the church further makes it an exclusive, narrow, and self-centred community, which is only interested in proclaiming the uniqueness of Christ and the Christian faith. This creates suspicion and a false notion in the minds of the other communities that the church is only interested in proselytisation. Relationships of mutual enriching, living dialogue with people of other faiths are yet to be practised widely in and through the churches.

Having given a general historical and critical overview of the character of the churches in India, let us now discuss some general Indian ecclesiological models.

## General Indian ecclesiological models

Let us begin this exploration with an insightful comment by T.V. Philip in one of his articles on Indian ecclesiology. He observes that "in the history of Indian Christian theology, there was no serious discussion on the doctrine of the church as such."[41] Philip argues that early Indian Christian theological responses developed in the background of Hindu philosophy where efforts were made to understand the Christian faith in terms of Hindu categories. Hindus did not have a parallel idea of a community akin to the church. For the Hindu, creeds, dogmas, and an organised religious community do not feature as part of their spirituality. Therefore, all those who theologised from a Hindu background during the formative periods of Indian Christian theology did not feel it necessary to develop a matured ecclesiology.[42] Indian Christians, moreover, were very critical of the organised church during the rise of nationalism and they struggled to envisage what it means to be an Indian church in the context of colonialism.[43] These factors discouraged Indian thinkers to give much thought to the church in India. However, from the nineteenth century onwards, rudiments of original ecclesiological thinking began to feature among Indian thinkers and theologians in the context of widespread criticism of the organised church.

The theological conversations surrounding the Indian church can be categorised variously, projecting various forms or shapes depending on the various ideas of what a church is and what it ought to be in the Indian

40 Das, *Church and the World*, 100.
41 Philip, "Ecclesiological Discussions," 72.
42 Philip, "Ecclesiological Discussions," 173.
43 Philip, "Ecclesiological Discussions," 173–174.

context. Most of the shapes of the Indian churches were determined by the contexts, concerns, and time-periods which the churches found themselves in. In the following, some of them are discussed.

### Church as a spiritual body

Sadhu Sundar Singh (1889–1929), a prominent Sikh convert and mystic, was not very interested in an organised church which is a visible institution. For him, the true church is a spiritual body constituted of those who are living and those who have departed. The Sadhu sought for the living Christ and did not bother if he belonged to a church or not.[44] Robin Boyd observes that the Sadhu had a tendency to reject the authority of the church and preferred the lead of personal revelation.[45] The Sadhu spread and popularised the ideal of the *sanyasi*, much akin to the Hindu ideal of gurus in search for spiritual knowledge. This kind of idea of the church can be categorised as the model or shape of *church as Spiritual Body*. This idea of the church has its disadvantages and advantages. On the one hand, it is individualistic and spiritualistic. This approach does not very much help in the furtherance of the church as a community of believers. This approach does not recognise that apart from the church being a spiritual body, it is also a human and visible institution. While individual spirituality is essential, this spirituality cannot be well-developed apart from the community of believers. However, Sadhu Sundar Singh's life and spirituality continues to be relevant in India in terms of the abundance of mystic understanding of religion and spirituality in India. As Boyd puts it, we will have always the need for such ministry to revitalise the church in its own way.[46] Another idea is that of the church being a new phase or new dispensation.

### "Church of the New Dispensation"

During the time of the Bengal Renaissance, one of the prominent figures of the *Brahmo Samaj* named Keshub Chunder Sen, who later split from the movement and started his own, experimented with the foundation of "the Church of the New Dispensation." This was an endeavour that sprung mostly out of his criticism of the organised church as it existed in his day. Sen thought that Indian Christians were actually denationalised and culturally alienated by being part of the Christian church still under foreign control. So, while his attraction remained strong for the person of Christ, he proposed a community modelled on the Christian church but

44 Boyd, *Indian Christian Theology*, 105.

45 Boyd, *Indian Christian Theology*, 105.

46 Boyd, *Indian Christian Theology*, 106.

without the trappings of the foreign domination.[47] Boyd notes that this Church of the New Dispensation, while construed as a syncretic organisation during his time, gained an image towards Christian orthodoxy as time went on, although this experiment was not successful in the end.[48] M.M. Thomas notes three aspects of Sen's understanding of the church: that Keshub sought to harmonise all religions under the supremacy of the God-man Christ; second, that this rises from the conviction that all religions are true; third, that Keshub understood himself as the divinely appointed leader of this church. His was a Christ-centred understanding of the church community under the new dispensation of the Holy Spirit.[49] This latter understanding was acknowledged by Boyd when he said that the Church of the New Dispensation, for Keshub, was intimately connected to the Holy Spirit as the end-product of the process of evolution which has been inspired by the Spirit.[50] Here, we see the brief role of pneumatology amidst a traditionally christocentric framework of the understanding of the church. Keshub understood that the church has to be decolonised and patterned so that it might create a christocentric community open to religio-cultural context, fully guided by the Holy Spirit under an inspired leadership.

Another model recalls what has been said earlier about Indian people's non-preference for a religious institution as a church.

### A noninstitutional shape of the church

The Indian thinkers of the nineteenth and twentieth centuries had serious reservations about the institutionalisation of the church. They had reservations about the Western nature of the church, its worship, liturgies, and administration of the sacraments and foreign control. They sought a church which is self-governed and Indian in nature, although it was not always clear what an Indian church would look like. They saw institutionalisation of the church as squeezing out the spiritual side of the same. Indian Christians did not want to sever connections with the Indian context and culture once they were converted. Manilal Parekh (1885–1967), a Jain convert to Christianity and a disciple of Keshub, was one who was totally against an institutional form of the Indian church. He had less links with the church as he could not reconcile with the Westernised non-vegetarian Christian community in India. Although he was a baptised convert, he thought that Christian discipleship need not cut one's ties with one's

47 Boyd, *Indian Christian Theology*, 35–36.

48 Thomas and Thomas, *Towards an Indian Christian Theology*, 46–47.

49 Thomas and Thomas, *Towards an Indian Christian Theology*, 46–47.

50 Boyd, *Indian Christian Theology*, 36.

family and the caste community. He was against every kind of Christian proselytism in India which he thought could lead to disintegration of the Indian nation.[51] In his opinion, baptism should be saved from being a mere ecclesiastical rite or instrument of proselytism to one that is integral to the destiny of spiritual salvation. Baptism should not severe ties by one's own community which is opposed to indigenous cultural traditions.[52] Manilal Parekh's line of thought was shared with a number of later thinkers and theologians in India who preferred a non-institutional and open form of the church. However, the Indian converts never forgot the ashramic and devotional character of religion, whether it was Brahmanic or otherwise. Thus, monasticism remained a prominent idea among the Indian people.

### Church as a monastic community or *ashrama*

Like Manilal Parekh, another prominent Indian thinker Pandipeddi Chenchiah (1886–1959) had a totally negative attitude towards the institutional church. He was one of the members of the *Rethinking Christianity* group in Madras (now Chennai) who expressed his deep misgivings about the institutional church. He found that the Christian church was Western, fraught with denominationalism, and more interested in administration than spiritual life. Chenchiah prioritised the kingdom of God as the Spirit-filled fellowship of people over the institutional church. Chenchiah went so far as to completely deny the need for the church and the sacraments.[53] He was also the one who proposed *ashramas* as the Indian form of the church. Chenchiah affirmed fellowships where both the Hindus and Christians can jointly form part of. Chenchiah was also the one who felt that the organised church is a hindrance to the work of the Spirit.[54] Chenchiah was also one who preferred a non-institutional form of the Indian church where the Spirit will be an animating force. The pneumatological basis of an open-bordered church which will be based on relationship with other religions and cultures is quite prominent in Chenchiah. His notion of an ashramite understanding of the church was quite radical in his times.

### A religio-culturally plural church

In the nineteenth century, there were Indian stalwarts who also had a different take on the church. There were people who were part of the

51 Thomas and Thomas, *Towards an Indian Christian Theology*, 160.

52 Thomas and Thomas, *Towards an Indian Christian Theology*, 161.

53 Boyd, *Indian Christian Theology*, 159–161.

54 Boyd, *Indian Christian Theology*, 159–161.

organised church and also had essentially no issues with it, but wanted a different form of the church so that the religio-cultural diversity of India could be reflected in the community. Of course, this did not assure that the church authorities agreed to such proposals in the first place. One of these pioneers of Indian thinking was Brahmabandhav Upadhayay (1861–1907) who had his own ideas about how an Indian church should look like. Boyd notes that he was different from other Indian Christians who were against the organised church. Brahmabandhav recognised the need for a "visible, organised church and for regular ministry of the Word and the sacraments."[55] He was uncomfortable with the Western garb of the Indian church and therefore envisaged a church dressed in Hindu garments and cultural elements.[56] He was the one who saw no difficulty to be a Hindu Christian, as he explained that we can be culturally and by birth Hindus, but by a second sacramental birth, we are Catholics or Christians.[57]

Another model is that of a missional church and a church which is interested in ecumenism. The Indian churches were always conscious of mission from the beginning although they had different views of the same.

### A missional and ecumenical church

The twentieth century was the age for missions and churches geared up with the vision of the Edinburgh Conference of 1910 to spread the gospel to the ends of the earth. The worldwide church became increasingly mission-minded and Indian Christians realised the essence of the church as mission. Bishop V.S. Azariah of south India saw the church as integral to mission. Church and mission are integrally related to each other. The corporate witness of the church is very important for mission. He emphasised on indigenous churches where foreign missions should only act as friends or co-workers. The unity of the church was of great importance to Azariah and he believed that a missionary church must move towards an organic unity, overcoming denominational boundaries.[58] One of the prominent non-Indian thinkers during this time who contributed enough to the missional thinking of the church was the ecumenical theologian and missiologist Bishop Lesslie Newbigin (1909–1998) who spent a good many years in south India, engaging with the churches. Veli-Matti Karkkainen observes that Newbigin's overall ecclesiological approach

55 Boyd, *Indian Christian Theology*, 83.

56 Boyd, *Indian Christian Theology*, 83.

57 Boyd, *Indian Christian Theology*, 83.

58 Thomas and Thomas, *Towards an Indian Christian Theology*, 118.

could be summarised in three ecclesiological streams. First, that the church is where the preaching of the gospel and right administration of sacraments are done. Second, it is the Catholic understanding of our participation in the sacramental identity of the church. Third, the experience or role of the Spirit in the church.[59] Newbigin sees a separation between the sacramental aspects of the church and the charismatic aspects which he lamented and hoped that these streams would continue to work together. Newbigin elaborates on the third stream in a booklet he wrote for the Indian church leaders, entitled *What is the Gospel?* Here in a small portion entitled *Fellowship of the Holy Spirit*, Newbigin affirms that the church is the new community of believers who have believed and received the Holy Spirit. In this short work, Newbigin discusses the work of the Holy Spirit in creating the new community of believers.[60]

Both Azariah and Newbigin had made significant contributions to ecumenism and unity of the church. As the church continued its mission in various ways, it continued to think especially in the post-Independent era about dialogical relationship with other faith communities. So, a dialogical approach also became necessary.

### A dialogical church

P.D. Devanandan (1901–1962), who led the movement for interreligious dialogue in post-Independent India, argued that the church is not totally understood by the Hindu community in the Indian soil. There is no idea among the Hindus regarding congregational worship and people gathered together as a church community.[61] Devanandan also criticised the organised church like the nineteenth century thinkers, but he did not lose faith in the church. On the other hand, he wanted to see the church as a transformed and transforming community. The church should be a healing and serving *Koinonia*, symbol of new creation, empowered by the Holy Spirit but centred on Christ.[62] M.M. Thomas is one of those theologians who had vigorously engaged in post-Independence reconstruction of the idea of the Indian church. Thomas's idea of the church grew both in the background of the criticism of the nineteenth century thinkers of the organised church and also the need for rethinking of the Christian community in the light of modernisation, secularisation, and the church's response to

59 Veli-Matti Kärkkäinen, *Introduction to Ecclesiology: Ecumenical, Historical & Global Perspectives* (Madison, WI: IVP Press), 155.

60 M.W. Goheen, "From a Christendom to a Missionary Ecclesiology (1909–1959)," accessed October 28, 2019, https://tinyurl.com/y63en6qq.

61 Boyd, *Indian Christian Theology*, 198.

62 Boyd, *Indian Christian Theology*, 198–199.

the Indian context. His reflections on the church come under his broader idea of the project of salvation as humanisation.[63] The church's mission under this project would mean the Indian church engaging in religions, cultures, and secular ideologies. The idea of an open church which would collaborate with people of other faiths and ideologies in the humanisation program and the rebuilding of the nation was of utmost importance to Thomas.[64] These concerns became quite pronounced when nationalistic fervours gripped India during the period of its struggle for independence. As mentioned earlier, there was an explicit critical attitude towards the organised church by the Indian Christians which was arguably shaped by the influence of Christianity and Western education and, of course, their nationalistic fervour. Springing from this were the concerns that bothered the Indian church since then.

### A charismatic church

Another prominent theologian of recent years, Samuel Rayan becomes significant in ecclesiological discussions in India. Rayan's thought of the church is grounded on the communitarian spirituality of sharing and caring of the early church based on Jesus's movement. Kurien Kunnumpuram, one of the prominent scholars on Rayan, observes that he understands the church as a countercultural movement. Jesus stood for human dignity and worth against the system of avarice and greed.[65] On the other hand, Rayan believes in the incarnation of the church in the culture of the people of this country so that we envisage a truly Indian church. He also believed in the church as a community of diversity and unity, with various charisms and ministry.[66] Kunnumpuram observes that Rayan acknowledges the reality of a Spirit-led church. The Spirit of God continues to speak to the churches and continues to animate the Christian community in various ways.[67]

---

63 See M.M. Thomas, *Salvation and Humanisation: Some Crucial Issues of the Theology of Mission in Contemporary India* (Madras: CLS, 1971).

64 See M.M. Thomas, *Ideological Quest within Christian Commitment, 1939–1954* (Madras: CLS, 1983).

65 Kurien Kunnumpuram, "The Beauty of the Church: An Investigation of Samuel Rayan's Ecclesiology," in *The Vision of a New Church and a New Society: A Scholarly Assessment of Dr. Samuel Rayan's Contribution to Indian Christian Theology*, ed. Kurien Kunnumpuram (New Delhi: Christian World Imprints, 2016), 129–131.

66 Kunnumpuram, "Beauty of the Church," 139.

67 There are some recent publications which dwell specifically on Samuel Rayan's ecclesiology. For eg., *Nature, Women and the Church: Indian Christian Reflections on Ecology, Feminism and Ecclesiology*, vol.1 of *Collected Writings of Samuel Rayan SJ*, ed. Kurien Kunnumpuram, SJ (Delhi: ISPCK, 2013).

## Conclusion

So far, we have done a historical-theological overview of the situation of churches in India, the ecclesiological conversations, and looked at various trends or models of the church in terms of its nature and shape. If we analyse the above models, we will find that Indian theology has conceived the church in various ways depending on the context and the age. It has developed from a narrow and exclusivistic one to more and more inclusivistic one. Inclusivity would always point towards a relational church while we can always find that the christocentric nature of ecclesiology is very well portrayed by most of the theological strands, which is its distinctive feature. Through this general survey, it is clear that the thinkers in India were not so much ecclesiologically conscious in the beginning. But, under the influence of Western colonialism and Christianity and in the wake of nationalistic fervour, gradually they were against a church which is Western and under foreign domination. They were all against an institutional church which is static, but favoured a church which is more in line with the Indian religio-cultural and philosophical traditions. There were strands noticeable which focussed on engagement of the church in secular realms and exploring questions of salvation and humanisation. It is noticeable that stalwarts like Chenchiah within the *Rethinking Christianity* movement reflects influential trends in nineteenth century Indian Christianity. He also has a prominent pneumatological orientation in his theology. M.M. Thomas has been already identified as a twentieth century Indian theologian who has prominent ecclesiological contributions. We have also identified that Samuel Rayan has an influential ecclesiology with a prominent pneumatological perspective. However, these have been general overviews and observations. An overview does not do justice to a wholesome engagement of Indian theology with the particular project in hand.

So now, we will move forward to discuss in detail, theologies and in particular, ecclesiologies of Pandipeddi Chenchiah, M.M. Thomas, and Samuel Rayan to launch a conversation regarding a permeable Spirit ecclesiological project we have in hand. We will critically assess their theological contributions to help us reflect on an ecclesiology which is Spirit-led but christologically-conditioned; in other words, with negotiable and porous borders.

# CHAPTER FOUR

# THE SPIRIT SHAPED CHURCH: ECCLESIOLOGIES OF SELECT INDIAN THINKERS

The previous chapter gave a brief overview about the various general models of the Indian church. The present chapter will seek to bring into conversation three theologians mentioned earlier in order to determine the shape of a Spirit ecclesiology for the Indian context with permeable or negotiable borders. In the second chapter, we arrived at a possible shape of permeable Spirit ecclesiology, but this has to be put into the framework of Indian thinking and Indian context. The Indian ecclesiologies will be discussed in terms of the relational-distinctive, Spirit-Word/Christ dialectics we have pointed out earlier and in terms of permeability of borders. It will be evident in due course that Pandipeddi Chenchiah falls within the category of ecclesiology with open borders, facilitated by the prominent action of the Spirit while still being christocentric. M.M. Thomas focuses on an ecclesiology of Christ-centered open fellowships; open to the plural contexts of religions and ideologies, while the role of the Spirit is unclear. Samuel Rayan's model will be argued to be the best model of a permeable Spirit ecclesiology which is truly permeable as characterised by its relational distinctiveness with the interworking of the role of the Spirit and Christ, and essentially combining the other two previous models and compensating for the deficiencies in the Western models.

## A borderless pneumatic ecclesiology from Pandipeddi Chenchiah

Pandipeddi Chenchiah (1886–1959) was born in Nellore, a city in the present state of Andhra Pradesh, which was part of the erstwhile Madras

Presidency during the British rule.[1] He converted to Christianity at a young age and later became a lawyer, but eventually began to engage himself in religion and politics; and to identify intellectually with the national movement of India's independence. He was a prominent member of the Madras Rethinking Group[2] and along with others sought to articulate an Indian understanding of Christianity. Chenchiah did not publish any books himself, so his theological writings have to be drawn from two chief books in which he collaborated, *Rethinking Christianity in India*[3] and *Asramas Past and Present*.[4] Chenchiah stood at the crossroads of the Indian history of pre- and post-Independence religious thinking. His original efforts at making sense of Christianity in a particularly Hindu context and in the context of nationalism remain challenging in the present times. Desiring to see an independent India, he stressed communion, fellowship, and collaboration between not only Christians but also other religious communities. In his writings, a passion to understand Christianity in the wider framework of the spiritual longing of India towards fuller humanisation is very prominent. Post-Independence, however, Chenchiah moved beyond the "philosophical-theological frameworks"[5] to develop a commitment to building an Indian Christian community. Chenchiah, in his later writings, was aware that post-Independence and the absence of the British Raj meant that "Christians must rely on the Holy Spirit" in looking for guidance.[6] Thus, his basic motivation was to build an inclusive community in the Spirit where people from all backgrounds could participate. Chenchiah was influenced by the evolutionary principles of French philosopher Henri Bergson (1859–1941) which led the former to have a theological approach which is fluid and always in process. He was also influenced by the Yoga guru Venkata Rao Venkatasami Rao of south India and Aurobindo, an Indian philosopher, which led him into his understanding of a Christian yoga of the Spirit and of the transformation of

1 D.A. Thangasamy, *The Theology of Chenchiah with Selection from His Writings* (Bangalore: CISRS/The Literature Department of the National Council of Y.M.C.As of India, 1966), vii.

2 Apart from Chenchiah, it included Vengal Chakkarai, A.N. Sundarisanam, G.V. Job, and others.

3 G.V. Job, D.M. Devashayam, and A.N. Sudarisanam, eds., *Rethinking Christianity in India* (Madras: Sudarisanam, 1938), https://archive.org/details/in.ernet.dli.2015.1112/page/n3.

4 P. Chenchiah, V. Chakkarai, and A.N. Sudarisanam, eds., *Asramas Past and Present* (Madras: CLS, 1996).

5 Chenchiah, "Christian Message in a Hindu Environment," *The Guardian* (February 9, 1950): 84–85, 100–101, cited in Nigel Ajay Kumar, *What is Religion? A Theological Answer* (Eugene, OR: Pickwick Publications, 2013), 122.

6 Kumar, *What is Religion?*, 122.

oneself through the Spirt into the image of Christ.[7] His theology shows a consistent pneumatological perspective. Chenchiah was convinced that the future of Christianity in India will depend on the discovery of the Indian church of the importance of the Holy Spirit.[8] Remarkably, his Christology, his interreligious concepts, and concepts of new creation are all influenced by his pneumatology. For him, the Holy Spirit is the universal Jesus, who indwells us all, and also the Spirit is the energy behind the new creation.[9] It will be evident that he was vehemently critical of the organised church and often considered it as a barrier to reaching Christ, though he himself was a church member until his death. This is another reason for making him one of our conversation partners. His criticism of the organised church can be taken as the basis of a broad paradigm for a decolonisation attitude towards the Indian church. Again, as a convert from Hinduism he can be said to represent the majority of Hindu intellectual views of the church and Christianity since pre-Independence times.

## Chenchiah's Indian ecclesiology in the Spirit

Before discussing Chenchiah's positive contributions regarding the church, ecumenism, and interfaith relationships, his criticisms about the church need to be highlighted. This is because he stands in the genre of those pioneering Hindu converts and intellectuals who have vehemently criticised the organised church for its Western nature and its relationship with colonialism. This is also crucial because he, along with others, blazed a trail that is now followed by contemporary Indian theologians in a bid to decolonise[10] the church and situate the church on the Indian soil.

### *A decolonisation approach to the Indian church*

Chenchiah is one of the precursors of the approach to decolonise the Indian churches because he is perhaps one of the most vehement and extreme in his criticism of the organised, institutional church. This is not to endorse Chenchiah's perspective in its entirety, but that he seems to provide an opportunity for us to rethink the nature and role of the church in India. One of his statements suggest that his criticism of the church did not lead to a compromise with his faith or devotion to Christ. Robin Boyd points out that he was unwilling to put Christ and the religion of

7 Christina Manohar, *Spirit Christology: An Indian Perspective* (Delhi: ISPCK, 2009), 151.

8 Thangasamy, *Theology of Chenchiah*, 218.

9 Thangasamy, *Theology of Chenchiah*, 217.

10 Here, the term is used in the sense of doing away with the influences of colonialism and colonial constructs in religion, society, culture, and political life.

Christianity with all its "trappings" or traditions on the same pedestal. Chenchiah writes,

> Let it be clearly understood that we accept nothing as obligatory save Christ. Church, doctrine, dogma, whether from the West or from the past, whether from Apostles or from modern critics, are to be tested before they are accepted.[11]

This christocentric statement is also very controversial regarding Christianity as a religion. Again, some of Chenchiah's other statements reveal that he is willing to accept the kingdom of God as the goal for Christianity rather than the church. He writes,

> Christianity took the wrong gradient when it left the kingdom of God for the church.. . . Christianity is a failure because we made a new religion of it instead of a new creation.[12] . . . The church arrested the kingdom when Peter added 3000 unto them—a fatal day for the kingdom and a glorious day for the church.[13]

Again, Chenchiah viewed the institutional church not as a spiritual reality, but as merely a human institution. He writes,

> When the Holy Spirit became a distant reality and then a dogma, when Jesus went to heaven and did not return, we thought of a church and built one.[14]

Chenchiah had also a thoroughly negative view of the rituals and sacraments of the church. He writes,

> There will be no baptisms, no confessions of faith, no creedal profession [The Hindu] will slowly and in different degrees come under the influence of the Spirit of Christ, without change of labels or nomenclature.. . . The change will be in the realm of the Spirit—not in the region of *nama* [name] and *rupa* [form].[15]

Chenchiah's criticisms of Christianity and the church, though extremely controversial, make available a broad parameter for the decolonisation project. In this broad parameter, nothing seems to be beyond scrutiny except the raw fact of Christ or specifically the Christ-event. The church with its traditions, confessions, creeds, sacraments, and rituals are

---

11 Thangasamy, *Theology of Chenchiah*, 2.

12 Robin Boyd quotes this in his discussion on the ecclesiology of Chenchiah. See Boyd, *Indian Christian Theology*, 159.

13 Chenchiah, "My Search for the Kingdom," *The Guardian* (February 8, 1951), in Boyd, *Indian Christian Theology*, 160.

14 Chenchiah, "The Church and the Indian Christian," in Job, Devashayam, and Sudarisanam, eds., *Rethinking Christianity in India*, 93.

15 Chenchiah, "Church and the Indian Christian," 93.

all to be rethought or reevaluated in the context of India and in terms of Christ. Rethinking Christianity becomes a crucial project for Chenchiah particularly because he himself was a convert from Hinduism and because he had strong nationalistic inclinations. His nationalistic fervour for the freedom movement guided his reactions to Christianity and the church. Following from his critique of Western Christianity and the church are his proposals for a religionless Christianity and an effort towards de-institutionalisation of the church.

*De-institutionalisation of the church and religionless Christianity*

Chenchiah's evolutionary ideas coupled with his pneumatological emphasis, his efforts to situate Christianity in the Indian milieu and Hindu worldview in the context of colonialism and nationalistic feelings, led him to conceive of the Christian community differently. His efforts were therefore towards a decolonised and de-institutionalised church. In contrast to an exclusive community on the Western pattern propagated in India, the Christian community would be conceived as belonging to the wider society where the secular-sacred divide would be nullified and interreligious communion would take place.[16] This is an effort to make it inclusive of the sociocultural reality of the people, because he realised that rigid institutionalisation is one of the problems of the Indian church. Here, the antidote is the power and presence of the Holy Spirit permeating not only people's religious, but social life as well. Chenchiah affirms that we are called to bring the motivating power of the Spirit into all levels of life and not only in the spiritual realm.[17] This is the power that enables us to live out our Christian life at the boundaries of the institutional church in our daily context. Consequently, Chenchiah is not in favour of segregation of the clergy and the laity and separation between people's religious and secular life. He argues that this segregation creates more institutionalisation. For instance, he points out that the laypeople's religion differs from that of the clerical in that the clerical seeks to uphold religion by preservation of truths through creeds and doctrines whereas the laypeople's religion finds fulfilment in action.[18] Here in the "non-clerical" religion, home becomes the temple and there is no division between the sacred and secular, and there is spontaneity of relations which might be missing in the church. Chenchiah's effort is to bring out the church into the daily life of

16 Chenchiah, Presidential address at a Laymen's Conference, *The Guardian* (1942): 28, in Thangasamy, *Theology of Chenchiah*, 43.

17 Chenchiah, "Kingdom of God in India," *The Guardian* (1939): 260, in Thangasamy, *Theology of Chenchiah*, 42.

18 Chenchiah, "Characteristics of Vanaprastha Asrama," 119, in Kumar, *What is Religion?*, 157.

the people and thus transcend the boundaries of the church. He contends that "we need a place of God outside the church where we work for him and with him, and this can only be the home and the *asrama*."[19]

*Asramas* were suggested as a model by Chenchiah as "non-authoritarian, non-traditional, non-ritualistic, non-sectarian, non-sacerdotal . . . and non-institutional"[20] communities. It is the place where the ideal of "realisation of religion" can be sought.[21] Nigel Ajay Kumar notes that this realisation is meant for harmony with *Brahman* (God) and all things involving the need for experimentation and inner purity. Thus, *asramas* would form a new "brotherhood" with peoples, animals, and nature.[22] This religion of the *asrama* is not renunciation. It is a religion of union, realisation, experimentation, and social reconstruction. It is achieved not by tearing oneself from life but placing oneself between God and the world.[23]

Consequently, Chenchiah calls for real engagement of Christians both in the church and in the secular world. In order to show that the Christian life can also be lived outside the church, he points out that the laypeople pray and practice their spirituality in their workplaces and through daily living which actually lie outside the church, or temple, or mosque. He continues that "the priest takes us into the temple of God; the laymen take God from the temple into our houses and social institutions."[24] Chenchiah was in favour of preaching and spreading the gospel, but that did not necessarily mean church affiliation for him. He claims that "a Christian movement within Hinduism without the umbilical cord being cut is a decided advantage to the Hindu and the Christian."[25] In other words, he meant that in order to be true Christians, affiliation to a particular institution is not absolutely necessary; it ought to be possible to follow Christ from within one's particular religion. Chenchiah argues that Christianity should be "communicated as life and power and not as an institution."[26] So, it is the inward dimension of realising our Lord in our hearts that ought to motivate our lives and actions which ought to be also the Indian church's pursuit for the "realisation of Christ."[27] Chenchiah

19 Chenchiah, "Characteristics of Vanaprastha Asrama," 157.

20 Chenchiah, "Characteristics of Vanaprastha Asrama," 157.

21 Thangasamy, *Theology of Chenchiah*, 254.

22 Kumar, *What is Religion?*, 156.

23 Kumar, *What is Religion?*, 157.

24 Thangasamy, *Theology of Chenchiah*, 44.

25 Chenchiah, "Christian Message in a Non-Christian World," in Job, Devashayam, and Sudarisanam, eds., *Rethinking Christianity in India*, 187.

26 Chenchiah, "Christian Message," 187.

27 Chenchiah, "Christian Message," 187.

wanted Christianity to permeate the society like a leaven without a particular community or church. Though he was baptised himself and was part of a church community taking part in the Eucharist, sacraments had become meaningless rituals to him because he thought that they did not carry the right meaning for India. Robin Boyd notes Chenchiah's argument that "the thought of having to undergo baptism has kept many a Hindu from open confession of his sincere faith in Christ."[28] Chenchiah thinks that the progress of Christianity should depend on its inherent appeal and not any external conditions, so he proposes a religion which has less of a formal structure, not "doctrine-bound, sacrament-affiliated, tradition-fixed."[29]

Practically speaking, Chenchiah tried to put into practice the openness of the church or the Christian community, in its engagement with the wider community. This was needed in terms of solidarity in common national concerns which at that time was the independence movement. Therefore, he was against the idea of the ghettoisation of the Christian community and the seeking of special privileges for Christians from the government.[30] This can be criticised nowadays from the perspective of Dalit rights of Christians in their struggle for gaining the Scheduled Caste status from the government; however, Chenchiah has to be understood from within his own context. In times of pre-Independence fervour, perhaps, it seemed more important for him to have national solidarity and equality than to have sectarian aspirations.

### Ecumenical relations

Chenchiah's idea of the openness of the Christian community draws within its purview ecumenical relationship among the churches, which is different in nature from the ecumenical discourses in the West. The difference begins with the scope of ecumenical interrelationship which is not limited to Christian denominations alone, but also in interrelationships among other faith communities. He actually wanted to unite Christians and people of other religions towards the common goal of India's national struggle for freedom. Keeping that goal in mind, he wanted to see Christianity as a movement rather than a consolidation of a community and it was in that spirit that he would seek expression in unity of fellowship amidst diversity. Thus, Chenchiah argued that Christian society ought not to be comprehended within the church alone. Here, the wider society is the broader field in which Christians should identify themselves. Within

[28] Boyd, *Indian Christian Theology*, 161.

[29] Thangasamy, *Theology of Chenchiah*, 234–245.

[30] The concerns and issues concerning the Dalits have been dealt with earlier.

this framework and interrelationships among the wider community, the Christian denominations should find their unity. He notes that Christians are bigger than the church and all unities, ideas, and reforms should flow from the wider society into the church.[31] This is a flow in a different direction. Ecumenical movements generally tend to work out relationships of unity among themselves and then seek to witness this oneness towards other communities. Instead, for Chenchiah, "the heart is in the society outside the church."[32] From this concept of the wider society, all Christians are one, a fluid society, not a historic church but a living soul. He affirms that "life is wider than devotion, soul greater than prayer, Christian people greater than church, the clergy, concepts, and institutions."[33]

Chenchiah thinks that there should be Christian action groups that are less bound by the church and more led by the Spirit, and also prayer groups to address the needs of the nation.[34] From here, Chenchiah takes us into the practical aspects of ecumenical relations. He points out that due to the difference between the churches in doctrine and practice, it is useful to start from our relations outside the church and gradually come to concerns that are common within the church. He suggests that we must start from the affirmation that we are all united in Christ and as Indians. He deplores the unfortunate fact that we are divided even though we are loyal to the same Christ we follow. He proposes,

> Let us be united because we are Christians and Indians. And then, let the church be one because Christians are one. If loyalty to Christ has no power to unite us, and loyalty to churches has power to divide us, there is something fundamentally wrong in the whole situation.[35]

Chenchiah spoke of church union not in terms of organisational structures or in terms of creeds and dogmas but in secular activities. He notes that it is the tragedy of the situation that it is "the church that separates Christians from Christians."[36] He points out that "the Protestant and Catholic mix in politics, combine in trade, work in municipalities and legislatures. The only place where they cannot work together is the church."[37] His idea of church union is to flow from the secular realm into

[31] Chenchiah, "Indian Christians: Problems and Privileges: Community or Movement?" *The Guardian* (1942): 28–30, in Thangasamy, *Theology of Chenchiah*, 307–312.

[32] Thangasamy, *Theology of Chenchiah*, 307–312.

[33] Thangasamy, *Theology of Chenchiah*, 307–312.

[34] Thangasamy, *Theology of Chenchiah*, 314–317.

[35] Chenchiah, "Problems of Indian Christian Community," *The Guardian* (1942), 40, in Thangasamy, *Theology of Chenchiah*, 28.

[36] Thangasamy, *Theology of Chenchiah*, 151–152.

[37] Thangasamy, *Theology of Chenchiah*, 151–152.

the religious. He further proposes that we first "bring laypeople together in secular activities, in trade, social work, in pleasure, before we attempt to join them in prayer."[38] Chenchiah affirms that there is an easy opportunity for us to unite in our secular lives where we meet everyday which can be exploited before seeking to unite as church members. He proposes,

> Let us unite together as men [and women] and country-men before we unite as Christians. Let us unite in the secular field before we unite as Christians.. . . Let us form common associations for all Christians in secular activities first. Let union begin outside the church and flow into it afterwards. This seems to be the easier way.[39]

The openness and relational character of the church which is not bound within any institution, but goes beyond into the wider community is poetically expressed by Chenchiah with the words:

> Let us get out of the incense-laden churches to the free air of plains. Let us go out of sects into vast spaces of community, let us leave candle-lit alters and pass into the sun-lit world that we may see without distraction plain facts in true proportion . . ..[40]

### Interfaith relations

Chenchiah believed that the solution to the communal problem in India could be cooperation between faith communities. He reflected on inter-religious and intercultural relationships being a privilege of the Christian to explore. For Chenchiah, Christians stand in a unique position to both Hindus and Muslims as they can allow those traditions to help reinterpret Christianity and also in turn bring to these communities the redemptive principles of Christianity. He writes that the "responsibility of a Christian [is] to transmit such portions of Western culture as are useful and helpful for national growth and freedom to his people and to transmit the living energies of his inherited culture to the West."[41] Chenchiah argued that Christianity is the gospel of new creation and in these terms, is a different religion compared to others, although he acknowledged the working of the Spirit in other religions, and because of this he thought building of bridges is possible. Moreover, spiritual insights from different religions can enrich the understanding of the person of Christ and Christian life and experience. He argues that "the negative plate of Jesus developed in a solution of Hinduism brings out hitherto unknown features of the

38 Thangasamy, *Theology of Chenchiah*, 151–152.

39 Thangasamy, *Theology of Chenchiah*, 151–152.

40 Chenchiah, "Problems of Indian Christian Community," 28.

41 Thangasamy, *Theology of Chenchiah*, xiv.

portrait [of Jesus] and these may prove exactly the gospel for our time. The same thing happens to Hinduism when developed in a Christian environment."[42]

Chenchiah showed that the influence of Christianity or Christ led to renewal of Hinduism on its own terms through the establishment of the *Brahmo Samaj*, *Arya Samaj*, and the *Ramakrishna Mission*, which were renewal movements within Hinduism. Chenchiah contends that it is possible that the truths of Christ can be brought to us by the adherent of another religion and it is also possible to follow Christ from outside the Christian faith. He tells of a person, Thiru V.K., who was led in devotion by a disciple of poet Ramalingaswami who himself had a vision of Christ. Chenchiah writes,

> It was Ramalingaswami that opened my friend's eye to the magnificence of Christ and the magnitude of his message. As he read the two hundred stanzas in which Ramalingaswami weeps for his sins, he awoke to a sense of sin and the need for repentance. As he saw Ramalingaswamy's portraiture of Siva, the face of Jesus flashed on him.. . . Christ came to him through Ramalingaswami. Both Ramalingaswami and Thiru V.K. remained Hindus, however, trying to imbue Hinduism with the spiritual values they had found in Christ.[43]

For Chenchiah, interfaith relationships are actually a quest of human beings for truth and in this quest, people in India cross religious boundaries. He contends that this crossing of boundaries is based on the shared understanding of God's presence as Spirit in faith communities. The pneumatology of Chenchiah here continues to be a major constitutive element. Chenchiah identifies that in India, there is a longing for understanding God as Spirit. He reminds us that the "central desire of the Hindu to approach God [is] in the realm of spirit"[44] and continues that the "inner needs of Hinduism . . . emphasize the need for the approach to Christ as a Spirit."[45] On the basis of shared experience of the Spirit, people of different faiths in India are driven towards other religions either in search of new hope and light or by despair from their own particular religiosocial situation.[46] Thus, Christianity is looked upon as being one of the many contributors to this search for reality for the Indians. Nigel Ajay Kumar points out that for Chenchiah, "Jesus stands in relation to the residuary

42 Thangasamy, *Theology of Chenchiah*, 36.
43 Thangasamy, *Theology of Chenchiah*, 40.
44 Thangasamy, *Theology of Chenchiah*, 214.
45 Thangasamy, *Theology of Chenchiah*, 214.
46 Chenchiah, "Who is Jesus?' A Study of Jesus in Terms of the Creative Process," *The Guardian* (1943): 352–353, in Thangasamy, *Theology of Chenchiah*, 100.

problems of other religions rather than satisfied longings of man. In other words, the relationship of Christ to non-Christian hearts and hopes lies in the unexplored regions of our Lord's life and not in the region already mapped out."[47]

Practically speaking, Chenchiah also made efforts towards intercommunity fellowships by bringing people together in prayer. He is said to have started small prayer groups consisting of Christians and Hindus. Chenchiah urged that a Hindu should pray for a Christian and a Christian should pray for a Hindu. He realised that "this sort of prayer group to relieve each other's distress really makes for sincere love and evidences mutual concern."[48] He was in favour of the spread of the gospel as inner change rather than change of communities or social groups outside Hinduism.[49] His ideology of conversion is that it would shift its emphasis from "mass to quality, from change to character."[50] He was also in favour of interreligious worship where both Christians and Hindus could join together and the best common worship would be monotheistic or non-idolatrous.[51]

The above discussion of Chenchiah's theology and ecclesiology shows clearly that he sought to develop a Christian theology on Indian foundations, drawing concepts from Indian philosophical and religious worldviews and practices. He clearly reflected the efforts of the Indian Christians of his period who searched for an Indian understanding of Christianity. The Indian or Hindu preference for a nondogmatic religion and spirituality in the Spirit, and the nationalistic fervour for freedom have influenced his ecclesiological understandings as well. He was thus in favour of a decolonised and deinstitutionalised Indian church. It was evident that Chenchiah's decolonising approach does not merely include critiquing European religio-cultural elements manifested in architecture, traditions, and customs, but goes to a deeper level. It questions the nature of Christianity itself couched in Western categories and includes the doctrines, dogmas, liturgy, worship, and sacraments which are central to the life of the church. Chenchiah's negative views about Christianity and the church urge us to rethink our theologies and ecclesiologies as many people still view the church in India today as foreign and imperialistic. This also provides a direction to critically rethink which elements of Christianity or ecclesiology need to be treated as core constituents and

47 Kumar, *What is Religion?*, 153.
48 Thangasamy, *Theology of Chenchiah*, xvi.
49 Thangasamy, *Theology of Chenchiah*, 38.
50 Thangasamy, *Theology of Chenchiah*, 39.
51 Thangasamy, *Theology of Chenchiah*, 41.

which of them could be treated as peripheral and need to be re-evaluated in the light of Christ and the Indian context. It also discourages a certain amount of complacency of the church regarding its colonial nature and its efforts towards meaningful projection of its faith through its doctrines and liturgical practices to those outside. It is wrong to think that Chenchiah proposed a total break from Western principles or cultures. He suggested healthy transaction of Indian values with Western traditions and cultures that promote mutual growth, but that also to ensure the freedom and autonomy of the Indian people. In other words, it is Christianity without its colonial bondage, at the same time with the freedom of the Indian people to interpret it from their own backgrounds.

It is evident that Chenchiah found pneumatology to be a driving force that has the potential not only to urge the Indian church towards decolonisation and de-institutionalisation, but also to accomplish a relational Christianity and relational church that would overcome the barriers of the secular and the sacred, Christianity with other religions, especially Hinduism, and the segregation of the clergy and the laity in the ministry of the church. We have seen how keen Chenchiah was to make Christianity the religion of the Spirit, to free it from the bounds of the institutional church so that both Hindus and Christians can participate in building up the kingdom of God. This also hints at new forms of Christian community in terms of dual or multiple religious belonging. The alienation that has been brought about among the Indian communities through a colonial Christianity is therefore hoped to be rectified through decolonisation, integration, and union through the Spirit. It is essentially in this perspective that he argues that the present denominational disunity of the church in India can be overcome through wider efforts of integration of Christians and people of other religions in their common response to sociopolitical issues. Chenchiah's conception of a relational church would hope to encourage mutual interreligious cooperation and common spirituality in prayer, worship, and action. The relational church of Chenchiah can thus be termed as a church without borders. Although Chenchiah was christocentric, this did not give his ecclesiology any particularistic or distinctive feature. Chenchiah's pneumatology, as we saw, gave freedom for free exchange of relationships and spirituality across religions and cultures. Now we come to another kind of ecclesiology, one that is both christocentric and distinctive with borders, but also open to other religions and ideologies. This is the ecclesiology of M.M. Thomas.

## *DIAKONIA* AND CHRIST-CENTRED *KOINONIA* WITH OPEN BORDERS: THE ECCLESIOLOGY OF M.M. THOMAS

M.M. Thomas (1916–1996), was brought up in Kerala in a Mar Thoma Christian household. He lived in a generation which had struggled under the impact of colonialism and had been critical about it. His deep interest was in the Indian independence movement and similar movements around Asia.[52] M.M. Thomas had encounters with various ideologies in his lifetime starting with Gandhism and Marxism, liberal nationalism, anti-caste movements like that of Jyotirao Phule and Ambedkar, and socialist humanism of Jayaprakash Narayan and Jawaharlal Nehru.[53] According to Hielke T. Wolters, Thomas himself identifies three stages of development in his theological thinking: The first period was characterised by a liberal theology and Gandhian ideology (upto 1941); in the second period, he combined neo-orthodox theology with Marxist ideology (upto 1948); and in the third period, he developed a Christ-centred model of participation collaborating with revolutionary changes in search for fuller humanity (beyond 1948).[54] T.M. Philip points out that Thomas was doing theology in the intersection between the church and the world. He sought to build bridges between them, "without falling into the twin dangers of either merging Christ and culture completely or separating them radically."[55] Thomas's theology suggests openness and participation of the church with other religions and secular ideologies. He proposes a wider *koinonia* in Christ which is wider than the church that will include people with various positive responses to Christ. On the other hand, he was supportive of a non-communal[56] Christian community which cares for secular ideals and nationalism built on peace and justice. His goal was humanisation of the society and the formation of a new humanity forged by God in Christ, both within and outside the church.[57] Thomas believed in the theology of what he termed as prophetic participation, which includes participation of the church and Christians in the society towards the struggle to achieve

---

52 Sunil M. Caleb, "M.M. Thomas' Engagements with Social Theories and Ideologies," in *Reclaiming Manyness: Re-reading M.M. Thomas in the Light of Indian Christian Theologies*, ed. P.G. George and Y.T. Vinayaraj (Serampore: SATHRI, 2015).

53 Caleb, "M.M. Thomas' Engagements," 23–27.

54 Hielke T. Wolters, *Theology of Prophetic Participation: M.M. Thomas' Concept of Salvation and the Collective Struggle for Fuller Humanity in India* (Delhi/Bangalore: ISPCK/UTC, 1996), 6.

55 T.M. Philip, "Preface" in *M.M. Thomas Reader: Selected Texts on Theology, Religion and Society*, ed. T. Jacob Thomas (Thiruvalla: CSS, 2002).

56 A community which does not discriminate on the basis of religion, caste, creed, etc.

57 Philip, "Preface."

fuller humanity. There is a balance in his writings between prophetic witness and participation in the wider community.[58] Thomas becomes important for our project because he guides Indian ecclesiology towards enlarging the borders of the church towards involvement and critical participation in the historical-social processes of the wider Indian community. He invites us to go beyond narrow, communal approaches of church engagement towards identification of the church with the religious, social, and ideological movements in the wider arena of the nation.

Let us now delve deeply into his ideas regarding the church and society so that we will be in a position to discern the kind of ecclesiological approach he had. Let me begin with what Hielke T. Wolters observed about Thomas's ecclesiology. Wolters noted that the dialectic between faith in the Christ-event and the struggle for fuller humanity strongly determines Thomas's understanding of the church. The relation between the church and the world, or church and society form the central themes of his ecclesiology.[59]

### A diaconal approach to the Indian church

M.M. Thomas is known to propose a diaconal approach to understand the role and character of the Indian church. *Diakonia* generally means the services, especially the social and charitable services, the church renders to the society. But, Thomas points out that as much as charitable services are important for the church, social *diakonia* is extremely important. He used the term *diakonia* in the sense of "social *diakonia*" borrowed from Masao Takaneka of Japan as distinguished from a charitable *diakonia*. This kind of social *diakonia* emphasises church's action to change the structures of the society in the direction of justice.[60] Thomas sees the importance of the diaconal approach as the starting point of thinking about Indian ecclesiology. This is the concept that Thomas hopes could make inroads for the church to be engaged in the wider society in various ways in the realm of religion or ideology. He regrets that this approach is something which is always relegated to the margins—the church's involvement in the socio-cultural and secular issues in the wider society.[61] According to him, the church should be engaged in service for the universality of human rights in society as well as peace with justice. In this sense, the church could

58 Wolters, *Theology of Prophetic Participation*, 5.

59 Wolters, *Theology of Prophetic Participation*, 232.

60 M.M. Thomas, *A Diaconal Approach to Indian Ecclesiology* (Rome/Thiruvalla: CIIS/CSS, 1995), 9.

61 Thomas, *Diaconal Approach*, 10.

be a prophetic sign to humankind as pointing to the kingdom of God.[62] Thomas emphasises that this *diakonia*, including "prophetic ministry and participation in the struggle for the humanisation of society and culture, becomes part of the essence of the church."[63]

Thomas points out that this *diakonia* should play out in India in the context of sociocultural transformation of our country in the secular realm with the influence of modernism. There has always been the legitimate demand that the Indian church should be grounded in Indian culture and traditions. However, according to Thomas, the *diakonia* of the church should deal with both the efforts of indigenisation and responding to modernisation. He contends,

> Many who are eager for an indigenous Indian church would emphasise rooting the church in the traditional religions and cultural life of India. But, since the traditional cultures of India are themselves in different stages of transformation under the impact of modernity, there is a strong case for affirming that it is necessary to relate the life and diaconic mission of the church to the contemporary reality of Indian life.[64]

Strikingly, Robin Boyd, writing much later after Thomas in *An Introduction to Indian Christian Theology* (2000), made similar arguments regarding the church's tension between indigenisation and secularisation and opted for an Indian church which is open to the secularising and modernising forces in the society. Boyd argues,

> Experiments along the lines of Christian ashrams, indigenous forms of worship, architecture and organisation are therefore of considerable value. But enthusiasm must be tempered with realism, for it is a sobering fact that many of those most enthusiastic for 'Indianisation' are now middle-aged and elderly...The Church must take care that the advancing mood of secularisation and modernising, particularly among young people, does not result in the marooning of a small island of "Indian Christianity" long since ceased to be current in the Indian society at large![65]

Boyd felt that post-Independence, Indianisation as inspired by nationalism is not the answer to develop a viable Indian church, but openness is one of the important factors. Drawing from D.T. Niles, Boyd is of the opinion that

> The (Indian) Church should simply be itself, living in "cultural kinship" with its non-Christian neighbours and drawing the dynamic of its development not from superimposed nationalism but from the Spirit of Christ

62 Thomas, *Diaconal Approach*, 10–11.
63 Thomas, *Diaconal Approach*, 11.
64 Thomas, *Diaconal Approach*, 12.
65 Boyd, *Indian Christian Theology*, 248.

> working within it, from the natural growth of the tree now firmly rooted in Indian soil. Such "indigenisation" need not conflict with openness in fellowship and sharing with the universal Church of Christ which knows no boundaries of nation, race or culture.[66]

Thomas rightly felt that we cannot totally neglect the wave of modernism in our world nor go back to a premodern situation. His hope is that we could search for a humanism in the present times of a more integral character which will be a participative endeavour with people of other faiths towards building up of our society in justice and peace. Thus, Thomas proposed the idea of an Open Secular *Koinonia* where the message of salvation in Christ is best communicated within the framework of humanisation of the modern world in dialogue with others and produces a diaconal witness in our society.[67] This leads us to the second important aspect of Thomas's ecclesiology, which is his Christ-centred wider *koinonia.*

### Church as Christ-centred wider *koinonia*

Thomas was always concerned that the Indian church has a narrow, communalistic character and that the church's fellowship with the wider world was limited. He envisaged a church which would be a *koinonia* or fellowship of believers, the secular society, and the wider community. The identity of this *koinonia* will however be determined by christocentricity. Christ continues to be the centre of M.M. Thomas's theology and ecclesiology. Thomas emphasises that "the religious fellowship within the church and the human fellowship in secular society are both within the reality of Christ and the history of salvation in the world."[68] The christocentricity provides the norm for Thomas's ecclesiology which is integrated in his theology to salvation and humanisation. Thomas's idea of a wider, christocentric *koinonia* in dialogical relationship with secular cultures, religions, and ideologies is based on his idea of Christ which is wider than the Jesus of Nazareth.[69] His idea of this wider *koinonia* beyond the visible boundaries of the church was reinforced somewhat, by his own admission, following Bishop Robinson's thought that in the New Testament, *koinonia* is expressive of the kingdom rather than merely the church. Thomas reiterates that recent documents of the World Council of

---

66 Boyd, *Indian Christian Theology*, 248.

67 Thomas, *Diaconal Approach*, 13.

68 M.M. Thomas, *Salvation and Humanisation: Some Crucial Issues of the Theology of Mission in Contemporary India* (Madras: CLS, 1971), 19.

69 M.M. Thomas, *Risking Christ for Christ's Sake* (Geneva: WCC, 1987), 114.

Churches (WCC) also go clearly in favour of this word being used in its wider sense.[70]

Thomas also follows Paul Devanandan and Raimon Panikkar, both of whom, according to Thomas, point to a redefinition of the church of Jesus Christ in relation to a wider people of Christ.[71] The open fellowship in Christ that M.M. Thomas is hinting at, is a community which constitutes different faith responses to Christ. He refers to one of the Vatican II documents (*The Dogmatic Constitution of the Church* and *Pastoral Constitution of the Church in the Modern World*) regarding the relationship of the church and the world, which is in terms of concentric circles. The groups in those circles range from baptised believers to those people who are unbaptised, but who acknowledge the Creator in some sense and those who do not acknowledge the source of goodness respectively, so on and so forth. Thomas notes that "there is no attempt to define rigidly the boundary of the people who are in communion with Christ."[72] Thomas makes it clear that apart from acknowledging a structured *koinonia* which is the church as we know it, we have to acknowledge a larger unstructured *koinonia*. He writes,

> We shall continue to speak of the community of those openly acknowledging the crucified and risen Jesus as the Christ and the gathered round the Lord's Table and the exposition of the word of God and scattered for witness and service, as the *church*, the "structured nucleus" of the people of Christ. But, we have to acknowledge a larger "unstructured stream" of *koinonia*-in-Christ or communion in the Messiah in human history, which is spiritually continuous and discontinuous with it.[73]

Elaborating on the idea of this Christ-centred wider *koinonia*, Thomas affirms that this fellowship is important so that rather than individualistic living, a community-centred living is possible.[74] This kind of wider *koinonia* will break down barriers of culture and religion, self-interests, and self-seeking, while seeking the formation of a community of common humanity based on justice, love, and forgiveness.[75] Moreover, according to Thomas, the significance of this type of *koinonia* is that

> it prevents the Church from a spiritual egoism which arrogates itself the right to decide who belongs to the messianic people...On the other, the

70 Thomas, *Diaconal Approach*, 13.

71 Thomas, *Risking Christ*, 113–114.

72 M.M. Thomas, *Man and the Universe of Faiths* (Madras: CLS, 1975), 136–137.

73 Thomas, *Risking Christ*, 114.

74 Thomas, *Man and the Universe*, 141.

75 M.M. Thomas, *The Church's Mission and Post-Modern Humanism: Collection of Essays & Talks, 1992–1996* (Madras/Delhi: CSS/ISPCK, 1996), 132.

> encounter with the Person of Jesus Christ will prevent commitments to the universal Christ-principle and the way of the Cross from being perverted into a legalism and used as an instrument of self-justification'.[76]

While Thomas's christocentricity is undoubtedly clear, he has very few references to the working of the Holy Spirit in his ecclesiology. However, in one instance, he cites the Vatican II documents by saying that the Holy Spirit makes it possible for different groups of people to be associated with the so-called paschal mystery of Christ. He finds this as inevitably pointing to the community of faith wider than the church.[77] In fact, Thomas agrees with the view of other scholars like Ioan Sauca who, on the basis of St. Maximus the Confessor, think that *koinonia* outside the church is possible because of the movements of the Holy Spirit who leads people to serve God even sometimes without their knowledge. Here, the church may seek to point out what the Spirit is doing outside the visible boundaries of the church, thus witnessing to the wider work of God in the world and creation.[78] Moreover, he believes that the open *koinonia* in Christ exposes the church to the "unexplored insights and facets of life in the Holy Spirit."[79] However, he does not explore nor theologise further regarding the role of the Spirit with respect to the church and how the Spirit works outside the church.

Returning to the concept of the wider *koinonia*, Thomas also discusses this in terms of the issue of baptism which has been generally construed as a criterion for determining membership in the churches. The wider *koinonia* that Thomas proposes includes fellowship between baptised and non-baptised believers. Thomas cites the Narsapur Consultation of church leaders held in 1966 for an emerging understanding of conversion and the meaning of being the church. He points out that the reports in this consultation agreed that there were converts in India who do not wish to go through baptism or identify with any particular church. In the light of this, a renewed understanding of baptism was called for. Baptism in India is generally taken to be one in which the person "repudiates his ancient cultural heritage and accepts an alien culture."[80] Thomas in his essay, "The Church—The Fellowship of the Baptised and the Unbaptised," cites many examples during the nineteenth century neo-Hindu period and also in present times of those who wished to belong to Christ but were

---

76 Thomas, *Man and the Universe,* 139.

77 Thomas, *Man and the Universe,* 139.

78 Thomas, *Diaconal Approach,* 13–14.

79 Thomas, *Man and the Universe,* 139.

80 Thomas, *Salvation and Humanisation,* 38.

not willing to be part of the organised church through baptism.[81] Thomas quotes Paul Lehman: "The difference between believers and unbelievers is not defined by church membership or even in the last analysis by baptism. The difference is defined by imaginative and behavioural sensitivity to what God is doing in the world to make and to keep human life human, to achieve the maturity of men (sic), that is, the new humanity."[82] Thomas's goal was a church which will be inclusive in nature and open to the diversity of Indian society. He approvingly cites Bishop V.S. Azariah in his emphasis that the church should not be a communal religious group only interested in its own. A communal church would prevent it from permeating the entire society across boundaries of caste, class, language, and race, a calling which can be fulfiled only through its members living alongside fellow-Indians sharing in public life with a concern for Christian principles.[83]

### A missional church

Thomas's ecclesiology cannot be conceived apart from his ideas on mission. Mission for Thomas includes evangelisation, construed beyond the usual narrow concerns of the growth of church membership to real concerns of human dignity and social justice.[84] Thomas is convinced that the church's mission is essentially about salvation and this salvation is integrally linked to humanisation.[85] In one of Thomas's writings, "A Social Manifesto of the Church 1942," certain lines of action by the churches (in Kerala) were suggested which include the idea of the church being involved in ministry to the whole person, including the person's environment.[86] Thomas suggests a dialogical approach to mission where the church must be in dialogical relation to both religions and ideologies. This relationship is supposed to be built up on the discovery of our common humanity. Thomas is, however, clear and categorical in stating that each culture or religion continues to maintain its uniqueness even as fundamental differences between them are affirmed.[87] The church's mission involves its engagement with sociopolitical issues of the society. Thomas

---

81 Thomas, *Church's Mission,* 155–160.

82 Paul Lehman, *Ethics in a Christian Context* (London: SCM Press, 1963), 101, 117, cited in Thomas, *Man and the Universe,* 136.

83 Thomas, *Church's Mission,* 152.

84 M.M. Thomas, *The Christian Response to the Asian Revolution* (Great Britain: SCM Press, 1966), 105.

85 Thomas, *Salvation and Humanisation,* 18.

86 M.M. Thomas, *Ideological Quest within Christian Commitment, 1939–1954* (Madras: CLS, 1983), 72.

87 Thomas, *Christian Response,* 115.

strongly stresses the church's need to address issues of social justice with the resources available in the world.[88] He strongly believes that

> the Churches dare not assume a purely passive, indifferent or neutral attitude towards crucial political and social issues of the times . . .. It is the responsibility of the Church to rediscover and proclaim both to its members as well as to those outside, the basic truths declared in the Bible concerning the life of men in society and in the State, which no individual or government can disregard with impunity.[89]

## Church's mission in a pluralistic context

M.M. Thomas is of the opinion that India had a plural context from the beginning, but it is in the contemporary times that pluralism is a phenomenon to be reckoned with in the background of the context of a secular democratic nation-state with its demands of liberty, equality, and justice.[90] Thomas contends that it is the "common historical responsibility of building a genuinely human community that brings peoples of all religions and culture within the dialogical framework of pluralism."[91] Thomas is convinced that the issue of pluralism is to be seen in connection with our joint struggle for humanisation of the world. He identifies the context of struggle as increasing technological advance and general mechanisation of human life along with impoverishment and marginalisation of a majority of the people.[92] In order to identify the nature of the gospel for such an engagement, Thomas stresses that it should be the humanity of the crucified Jesus where the cross in the Indian setting is taken as God's identification with human suffering rather than Paul's emphasis on the atonement for human sin.[93] Thomas connects the church's mission to his idea of the Christ-centred *koinonia* where the church transcends all communities defined by type, culture, and even ideology and religion and opens people for interpersonal communication with each other.[94] In this way, Thomas contends that a sort of secular *koinonia* outside the church is possible at the local, national, and world levels in the modern pluralistic society of many religions and cultures.[95] Thomas identifies that communalisation (segregation on the basis of caste, religion, creed, etc.) of society is a problem in India which the church also

88 Thomas, *Ideological Quest*, 72–73.
89 Thomas, *Ideological Quest*, 224.
90 Thomas, *Church's Mission*, 129.
91 Thomas, *Church's Mission*, 129.
92 Thomas, *Church's Mission*, 129.
93 Thomas, *Church's Mission*, 130–131.
94 Thomas, *Church's Mission*, 132.
95 Thomas, *Church's Mission*, 132.

is very much part of. His theology of humanisation therefore entails a vision of the church which is non-communal in the context of separation of the Indian society into narrow communities based on various religions and cultures. He seeks to find a solution to get out of such a church. He states,

> Along this approach may lie the solution of our finding in India, a non-communal form of the church in a situation where religious communalism has become a serious national problem; and the church organised as a minority community separate from the majority and other minority communities, each safeguarding its numerical strength and its own traditional personal law and seeking communal prestige and communal political power in the body-politic, makes conversion of groups and even individuals a problem of intercommunal relations.[96]

M.M. Thomas highlights why the dialogical approach to mission helps. The dialogical approach, according to Thomas, can help in various ways: First, "it will help us distinguish the essential unchanging core of our faith from the historical expressions of that core in doctrine and life."[97] Second, "it brings new insights which illumine and enrich our understanding of God and his Christ and leads the church to a greater catholicity."[98] Third, "we come to realise in a new way that the mission is Christ's, not ours, that evangelism means meeting Christ who is already at work in the situation."[99] Thomas's concern for participation of the church in every aspect of religious and secular life is geared towards building up of the nation. Thomas urges us to shed the minority consciousness that is so prevalent among the Christian community and asks us to work together towards nation-building. The church must seek to serve the larger human community as its servant and, thus, it can be an open community. The church would become a prophetic voice only when it participates with the larger struggles of the community. Thomas famously said that "Only participants can be prophets."[100] For M.M. Thomas, participation of the church in nationbuilding with people of other faiths and no faiths is one of its true mission and ministry. This participation of Christians in the life of the nation and its people could be taken as an expression of Christian discipleship.[101]

---

96 Thomas, *Church's Mission,* 134.
97 Thomas, *Christian Response,* 117.
98 Thomas, *Christian Response,* 117.
99 Thomas, *Christian Response,* 117.
100 Thomas, *Christian Response,* 108.
101 Thomas, *Christian Response,* 104.

## Structure or shape of the church

For Thomas, the structure or shape of the church is determined by the concerns that the Indian church needs to attend to. He fears that the church of today is narrow and concerned only with itself instead of wider engagement with society and culture. Deliberating on the new shape or form of the Indian church, Thomas contends that the question of shape of the church is of radical importance in this secular age.[102]

He understands that the "being, functions, and forms of the church" should be seen within the setting of the Christian solidarity with all others in the larger human community.[103] He is of the opinion that for the church to meet the needs of the society, it needs the resources and participation of people from all faith communities.[104] According to him, the form or shape of the church should be such that the congregation may be oriented to the mission for the secular humanity beyond the church.[105] In all these instances, it is evident that Thomas is in favour of a church with open borders.

Thomas's ideas are thrown into sharp relief with the ideas of Lesslie Newbigin, the well-known missionary statesman, who spent a good part of his life in south India and became bishop in one of its dioceses. Their exchange of thoughts mostly centred around the church and its relationship with the world. Thomas had quite a bit of disagreement with Bishop Lesslie Newbigin's position about Christianity and the church's response to the human community outside the church in its secular and religious contours. Thomas points out Bishop Newbigin's concern about the ecumenical movement's stress on engagement with humanity; that human beings cannot be the object of ultimate loyalty and humans cannot be understood by other humans, all of whom are mortals. He questions this by saying that though Bishop Newbigin had a point, yet, we must understand that the kingdom of God does not start with death, but begins and is partially realised here and now within history and the pangs of death and disintegration.[106] Thomas also cites Newbigin to say that the latter stood for a church which should be more ready to identify itself thoroughly with the life of the nation.[107] But, there is Newbigin's objection to any special treatment of a particular context for the proclamation of the gospel because the latter thinks that the gospel will make itself relevant for any particular

[102] Thomas, *Salvation and Humanisation*, 59.
[103] Thomas, *Christian Response*, 114.
[104] Thomas, *Christian Response*, 113.
[105] Thomas, *Salvation and Humanisation*, 58.
[106] Thomas, *Salvation and Humanisation*, 9.
[107] Thomas, *Salvation and Humanisation*, 17.

situation, time, or context. Thomas objects to this by rejecting any kind of universalism or biblicism inherent in such a suggestion. He refers to the issue that God is here understood in too static terms, and also that the biblical realities and truth need interpretations in a secular context and cannot be taken literally.[108]

Deliberating on the new shape or form of the Indian church, Thomas contends that this question of shape of the church is of continuous importance in this age and especially in India. In a context now where the church does not control society and politics, the danger is of having a church which is interested in its own narrow interests, leading to a secluded or narrow existence unconcerned about public life and the world. It leads to an exclusively individualistic life of piety.[109] Thomas proposes the idea of a participatory church in the secular world where the church will play the role of a suffering servant like that of the Confessing Church in Germany which involved itself in the political situation of the country.[110] Thomas says,

> We have to find a more proper form for the Church in India than the very unsatisfactory form of an Indian religious community. The goal should be its capacity to witness to Christ as Saviour, Servant and Perfector of all men (sic) not merely isolated individuals, but as persons in and with their various secular and religious group-ties and longing for fuller life... We need a new pattern of combining Christian self-identity and secular solidarity with all men.(sic)[111]

Thomas's ecclesiology is clearly geared towards wider engagement of the church in the sociopolitical arena of the Indian society. What is significant is Thomas's stress on prophetic participation of the church in the historical processes of the wider society. His ideas of the church to go beyond narrow confines of one's religion, culture, and ideology calls the Christian community towards living and acting together in solidarity for common issues. On the other hand, the christological commitment of the churches lays out distinctive borders for the church although it is open to engagement and interaction. One of the striking observations of Thomas is that in the context of India's development in terms of modernisation and secularisation, the church should be able to adjust and coordinate boundaries with secular cultures, communions, and society. In this sense, the secular fellowship which Thomas proposes, although Christ-centred, offers a viable way towards wider engagement

[108] Thomas, *Salvation and Humanisation*, 47.
[109] Thomas, *Salvation and Humanisation*, 59.
[110] Thomas, *Salvation and Humanisation*, 59–60.
[111] Thomas, *Salvation and Humanisation*, 60.

of the church. His ecclesiology is therefore relational, but has distinctive boundaries. However, it is not clear how Thomas bases his relational church on a christocentric paradigm without adequate employment of pneumatological motifs. As it is shown earlier, Thomas's pneumatological reflection is scarce and he has very little to say about the role of the Spirit in the church which seeks to engage and enlarge its borders.

## Ecclesiologies of Chenchiah and M.M. Thomas: Comparative appraisal and Spirit's role in the Indian church and its borders

In the preceding discussions, we have found two insightful perspectives from two prominent Indian thinkers who have tried to make sense of the church from an Indian context. We can find both similarities and contrasts in their approaches. While we point them out, we will also evaluate whether their ecclesiologies have adequately taken with seriousness the Spirit's role in the church and how far they are suitable to develop a permeable Spirit ecclesiology for India.

It is evident that both Chenchiah and Thomas were critical of the organised church, as found in India, reflecting the general trend of the pre- and post-Independence period theological thinking. However, Chenchiah's blunt rejection of the essence of the church with respect to its rituals and sacraments stands in contrast to Thomas's subtle critique of the same. Hailing from a Hindu background, Chenchiah did not find the organised Christian church very relevant for the people in India. He was more in favour of the shape of the church with essentially no divisions or borders between various religious communities. The church, in this sense, would overcome the divisions of creed and religion, spiritual and secular, and barriers of doctrine and practices, and spread like leaven. On the other hand, Thomas partly advocates open borders where the church would engage with various religions and ideologies in a secular fellowship, but will be defined christologically. The church's mission in this sense would include its engagement in social, cultural, economic, and political life of the people. Thomas's church would engage with the wider society and seek to get involved in issues of justice and peace. This last was, however, not the forte of Chenchiah's church's engagement with sociopolitical justice issues. Chenchiah's was much of a religious endeavour to bring all communities together in a common spirituality with a nationalistic motivation.

Both Chenchiah and Thomas were christocentric to their core. To Chenchiah, as we have seen, Christ matters more than churches, or institutions, or rituals and dogmas. This is not surprising, though, because of the Hindu religion's generally nondogmatic stance, although not non-ritualistic. For Thomas, Christ is the central identity for the church or for any secular fellowship. This is what ensures that Thomas's church is open but bordered as it is defined by its christocentricity. On the other hand, while Chenchiah is christocentric, his church is an open, or a borderless community where people of various religious backgrounds can be united into a common spirituality. Chenchiah's christocentricity does not encompass the church with distinctive borders.

What greatly separates them is the pneumatological emphasis in Chenchiah's ecclesiology and the corresponding significant lack in Thomas's of the role of the Spirit in the church. It can be clearly pointed out that the notion of the Spirit plays a great role in fostering openness and vitality in the ecclesiology of Chenchiah. Chenchiah's efforts were towards bridging the religious-social, sacred-secular divide in the power of the Spirit and practicing spirituality even beyond the church in and through daily lives. This brings him to the concept of a noninstitutional religion and even a churchless Christianity, where there is no need for liturgy and sacraments. Christianity is supposed to spread like a leaven without a particular church structure. Although Thomas indicates at some points that the Holy Spirit enables us to form inclusive communities, he fails to give adequate role to the Spirit in the church's life. While the Spirit forms the principal animator and basis of the open church, Thomas could not elaborate on how Christ, without the action of the Spirit, can be instrumental in creating open secular fellowships. The pneumatological perspective in Chenchiah's ecclesiology can be said to provide relationality in terms of making the particular universal and in providing a sort of openness and inclusivity. Here, it is clearly evident that Chenchiah qualifies the christological dimension with a pneumatological perspective. His pneumatological perspective renders his ecclesiology relational. However, this relationality is not qualified with the particularity and distinctiveness of the Christian community. While decolonisation is important, the distinct identity of an Indian church as a Christian community is not clearly dealt with. For Thomas, however, the mark of distinctiveness is Christ himself who defines the church and gives to it its particularity although it seeks to be open.

So, for the purposes of the central argument of the present book, it can be noted that while Chenchiah's ecclesiology is pneumatologically influenced which leads to its open and borderless character, it fails in maintaining its distinctiveness. On the other hand, while Thomas's ecclesiology is christocentric and particular, it still remains a church with open borders.

However, he fails in maintaining the dialectics of the role of Christ and the Spirit which should have formed the basis of the church with open borders. One thing worth pointing out is that, for both the theologians, there is a lack of the dialectical relationship between relationality and distinctiveness in terms of a balance between universality and particularity, unity and diversity, the joint action of the Word and Spirit, the spiritual and the material, and so on.

Thus, in the following pages, we look forward to engaging with the Spirit ecclesiology of Samuel Rayan to address the issues of these dialectical relationships and to arrive at a permeable ecclesiology for the Indian context in conversation with other theologians dealt with so far, both Western and Indian.

## The Spirit ecclesiology of Samuel Rayan with permeable borders

The arguments that will follow will be an attempt to offer a suitable Spirit ecclesiology that fulfils, on the one hand, the criterion of relational-distinctiveness, and on the other hand, the particular demands of the Indian context. The Spirit ecclesiology of Samuel Rayan is offered as a suitable alternative. It will become clear that what is lacking in Amos Yong's ecclesiological project is supplemented by Rayan's project. Rayan's project will also show in what areas he is more suitable than his counterparts Chenchiah and Thomas for the development of a permeable Spirit ecclesiology. We will start with a brief introduction of Samuel Rayan.

Samuel Rayan SJ, born in 1920, is an Indian theologian, broadly characterised as a liberation theologian. However, he is a liberation theologian with a difference as his pneumatological perspectives guide his theology of liberation.[112] He entered the *Society of Jesus* in 1939 and then studied philosophy at Shembabanur, Tamilnadu, from 1942–1945. Following his philosophy degree, he studied theology at De Nobili College, Jnana-Deepa Vidyapeeth, Pune. Rayan was ordained as a priest in 1955 and thereafter, he pursued his doctoral studies in theology at the Gregorian University, Rome, from 1958–1960. In the year 1961, he became the chaplain of AICUF (All India Catholic University Federation) in Kerala.[113] This led him into his engagement with Marxism regarding concern for

[112] Kirsteen Kim, *Mission in the Spirit: The Holy Spirit in Indian Christian Theologies* (Delhi: ISPCK, 2003), 139.

[113] Kurien Kunnumpuram, ed., *Jesus: The Relevance of His Person and Message for Our Times*, vol. 1 of *Selected Writings of Samuel Rayan SJ* (Bombay: St. Paul's, 2011), 7.

humanisation and development.[114] Kirsteen Kim points out that Rayan's liberation theology was also influenced by the Sri Lankan Jesuit Aloysius Pieris SJ.[115] From 1968 to 1982, he was one of the first invited Catholic members of the WCC Faith and Order Commission. This ecumenical engagement equipped him to serve as the principal of the Indian School of Ecumenical Theology in Bangalore from 1988 to 1990. He also served as a professor and Dean of Vidyajyoti College of Theology in Delhi.[116] In a context where socioeconomic and religio-cultural oppression and marginalisation continues, Rayan's theology provides the church with tools to engage broadly in the Spirit with liberation of the oppressed. For Rayan, theology is "faith seeking justice."[117] Moreover, his pneumatological perspective has led him to take the concrete, cultural, and religious realities into account in his theology.[118] Theology ought to address the struggles, problems, and potentials of a community. It is the theology of everyday life not as practised by professionals, but out of the lived experiences of the common people.[119] Rayan's thoughts can be explored through one of his published books[120] and various articles in different journals.[121]

### Overview of Samuel Rayan's theology

Samuel Rayan's theology and ecclesiology can be described as the dynamic combination of twin images, *bread* and *breath*. In fact, the title of a *Festschrift* for Rayan's seventieth birthday contained the phrase *bread and breath*.[122] In the introduction to this book, *bread and breath* are referred to as the "two poles" around which Rayan's theological reflections

114 Kim, *Mission in the Spirit*, 140.

115 Aloysius Pieris, *An Asian Theology of Liberation, Faith Meets Faith Series* (Maryknoll, NY: Orbis Books, 1988), 45–50, cited in Kim, *Mission in the Spirit*, 157.

116 Kim, *Mission in the Spirit*, 138.

117 Samuel Rayan, "Doing Theology in India," in *Doing Theology: Indian Christian Reflections on Theologizing in India Today*, vol. 2 of *Collected Writings of Samuel Rayan SJ*, ed. Kurien Kunnumpuram (Delhi: ISPCK, 2013), 22.

118 Kim, *Mission in the Spirit*, 139.

119 Rayan, "Doing Theology in India," 23.

120 Samuel Rayan, *Breath of Fire—The Holy Spirit: Heart of the Christian Gospel* (London: Geoffrey Chapman, 1979). First published as *The Holy Spirit: Heart of the Gospel and Christian Hope* (Maryknoll, NY: Orbis Books, 1978); and later published as *Come Holy Spirit* (Delhi: Media House, 1998).

121 Journals namely *Jeevadhara, Religion and Society (RS), Indian Journal of Theology (IJT)*, and *Vidyajyoti Journal of Theological Reflection (VJTR)*.

122 T.K. John, ed., *Bread and Breath: Essays in Honour of Samuel Rayan SJ*, Jesuit Theological Forum Reflections 5 (Anand, Gujarat: Gujarat Sahitya Prakash, 1991). Rayan himself derives this phrase from a poem by Gerard Manley Hopkins entitled *Giver of Breath and Bread*.

turn.[123] The phrase *bread and breath* in Rayan's theology expresses the dynamics of our human life in many facets and maintains the dialectics of the joint action of Christ and the Spirit. *Bread and breath* in Rayan's theology brings together various meanings. *Bread* for him signifies food for all, along with the need for justice when considered in the context of marginalisation and poverty perpetuated by the powerful. *Breath* signifies the role of the Spirit that inspires us through faith to provide for the hungry.[124] The *breath* of God helps us to live by the Spirit while the Spirit also inspires us through Christ to share the materials we possess. Our human life is the dynamic interplay of the spiritual and the material.[125] The dialectics of *bread and breath* is more nuanced in Rayan as Kirsteen Kim points out that "*bread and breath* are even more integrated . . . not only breath but also bread is a symbol of the Holy Spirit."[126] Again, *bread* is the person of Jesus Christ, the Bread of Life who breathes the Spirit of God. Kim observes the dialectics further. She writes,

> Bread and the breath is a richly poetic way of combining two natures of Christ, the secular and the sacred, the immanence and transcendence of God . . . to motivate mystics to seek human well-being and encounter the Spirit in their neighbours . . .. Conversely, bread and breath expresses to activists the role of the contemplative and to historians the validity of the mystical.[127]

The above *breath and bread* dialectic represented in one of the connotations of the joint working of Spirit and Christ can be seen in Rayan's description of Spirit Christology. Although his Christology can be primarily classed as Spirit Christology, he admits that this cannot be done without a corresponding Logos Christology.

## Spirit Christology

Rayan's Christology is distinctively pneumatological and liberationist. Jesus is the "symbol of the Holy Spirit,"[128] but this Spirit "is the non-conformist manner in which Jesus moved with bad characters, and ate with social outcasts [and] in the concern for bread for the hungry."[129] This is its liberationist aspect. The Spirit-Christ dialectic is further evident as he

123 John, *Bread and Breath*, xii.

124 John, *Bread and Breath*, xii.

125 Kim, *Mission in the Spirit*, 192.

126 Kim, *Mission in the Spirit*, 192.

127 Kim, *Mission in the Spirit*, 193.

128 Rayan, "Symbols of the Spirit," in *God's Hope Becoming Visible: Indian Christian Reflections on Some Relevant Issues of Our Times*, vol. 3 of *Collected Writings of Samuel Rayan SJ*, ed. Kurien Kunnumpuram (Delhi: ISPCK, 2013), 120.

129 Rayan, "Symbols of the Spirit," 120.

contends that "at the beginning of Christianity stand two events: the Christ event and the Spirit event. [. . .] Without the experience of the Spirit, Jesus could not have moved men and women of his time as he did."[130] Rayan clearly explains the relationship between pneumatological Christology and christological pneumatology. He writes: "Jesus is Christ and Lord only through the Holy Spirit. This is pneumatological Christology. But the Holy Spirit is only given, and in this sense, 'there is a Spirit at all only if Jesus is Christ and Lord.'"[131] Here, we have christological pneumatology. He argues that it is not possible to develop pneumatology separately from the Word.[132] On the other hand, Rayan does highlight the importance of Spirit Christology, which he claims has been neglected in favour of Logos Christology in the West. He writes,

> Spirit Christology presents an interpretation of Jesus in a way analogous to Logos Christology which has been dominant since the second century. The main difference is that Spirit Christology functions in an inclusive way, open to other New Testament Christologies, ready to consider, interpret, and appropriate them, while Logos Christology has tended to be exclusive, throwing other Christologies in a shadow.[133]

Rayan argues for the importance of Spirit Christology as its capacity to highlight Jesus's humanity in his "subjectivity, personhood, freedom, and obedience,"[134] which reveals him as a person of history. This aspect of Jesus has been neglected by Logos Christology.[135] Spirit Christology also determines the aspect of salvation for Rayan and makes it universal. He writes,

> God as Spirit has been effecting salvation from the beginning of world history. Salvation did not begin with Jesus. Jesus reveals it, realises it historically, and becomes its perfect exemplar . . .. Since no less than God acts in Jesus for the salvation of the world, this salvation is universally relevant for humankind.[136]

Rayan's Spirit Christology is expressed in terms of annunciation, baptism, resurrection, and Pentecost. In the annunciation, the Virgin Mary was hovered over by the Holy Spirit resulting in the New Man, Jesus Christ. When we offer ourselves similarly to the Spirit, "God's Word will

---

130 Rayan, "New Efforts in Pneumatology," in Kurien Kunnumpuram, ed., *God's Hope Becoming Visible,* 99.

131 Rayan, "New Efforts in Pneumatology," 98.

132 Rayan, "New Efforts in Pneumatology," 98.

133 Rayan, "New Efforts in Pneumatology," 98.

134 Rayan, "New Efforts in Pneumatology," 100.

135 Rayan, "New Efforts in Pneumatology," 100.

136 Rayan, "New Efforts in Pneumatology," 100.

become flesh in us."[137] Rayan affirms that from the moment of baptism, the Spirit took charge of Jesus's ministry and similarly, the work of the Spirit begins in our hearts with the coming of the Spirit.[138] For Rayan, the death and resurrection of Christ are bound up together. While death symbolises the commitment of Christ towards the oppressed and exploited and is a resistance towards evil, the resurrection symbolises the beginning of new birth and new creation.[139] Rayan agrees with M.M. Thomas that resurrection is an eschatological event, which signals the entry into new creation. It is through the Spirit that Jesus is made contemporary and ever present with us. It brings out the possibility of a new order in our present times and makes history present. He links this to our daily life and concern for justice through the effect of Christ's resurrection for all humanity. He concludes that Christ is present because of resurrection, "not only in the church, not only in the sacraments, but in the care people give for one another, in the struggle for justice, solidarity, and friendship and the toil for daily rice. Jesus is there with them participating in their liturgy of life."[140] Rayan argues that through Christ's resurrection, the Spirit is breathed in us and we are encouraged to communicate that Spirit among others. This makes the "Spirit of God, a Spirit of befriendedness and reconciliation."[141] He claims that we can all share in the resurrection of Christ through the communication of the Spirit, building a community of justice and love.[142] At Pentecost, referring to the pouring out of the Spirit with tongues of fire, Rayan affirms that "the Spirit is the Communicator of the Word. The creative Spirit and the creative Word work together."[143]

What is evident in Rayan's Spirit Christology is the dialectic of the working of the Spirit and the Word/Christ together with an added liberationist perspective. It is seen that the Spirit, on the one hand, ensures the relevance of salvation of Christ universally among humanity, and on the other hand, ensures the particularity of that salvation through the Logos made flesh historically. Salvation in Rayan always has liberation of the oppressed in focus. Again, the resurrection of Christ, on the one hand, signifies new creation through the Spirit, while the eschatological Spirit

137 Rayan, *Come Holy Spirit*, 14.

138 Rayan, *Come Holy Spirit*, 15.

139 Rayan, "Jesus and the Poor in the Fourth Gospel," in *Jesus: Relevance of His Person and the Message for Our Times*, ed. Kurien Kunnumpuram, vol. 1 (Mumbai: St. Paul's, 2011), 145.

140 Rayan, "Decolonization of Theology," in Kurien Kunnumpuram, *Doing Theology*, 43.

141 Rayan, *Come Holy Spirit*, 76–77.

142 Rayan, *Come Holy Spirit*, 76–77.

143 Rayan, *Come Holy Spirit*, 19.

makes the resurrected Christ ever present with us. Furthermore, the Spirit helps the liberation of Christ to be witnessed in our everyday lives and in the building of communities of justice and peace. Thus, there is also the dialectics of the Spirit and Christ, the spiritual and the concrete, working here along with the liberationist perspective.

**Decolonisation of theology and theology of life**

Along with the above dialectic working in Rayan's theology, it must be highlighted that it has a strong decolonisation approach, which leads him to a theology of life from the liberationist perspective. In his article, *Decolonizing of Theology*, Rayan admits that such an effort of decolonisation is neither new nor confined to India, but emphasises that it is absolutely necessary in India. In this article, he outlines the problems with colonial theology: He contends that since colonial theology failed to acknowledge that God has been working through the Spirit even before the colonial era in India, it failed to acknowledge the richness of India's culture and religion, its thought-world and symbols. Subsequently, it opted for importing the traditions and cultures of the West, which ended up making God a stranger in the land and the churches mere "replicas of Western churches."[144] Colonial theologies manufactured in the Western academies and monasteries stressed hierarchy, power, submission, and otherworldly salvation and failed to be prophetic in proclaiming a gospel of liberation for the poor.[145] Following Balasundaram,[146] Rayan further notes that classical traditional theology is a "handmaid of Western expansionism" and, therefore, has been primarily church-centred and usually equated the kingdom of God with the church making it the sole vehicle of salvation.[147] It has been nonrevolutionary and ignorant of the conditions of workers and the poor, being bereft of social analysis, "individualistic in orientation,"[148] and presents Christ, in the words of Aloysius Pieris, as "the Western colonizer's tribal god seeking ascendency in the Asian pantheon."[149]

In response to this colonised theology, Rayan offers a theology of life, of praxis; rather "ortho-theo-praxis,"[150] that rescues faith from being merely an "intellectual assent" of the patristic and scholastic system to a

144 Samuel Rayan, "Decolonization," 29–34.
145 Rayan, "Decolonization," 29–34.
146 Rayan, "Decolonization," 32.
147 Rayan, "Decolonization," 34.
148 Rayan, "Decolonization," 34.
149 Aloysius Pieris, *An Asian Theology of Liberation* (New York: Orbis Books, 1988), 59, cited in Rayan, "Decolonization," 34.
150 Rayan, "Decolonization," 39.

theology that concretely connects with hope of the kingdom.[151] He writes that theology ought to "connect hope and freedom in history; connect eschatology and struggle for justice now; connect Reign of God and social change."[152] As a concrete theology of praxis and life, Rayan's theology seeks to speak from the perspective of the oppressed, springing from the suffering and struggles of the victims of oppression; in other words, from the "underside of history."[153] Such a theology from the perspective of the oppressed people becomes a "people's theology"[154] that critiques the structures of society that oppress the poor and the marginalised. Further, this kind of theology affirms a theology of religions not only from the perspective of Christians, but from the perspective of neighbours of other faiths. Rayan argues that since in India or Asia, the majority of the poor are from other faiths, "theology has to speak to and speak through non-Christian peoplehood."[155] Citing Aloysius Pieris, Rayan notes the importance of "theology of religions that will expand the existing boundaries of orthodoxy as we enter into the liberative streams of other religions and cultures."[156] In other words, this liberationist theology would affirm unity in diversity, theological pluralism and not dead uniformity, and this unity would be "woven out of diverse ethnic groups, cultures, languages, religions, myths, and sacred texts and symbols."[157] Finally, such a theology itself would be open to be challenged, judged, and evaluated from different perspectives and especially from the perspective of the victims.[158]

The above are the features of a theology of life that Rayan seeks to offer, but how does he actually attempt to do it? His primary strategy to get rid of much of colonial theology's abstract and metaphysical emphasis and theoretical articulations is to give bodily language to theology. This would be a language of "art, of poetry, drama, painting, sculpture and dance, of the novel and the short story, or even of architecture," a language close to the earth and one that has the capacity to carry our struggles and celebrations.[159] In these terms, symbols, myths, imagination, and memory become vital vehicles of faith. Rayan makes a plea to use symbols "for the creation of a living and vigorous theology."[160] He claims that myths expressed

151 Rayan, "Decolonization," 39.
152 Rayan, "Decolonization," 39.
153 Rayan, "Decolonization," 41.
154 Rayan, "Decolonization," 41.
155 Rayan, "Decolonization," 41.
156 Pieris, *Asian Theology*, 87, cited in Rayan, "Decolonization," 41.
157 Rayan, "Decolonization," 35–43.
158 Rayan, "Decolonization," 35–43.
159 Rayan, "Theology as Art," in Kurien Kunnumpuram, *Doing Theology*, 8.
160 Rayan, "Theology as Art," 8.

through rituals and stories lead us into participation with a particular religion or culture and hold together the sacred and the profane. So, he calls for the re-mythologisation of religion and theology that would open up avenues to explore and appreciate the mythical richness of religious traditions of India. Imagination and collective memory of the community again are the bedrock of myths and symbols, which continue to connect us to God and the entire creation.[161] Again, to counteract the theologies of the dominant, he does *people's theology* as mentioned above. The source for people's theology is the life of the people and the stories that narrate people's movements, struggles, and generosity of ordinary people. It is a theology of the ordinary people and not simply about learned propositions to be discussed in academia. It is a people-centred theology using the narratives of ordinary people.[162] This includes doing theology as a disciple. In other words, the call to discipleship is a call to theologise as well. The call for commitment to Christ is a call to critically analyse the forces at work in the world, to be open for God's kingdom, and to discern movements of liberation in the world.[163] This theology rooted in praxis looks forward to history being humanised and transformed. Rayan maintains that our faith in God and the coming reign should be correlated with a praxis that critically evaluates history and also transforms it.[164] One of the aspects in which Rayan expresses his theology of life is through his theology of creation and the earth.

## Theology of creation and the earth

Rayan's theology of creation and the earth holds in tension the dialectics of the unity in diversity, spiritual and the concrete, and the role of the Spirit and Christ with his own characteristic liberationist perspective. Rayan claims that "the Holy Spirit is the author of all dynamism in nature, all the chemisms and tactisms . . . movements, colours, sounds, freedoms, and spontaneities. It is the Spirit that holds this diversity together, weaving them into cosmic harmony."[165] In this web of interrelatedness, "God is here not as the proprietor of nature and of men and women but as Source

161 Rayan, "Theology as Art," 3–13.

162 Rayan, "People's Theology," in Kurien Kunnumpuram, *Doing Theology*, 79–103.

163 Rayan, "Theologian as Disciple—Disciple as Theologian," in Kurien Kunnumpuram, *Doing Theology*, 46–52.

164 Rayan, "Indian Theology and the Problem of History," in Kurien Kunnumpuram, *Doing Theology*, 192–221.

165 Rayan, "New Efforts in Pneumatology," 107.

and Goal and Friend and Home."[166] Rayan thinks of this interrelatedness as otherness. He writes,

> the otherness is a reality within interrelatedness. All otherness is intrinsically for-one-anotherness.. . . There is a unity of the human, the cosmic, the technical, and the divine. Without nature, the human being is nothing; without the human being, nature is nothing.[167]

The above shows the unity in diversity that is brought about by the Spirit in and through creation. Rayan uses this aspect of interrelatedness and gives it his own liberationist perspective. He explains that through this interrelatedness brought about by the Spirit, we are encouraged to resist dehumanisation and oppression and are urged to fight for justice and freedom.[168]

Rayan links this interrelatedness to new creation with a liberationist perspective. He affirms that the Spirit brings new creation in terms of providing power and energy to the weak and the oppressed.[169] The new creation not only energises the weak and the oppressed but also renews the whole earth, as Rayan believes that the whole creation and our whole lives are "bathed in the Holy Spirit."[170] The Spirit renews the world. Rayan contends that the Spirit's work has to be affirmed both in our hearts and in the wider outreaches of the cosmos of God's creation. The involvement of the Spirit in creation takes up the issues of renewal of the earth, regeneration of society, and rebuilding our value systems.[171] Rayan claims that "all the beginnings, all fresh stirrings of life in particular, all creativity and development, all lushness and blossoming, is associated with and attributed to the action of the Holy Spirit!"[172] The Spirit pleads with us to be befriended by God and nature, to restore God's beautiful creation.[173] While the Spirit inspires and creates, the earth becomes the concrete locus of such renewal as it is considered an embodiment of Christ's body. Rayan thinks of the earth as the "primordial sacrament"[174] of God because

---

166 Rayan, "Theological Perspectives on the Environmental Crisis," in *Nature, Woman and the Church: Indian Christian Reflections on Ecology, Feminism and Ecclesiology*, vol. 1 of *Collected Writings of Samuel Rayan SJ*, ed. Kurien Kunnumpuram (Delhi: ISPCK, 2013), 89.

167 Rayan, "Theological Perspectives," 89.

168 Rayan, "Symbols of the Spirit," 135.

169 Rayan, "Symbols of the Spirit," 135.

170 Rayan, *Come Holy Spirit*, 10.

171 Rayan, *Come Holy Spirit*, 10.

172 Rayan, "Ecology and Theology: A Theology of Nature, a Theology of Life," in Kurien Kunnumpuram, *Nature, Woman and the Church*, 64.

173 Rayan, "Ecology and Theology," 65.

174 Rayan, "'Ecology and Theology," 59.

the earth is the ground of our existence; "the giver of breath and bread and like God, immensely resourceful."[175] He finds in nature and earth the extension of "Christ's bodiliness."[176] In the incarnation, the universe's evolutionary pilgrimage attains its fulfilment. In Christ, all matter and all its forms and processes seem to draw in the divine and endow everything with new sanctity and dignity. The "whole of nature is the Mother of the Son of God."[177]

Having discussed the basic framework of Rayan's theology, we will now proceed to discuss his Spirit ecclesiology. We hope to show that his Spirit ecclesiology is a permeable Spirit ecclesiology that shows the relational-distinctive dialectics. It will be shown how Rayan's ecclesiology is both similar to and different from Yong's, Chenchiah's, and Thomas's and thereby argue that Rayan's theology and ecclesiology are appropriate for a permeable Spirit ecclesiology in the Indian context. We will discuss Rayan's ecclesiology in terms of the nature, ministry, and mission of the church.

## The permeable Spirit ecclesiology of Samuel Rayan

### The nature of a permeable Spirit ecclesiology

#### *A pneumatic and liberationist community with a critical edge*

Ecclesiology, for Rayan, is essentially constituted by the Spirit, but he thinks that the Spirit-experiences of the people help build the church community. Distinctively, Rayan's focus is on the Spirit-experiences of those people who are poor and marginalised, expressing the liberationist dimension. This liberationist dimension also carries with it a distinctive critical character which is both self-critical and a critique of the oppressive forces in and beyond the church that perpetuate such marginalisation. Rayan affirms that the "church is radically pneumatic"[178] in the sense that it is constituted out of the people's Spirit-experience, mediated through the Spirit's presence and gifts to them.[179] One might ask, what is the content of this Spirit-experience? Rayan writes, "The Spirit works primarily by generating awareness and communion . . . by giving us vision and urging us to build community."[180] Rayan contends that this kind of Spirit experience ensures participation by the ordinary people, especially

175 Rayan, "'Ecology and Theology,'" 59.
176 Rayan, "'Ecology and Theology,'" 62.
177 Rayan, "'Ecology and Theology,'" 62.
178 Rayan, *Come Holy Spirit*, 90.
179 Rayan, *Come Holy Spirit*, 90.
180 Rayan, *Come Holy Spirit*, 91.

the marginalised, and helps them to work for their freedom, to speak for their rights, and to form communities.[181] The Spirit enables the church to take the side of the weak and the oppressed, which is a critique of the notion of the catholicity of the church that compromises with the colonial church.[182] The Spirit, who is the genuine authority of the church, redistributes power to all and offers a critique of a narrow view of apostolicity, authority, and charism that is often limited to the offices of the church. On the whole, it makes the church active towards affirming life itself.[183] Rayan's pneumatic church, therefore, maintains its spiritual character by affirming that it is constituted by the Spirit and also in its concrete character by including the Spirit-experiences of the people. It is, on the one hand, egalitarian and inclusive in its notion of catholicity and apostolicity while, on the other hand, it also qualifies such criteria by critiquing the colonial and hierarchical character of the church.

### *The church of the kingdom of God*

In the church's relationship to the kingdom of God, Rayan shows similar dialectics. Rayan's church of the kingdom is universal and inclusive through the Spirit as the church operates in the horizon of the kingdom of God. Rayan contends that the church is actually the consequence of the kingdom of God, a provisional sign, whereas the kingdom is the definitive eschatological reality. The church is always a small-group movement, but the kingdom is involved with the whole of human history and its ultimate meaning and completion.[184] On the other hand, the church of the kingdom is particular in that it operates on the principles of Jesus's conception of the kingdom. The reign of God, for Rayan, involves Jesus's invitation of fellowship with outcasts and marginalised people. The "compassion of Jesus breaks down walls of class and caste barriers, elitist pretensions, and rebuilds the honour and pride of the marginalised and despised."[185] This creates an inclusive, egalitarian, and casteless community, which is so important for the caste-ridden church of India. It creates opportunities for all in the church without discrimination on the basis of caste or tribe. Both Spirit and the Word/Christ operate in such a church of the kingdom together to build a relational community of sharing. Rayan claims that the new humanity within the kingdom of God will not be a "relationship

---

[181] Rayan, *Come Holy Spirit*, 93–94.

[182] Rayan, *Come Holy Spirit*, 102.

[183] Rayan, *Come Holy Spirit*, 93–94.

[184] Rayan, "Theology of the Church," in Kurien Kunnumpuram, *Nature, Woman and the Church*, 299.

[185] Rayan, "Jesus: A Flesh-Translation of Divine Compassion," in Kurien Kunnumpuram, *Jesus: The Relevance of His Person*, 82–83.

based on human biology but on the new biology of the shared blood of Jesus and his shared Spirit."[186]

Furthermore, Rayan concretises the church of the kingdom with the liberationist viewpoints of the need for sharing of bread and love with all. Thus, the kingdom of God is linked with a community of people living in openness, love, and care, and in the bread that we eat. These are the bases of life and the foundational sacrament of God.[187] Rayan further concretises aspects of the kingdom of God with his notion of history. Rayan's notion of history is both eschatological in the Spirit and grounded on building up of a new humanity in Jesus. Rayan's eschatological history, on the one hand, unites the sacred and the profane, in other words, the religious and the secular; and on the other hand, grounds it in the responsibility of human beings to build human communities based on love.[188] The church is therefore part of the realised eschatology founded on the love for its neighbour. The eschatological universality of the Spirit can build communities beyond the church since it unites the sacred and the profane; yet, Rayan thinks that this history is the "history of the Spirit" made particular in the risen Christ.[189] The church of the kingdom, which is related to the history of the Spirit, leads to Rayan's understanding of the church as a dynamic movement.

*The church: A dynamic movement*

Rayan seeks to address the problem of the institutionalisation of the church through a pneumatological perspective. He argues that over-organisation or over-institutionalisation fails to maintain the spiritual nature of the church. This leads to what he calls "despiritualisation and impoverishment"[190] where "centralised bureaucratic control contradicts the characteristic of spiritual existence."[191] He further contends that this institutional nature of the church prevents it from being open and creative. Some of the reasons for such a state, Rayan argues, are the church's tradition, longing to keep the status quo, excessive legalism, its foreign character, and its incapacity to keep up with change. Rayan agrees with John V. Taylor that the church has tried to tame the Holy Spirit through this kind of institutionalisation. Instead of the Spirit being the creative

186 Rayan, *Come Holy Spirit*, 54.

187 Rayan, "The Praxis of Subversive Prayer," in Kurien Kunnumpuram, *Jesus: The Relevance of His Person*, 74.

188 Rayan, "Mission after Vatican II: Problems and Positions," *International Review of Mission* 59 (October, 1970): 419, cited in Kim, *Mission in the Spirit*, 155.

189 Rayan, "Mission after Vatican II," 421–22, cited in Kim, *Mission in the Spirit*, 156.

190 Rayan, "Theology of the Church," 313.

191 Rayan, "Theology of the Church," 313.

Lord and initiator of communal responses in the church, she became a thing to be manipulated by the office of the church and dispensed with sacramentally.[192] The basic issue, says Rayan, is that we have not "yet succeeded in incarnating the church redemptively in the concrete life of the people."[193] According to Rayan, the institutionalisation of the church has led to

> the separation of the Spirit's mystery and institutional aspects, laity from clergy, marginalisation of women, distinction of spirit from matter, death of prophetism in the church, rejection of democracy and religious liberty, mentality that is suspicious of mysticism and inclined to positivism and rational order.[194]

Instead, Rayan prefers the church to be a movement, which he thinks is more suitable for India. In a movement there is no fixed membership, people can "belong" or participate in many different ways. For example, this can be done though "participating in gatherings and meetings, reading literature, contributing to thinking, assuming responsibility in some form."[195] Drawing on Karl Rahner, Rayan's notion of de-institutionalising the church also includes decentralisation of control and openness in the Spirit to adapt to new situations, but at the same time emphasising the loyalty of the individual Christian to the church. He writes that the church should be "practicing decontrol in favour of larger freedom and guidance of the Spirit . . . and the loyalty of the individual Christian, and by adapting itself continually to situations that evolve from day to day."[196] For the same reason, Rayan urges the church along with other faith communities to be involved in the sociopolitical struggles of the people. He thinks that religions must not be disconnected from the sociopolitical situations and problems because religion has both served to justify oppression on some occasions and also has liberationist potential.[197]

Thus, Rayan's project of de-institutionalisation of the church opens the way for the church to move out of its colonial assumptions and reform itself in terms of upcoming challenges, and also allows the church to be concretely situated within its context. It not only holds to the core

192 J.V. Taylor, *The Go-Between God: The Holy Spirit & Christian Mission* (London: SCM Press, 1972), 208–209, cited in Rayan, "New Efforts in Pneumatology," 83.

193 Rayan, "Theology of the Church," 286–287.

194 Rayan, "New Efforts in Pneumatology," 83–86.

195 Rayan, "Theology of the Church," 313.

196 Rayan, "Responsibility of the Church in India Today," in Kurien Kunnumpuram, *Nature, Woman and the Church*, 322.

197 Rayan, "Commonalities, Divergences and Cross-fertilization among Third World Theologies," in Kurien Kunnumpuram, *Doing Theology*, 322.

elements of Christianity and concrete participation, but it also allows different ways of understanding itself in the Spirit and allows different ways of participating in the church. This also opens the way for people who do not officially belong to the church, but seek to participate in different ways.

*The ecumenical church: Unity in diversity*

In terms of ecumenical relations, Rayan finds that unity in diversity of the Spirit is a helpful criterion. He claims that the Spirit helps the church to transcend borders of our narrow ecclesiastical boundaries. Rayan argues that the Spirit "breaks walls of divisiveness and transcends barriers between churches since the Spirit cannot be the monopoly of any church, religion, culture, race, or epoch."[198] The Spirit is universal in presence and as such cannot be bound by sacraments and structures.[199] This shows that Rayan is in favour of unity of the churches that can transcend the barriers of liturgy, sacraments, and structures. Rayan takes up the model of Pentecost and the outpouring of the Spirit to point out that the Spirit brings new approaches, new living, and new being to the conception of the church.[200] He argues that if "we accept the different [or the other] which the Spirit of God continually creates, we will be able to collaborate, and thus build unity from variety."[201] We are invited "to think out new styles of Christian living, new forms of religious life, [and] new kinds of church structure that will be expressive of the community the Spirit gathers and serve the brotherhood he builds."[202] According to Rayan, in today's plural world, ecumenical sensitivity would demand that Christian churches should lead in reflections on formulations, symbols, and practices of catholicity and unity of all life.[203] This shows that Rayan is in favour of moving beyond the barriers of unity in diversity built upon conformity of sacraments and liturgies to unity based on the acceptance of diversity.

## Ministries of a permeable Spirit ecclesiology

### The incarnated ministries of the church

Rayan's views on the ministries of the church reflect his notion of an "incarnated Christian spirituality." In this sense, local cultures become

198 Rayan, "Symbols of the Spirit," 123.
199 Rayan, "Symbols of the Spirit," 125.
200 Rayan, *Come Holy Spirit*, 16, 19.
201 Rayan, *Come Holy Spirit*, 94.
202 Rayan, *Come Holy Spirit*, 23.
203 Rayan, "How Will the Hindu Hear?," in Kurien Kunnumpuram, *God's Hope Becoming Visible*, 233.

"instruments of incarnated Christian spirituality."[204] Rayan's spirituality does not discard the potential of the different strands of Indian tradition, like the *Advaita, Bhakti,* and *Shakti,* yet he thinks that Indian or Asian spirituality should take into account the concerns of the marginalised and consider the Dalit, feminist, and tribal criticism of brahmanical traditions like *Advaita.* He prefers the *Shakti* tradition which represents the freedom and power of the Spirit in India. However, he also realises the potential of the *Bhakti* tradition for reflecting Indian experiences.[205] Highlighting Rayan's spirituality, Kim finds that Rayan favours, on the one hand, the contemplative life and, on the other hand, a spirituality of the struggle for liberation.[206] This spirituality is liberationist in terms of releasing the church from symbols of colonisation and searching for new symbols from the culture of the people and relating to concrete struggles of the oppressed.[207] This accounts for Rayan's understanding of ministries of the church as both spiritual and concrete. Accordingly, Rayan holds that the church should be given the freedom to experiment with different kinds of liturgy, all rooted in the particular ethno-linguistic-religious culture of the people. The local church should be able to use particular gestures, elements, symbols, and lyrics that are compatible with the culture of the people. Rayan suggests that "In India . . . there will be Tamil, Telugu, Hindi, Bengali rites and liturgies" if the logic of an *incarnated spirituality* is to be followed.[208] Moreover, he suggests that to make worship more concrete, the use of less verbal forms and more nonverbal expressions like gestures, postures, movements, dance, and use of pictures could be more effective.[209] Rayan proposes a more egalitarian church order, which is hoped to bring unity among the members and offices of the church.

In terms of offices of ministry, both the clergy and the laity belong to the church, and hierarchy only means that the church has a sacred beginning. The church's unity and freedom is expressed through prophetic witness of love, which prevents "absolutising of offices, organisations,

---

204 Rayan, "Local Cultures: Instruments of Incarnated Spirituality," in Kurien Kunnumpuram, *God's Hope Becoming Visible,* 295.

205 Rayan, "Review of S. Samartha, The Hindu Response to the Unbound Christ," *IRM* 66, no. 262 (April 1977): 189; "Spirituality for Interfaith Social Action," in Xavier Irudayaraj, ed., *Liberation and Dialogue* (Bangalore: Claretian Publications, 1989), 69, cited in Kim, *Mission in the Spirit,* 163.

206 Rayan, "Nairobi Experience," *VJTR* 40 (March 1976): 116–120, cited in Kim, *Mission in the Spirit,* 150.

207 Rayan, "Local Cultures," 295–308.

208 Rayan, "Sociological Factors and the Local Church as a Eucharistic Community," in Kurien Kunnumpuram, *Nature, Woman and the Church,* 78.

209 Rayan, "Sociological Factors," 179.

rituals, customs, and laws while marginalising life."[210] Rayan shows that through the practices of the early church as a "Jesus Movement it was more sociological than religious, through four shared realities," namely, "shared faith, shared prayer, shared or broken bread," and "shared material resources."[211]

Rayan's understanding of the sacraments features inclusivity, but is grounded in the social reality of the Indian context. It is liberationist and also a critique of the social and economic structures that perpetuate poverty and dehumanisation. Rayan seeks to build the church's relations on the inclusive and liberationist structure of the Eucharist. He explains that the current structure of the church in India shows a feudalistic character: the divisions of class and caste, the division of labour, the exclusion of certain groups, and so on.[212] For Rayan, the Eucharist has definite socio-political implications.[213] He writes,

> The bread of the Eucharist is a social reality made by the labour of hundreds of people, men and women. It is an economic reality, bought and sold in the market, around which treatise can be signed between nations. It is a political reality around which battles have been fought and still are fought.[214]

Rayan believes that the Eucharist can "become the starting point of an ever-widening activity of sharing bread and wealth in all areas of life, making for a fraternal, Eucharistic, socialist community of peoples."[215] He interprets this in relation to the earth where the earth becomes the Lord's Table. It is God who lays down the table for all; "it is a round loaf of bread and a big bowl of rice to be shared by all men and women. All are invited to this feast of the Lord."[216] The openness in the Spirit is matched by the paschal mystery of Christ. Rayan contends that the Eucharist points to the paschal mystery and its relationship with the outpouring of the Holy Spirit, which urges us to struggle against dehumanisation of particular communities.[217] Rayan believes that the Eucharist is the sacrament of

210 Rayan, "Hierarchy-Religious Relationship," in Kurien Kunnumpuram, *Nature, Woman and the Church*, 374–380.

211 Rayan, "Sociological Factors," 182.

212 Rayan, "Ecclesiology at Work in the Indian Church Today," in Kurien Kunnumpuram, *Nature, Woman and the Church*, 166.

213 Rayan, "Sociological Factors," 173.

214 Rayan, "The Church-The Jesus Movement," in Kurien Kunnumpuram, *Nature, Woman and the Church*, 183.

215 Rayan, "Indian Theology and the Problem of History," 217.

216 Rayan, "The Earth is the Lord's," in Kurien Kunnumpuram, *Nature, Woman and the Church*, 7.

217 Rayan, *Come Holy Spirit*, 63, 75.

the body of Christ and this body especially constitutes the poor and the downtrodden. It is a call to commit to justice and equality for all and a celebration of unity and oneness in the one Lord and one table. So, he believes that to bring in discriminations and divisions in the table of the Lord would slow the growth of the church.[218] Rayan contends that,

> in the Eucharist as the sacrament of that Body which we are, and as the meal of the new fellowship which cuts across all lines of race and colour, all purity laws and separatist traditions, and all self-righteous pretences; in the Spirit as abiding in all and enveloping all and especially empowering the weak; in Jesus's option to be Flesh, and poor, and socially lowly and powerless; in Jesus's mission as liberation of the downtrodden.[219]

Rayan also understands baptism in terms of an event which is spiritual, but which is grounded in history and the concrete life of the people. It is liberationist as it helps to build new communities and demands commitment to freedom of the oppressed. He relates it to "concrete processes of history," which should "awaken us to the urgency of the call for dignity and freedom."[220] In other words, our baptism should make us realise the harsh realities of life and respond to them. He contends that the Lima text[221] regarding sacraments has been primarily christological in focus while neglecting the trinitarian understanding with an emphasis on the work of the Holy Spirit and a lack of historical and sociopolitical implication.[222] Although Rayan does not discard the traditional meanings of baptism like remission of sins, belonging to the Lord, entry into the new people of God, dying and rising with Christ, rebirth to become a new creation,[223] his position is especially that of liberation. Rayan believes that his perspective on baptism links us through the power of the Spirit to the realities of the poor and the marginalised. He believes that through baptism, Jesus showed solidarity with the oppressed and the exploited of the earth. It shows a commitment to working for freedom of the oppressed.[224] He claims that the core meaning of baptism should be immersion into the Christ-event and "commitment unto death to the cause of liberation in

218 Rayan, "The Challenge of the Dalit Issue: Some Theological Perspectives," in Kurien Kunnumpuram, *God's Hope Becoming Visible,* 196.

219 Rayan, "Challenge of the Dalit Issue," 197.

220 Rayan, "Baptism and Conversion: The Lima Text in the Indian Context," in Kurien Kunnumpuram, *God's Hope Becoming Visible,* 215.

221 World Council of Churches, *Baptism, Eucharist and Ministry,* Faith and Order Paper no. 111 (Geneva: WCC, 1982).

222 Rayan, "Baptism and Conversion," 216.

223 Rayan, "Baptism and Conversion," 215–216.

224 Rayan, "Baptism and Conversion," 217.

given historical situations."[225] Rayan reinterprets baptism along with conversion. He writes that baptism means

> conversion from individualism in religion and society to corporate existence; from spiritual and economic selfishness to the truth of the community and of the world which God loves; from rigid doctrines of private property to the original purposes for which God gave his earth to his human family; from privatization of life to trinitarian communion; from ritual preoccupations to pursuit of justice from law to grace and from sacrifices to mercy.[226]

Thus, baptism for him is an event that involves the working of Spirit and Christ to build communities of justice and peace. This is not simply a spiritual event, but one that is concretised in the struggle of the people.

### The mission of a permeable Spirit ecclesiology

Kirsteen Kim observes that Rayan's understanding of the mission of the church is pneumatological. Rayan identifies the Holy Spirit's presence and work in the world as God's redemptive call for universal salvation through the particularity of the gospel of Christ.[227] Here, one can find that the mission of the Spirit is integrally linked with the mission of Jesus. Jesus's mission is the model for the church's mission.[228]

#### *Mission to people of other faiths*

Rayan finds that other religions are "sacraments of salvation" through the presence of the Spirit.[229] In relation to other religions, the church becomes symbolic of the salvation brought about by Christ. It makes the church "the sacrament of universal salvation" rather than "the universal sacrament of salvation."[230] Kim observes that Rayan has an inclusivist theology of religions with Christ at the centre, but it is modified by his pneumatological perspective. She points out Rayan's belief that "the genius of India seeks the Universal Spirit"[231] and "the historical particularity of Jesus has been a difficulty in the way of accepting him as the Universal Spirit and the Saviour of all."[232] Thus, Rayan suggests a theology of religions focus-

---

225 Rayan, "Baptism and Conversion," 216.

226 Rayan, "Baptism and Conversion," 220.

227 Kim, *Mission in the Spirit,* 188.

228 Kim, *Mission in the Spirit,* 189.

229 Rayan, "Mission after Vatican II," 422–25.

230 Rayan, "Mission after Vatican II," 422–25.

231 Rayan, "Interpreting Christ to India: Contributions of Roman Catholic Seminaries," *Indian Journal of Theology* 23, no. 4 (1974): 223–231.

232 Rayan, "Interpreting Christ," 223–231.

sing on the history of the Spirit.[233] Rayan's pneumatological theology of religions is life-centred and community-centred. In his article, *How Will the Hindu Hear?* he argues that Hindus or the people of other religions can only connect to Christianity if it proclaims the message of life; life out of struggles and sufferings. He notes that theoretical proclamations cannot be as effective as the life that is lived out by the believers for all to see. It is the witness of the lives lived in Christ by the power of the Spirit that lends credibility to the message for others.[234] In his article, *Dialogue with Hinduism*, Rayan notes that Hinduism has "little or no juridical structures, organizations, or persons in authority," and therefore finds it hard to accept an institutional church expressed through power, wealth, and centralised control.[235] Rayan's plea is for the church to proclaim its gospel in terms of "free and unorganized witnessing . . . prophetic and charismatic [and] responsible lay initiative."[236] He thinks the best way of communicating the gospel is to use the language of love, a language that is down-to-earth, of freedom and renouncement.[237] Rayan's theology of religions therefore centres on a spirituality that crosses religious boundaries, yet is grounded concretely in the cultures and struggles of the people, especially the marginalised.

### *Mission towards the Dalits*

Rayan's theology and ecclesiology are prominently liberationist and so far this has been clearly proven; however, his response to the question of the Dalit issue should be highlighted here as the church in India continues to be caste-ridden. Rayan strongly denounces caste in the church. He writes, "For the church to make room for, approve of, tolerate, or perpetuate dalitness and discriminations based on caste or class or gender would amount to apostasy from the Christian faith."[238] In responding to the Dalit predicament in his article, *The Challenge of the Dalit Issue*, Rayan urges us to follow the praxis of Jesus. This praxis was exemplified in Jesus's baptism with his identification with the masses and his table fellowship with the outcastes of his day. Through the parable of the last judgement (Matt 25:31–46) and the parable of the good Samaritan, Rayan identifies Jesus with the oppressed Dalits where his crucifixion is the culmination of his

---

233 Rayan, "How Will the Hindu Hear?," 235–236.

234 Rayan, "How Will the Hindu Hear?," 235–236.

235 Rayan, "Dialogue with Hinduism," in Kurien Kunnumpuram, *God's Hope Becoming Visible*, 370–371.

236 Rayan, "Dialogue with Hinduism," 370–371.

237 Rayan, "Dialogue with Hinduism," 371.

238 Rayan, "Challenge of the Dalit Issue," 194.

"dalitness,"[239] so Jesus was a Dalit from "cradle to the cross."[240] This fact of Dalit segregation and oppression is a human creation and is considered by Rayan as "a radical evil like sin and death."[241] Rayan challenges the church to "go outside the camp" like Jesus to identify ourselves with the Dalits and recommit ourselves through baptism and the Eucharist, in liberating service of justice and love, to the oppressed and the outcaste.[242]

### *Mission in terms of creation-care*

Rayan's response to the earth's ecological crisis is his effort towards an ecological theology of creation. In attempting an ecological theology, Rayan forwards the notion of belongingness of the earth and combines the spiritual-sacramental approach with concrete images of the earth. It combines the work of the Spirit since creation and the earth is understood as Christ's body. Further, his liberationist perspective adds the socioeconomic oppression of the earth and commends care for creation. In his article, *The Earth is the Lord's*, he affirms that the earth belongs to God because it was created by the power of the Spirit of God hovering over the waters. Thus, the earth is the "Lord's self-manifestation" and a sacrament that reveals God, his generosity and tenderness, and it is the Lord's Table that provides for the hungry.[243] However, he also affirms that the earth belongs to us and that we have an integral relation to it in terms of "work, food, knowledge, contemplation, and gift-giving."[244] Rayan raises concerns about the ecological crisis, which includes a liberationist socioeconomic critique. He puts it in terms of the "commercialization of the earth,"[245] the "global imbalance in land/population proportion"[246] and "the ecological crisis."[247] In response to these, Rayan believes that nature or the earth is integral to our faith and pleads for a "mystical view of nature and a reverential approach to it, for a sacramental vision of the world, and for a culture of gentleness and poetry which can also act as a corrective to and a source of resistance against that kind of scientism and technology"[248] responsible for this crisis. This response is a matter

239 Rayan, "Challenge of the Dalit Issue," 184–188.
240 Rayan, "Challenge of the Dalit Issue," 189.
241 Rayan, "Challenge of the Dalit Issue," 189.
242 Rayan, "Challenge of the Dalit Issue," 187.
243 Rayan, "Earth is the Lord's," 2–9.
244 Rayan, "Earth is the Lord's," 2–9.
245 Rayan, "Earth is the Lord's," 16.
246 Rayan, "Earth is the Lord's," 16.
247 Rayan, "Earth is the Lord's," 16.
248 Rayan, "Ecology and Faith: The Mystery of the Earth," in Kurien Kunnumpuram, *Nature, Woman and the Church*, 25, 36.

of God's justice related to the establishment of the kingdom of an egalitarian society, a countercultural praxis that subverts the ideology of resources in the hands of the few.[249] Rayan contends that the ecological crisis can only be responded to not simply through a mystical theology of creation, but through christological and pneumatological perspectives. Christologically, creation is seen as rooted in the Christ-event, in being included within the family of God through Christ, in being the bodiliness of Christ. Pneumatologically, creation is birthed by the Spirit, carries the "grief of the Spirit" in its plight and looks forward to new creation and transformation in the Spirit.[250] Thus, the mission of the church in Rayan is all-inclusive in Spirit and Christ.

## Conclusion

### Samuel Rayan's Spirit ecclesiology is comparatively appropriate in terms of permeability and the Indian context

In the preliminary chapters, we had discussed the criterion of relational-distinctiveness as expressing the feature of permeability. We explored various models of the church from the West and found that Yong's ecclesiology comes closer to featuring the dialectics of relational-distinctiveness in its borders, which is the feature of permeability. This dialectic is expressed in terms of universality-particularity, the spiritual and the concrete, the static and the dynamic, unity and diversity, the one and the many, and the joint working of the Spirit and the Word/Logos/Christ. However, in order to conceive of a permeable Spirit ecclesiology in the context of India, recourse to Indian perspectives and theologies was essential. Conversation with the theologies and ecclesiologies of Chenchiah and Thomas showed that Indian ecclesiology requires orientation towards Indian plural, cultural, and social-political contexts. The particular contexts of India in terms of its religio-cultural background, its socioeconomic condition and situations of marginalisation, demand that the Indian church engage with the concrete life of the people. An awareness of the history of the church in India and colonisation, its unique heritage, and the life of Christians and people of other faiths and situations of oppression and dehumanisation, is needed. This calls for perspectives of understanding the church in the context of liberation from marginalisation, oppression, and efforts at humanisation of people. For India, ecclesiology cannot simply be an intellectual affair, but it ought to

249 Rayan, "Seek First God's Kingdom and His Justice," in Kurien Kunnumpuram, *Nature, Woman and the Church*, 37–44.

250 Rayan, "Ecology and Theology," 46–76.

deal with real life struggles, questions of identity, and survival. Even unity of the churches cannot be looked into while disregarding issues of life and liberty. Although the Western ecclesiologies seek to be permeable in terms of relational-distinctiveness, they fail to address the particular issues and contexts that the Indian church faces. Therefore, while appreciating their ecclesiologies for giving us a framework to conceive of a permeable Spirit ecclesiology, we sought to enrich this framework and ground it in our context through contributions of Indian theologians. Even among these Indian theologies or ecclesiologies we have shown as in Chenchiah and Thomas, there were deficiencies that we had sought to fulfil with the Spirit ecclesiology of Samuel Rayan.

We have shown that Samuel Rayan's permeable Spirit ecclesiology is theologically based on the *bread and breath* metaphor, broadly representing the joint working of the Spirit and Christ. This is parallel to Yong's basis of the Irenaeus's metaphor of the two hands of the Father. Rayan's *bread and breath* metaphor, like Yong's has given the former much leverage in articulating the relational-distinctive dialectics in terms of universality-particularity, spiritual-concrete, static-dynamic, and unity-diversity characteristics. Yong's Spirit ecclesiology, though permeable, is inadequate for the Indian context as it understandably fails to include the particular concerns of India. In particular, Yong's ecclesiology does not grapple with the concerns of colonisation and related approaches of decolonisation and de-institutionalisation, which are important aspects in Indian ecclesiology. Yong's ecclesiology also does not draw on Indian religio-cultural resources to be particularly grounded in the Indian context. His ecclesiology does not concern the dilemma of Indian Christian identity, and the reality of multiple religious belonging as faced by the marginalised. Yong's theology of religions can also be put into the category of being metaphysical and intellectual. Yong also lacks a prominent liberationist aspect and a critique of the socioeconomic and structural forces that perpetuate marginalisation. Rayan's ecclesiology fulfils many of the above criteria for an Indian permeable Spirit ecclesiology.

Rayan's theology and Spirit ecclesiology reveals many similarities to Chenchiah's and Thomas's, but it also differs from them considerably. Chenchiah and Rayan have pneumatological perspectives and emphases needed for a Spirit ecclesiology, but Rayan's is distinctive because he highlights the potential of concreteness and diversity in contrast to mere universality accorded to the Spirit as in Chenchiah's. Rayan's theology and ecclesiology includes the decolonisation aspect which both Chenchiah and Thomas have, but Rayan includes a positive aspect of a theology of life in his project, which Chenchiah fails to develop, but

Thomas seeks to compensate with a theology of humanisation. In other words, the decolonisation project that the Indian church needs is turned from a negative exercise into a positive one, towards building a human community on the theology of life. Further, Rayan's project helps to ground the largely elitist interfaith relations into the concrete life of the people so that it becomes a community exercise rather than an intellectual one. His pneumatological theology of religions includes the Spirit-experiences of ordinary people, especially the marginalised. Finally, Rayan has an edge over both Chenchiah and Thomas due to his liberationist perspective, which caters to the Indian situation of the Dalits, tribals, and other oppressed groups. Rayan's theology and ecclesiology also has a self-critical aspect and critical approach towards the socio-economic-political dimension of India which Chenchiah lacks, but which Thomas addresses to an extent. Rayan's project, being pneumatological, succeeds to find a basis for the permeability of the church which Thomas lacks.

However, it is important to admit here that all the theologians discussed in this project contribute somehow either directly or indirectly to ecclesiological conversations. From a Western perspective, while Moltmann gives a reasonable, although debatable basis of relational aspects of the church on the foundation of the Trinity, Hauerwas highlights the distinctive aspect and Tanner the christological aspect. All this is well-balanced with the pneumatological theology of Amos Yong who keeps the relational-distinctive dialectics quite successfully with bringing together the dynamics of the Spirit and the Word at play. This highlights a significant understanding that ecclesiology cannot be only based on Christology, but also on the joint action of the Word and the Spirit. Also, the dialectics of the spiritual-concrete, unity-diversity, universal-particular, and one and many aspects of the church become very important. From an Indian perspective, while Chenchiah sharply highlights the importance of decolonisation and self-critical understanding of the Christian church in India and proposes ways for an open borderless church based on the Holy Spirit's work, Thomas rightly maintains the borders of the church christologically while trying to engage with religions, cultures, and ideologies seeking to propose a secular fellowship of people. Thomas's major contribution is in terms of pointing out that the church has to be engaged with the secular and increasingly modern world. The church needs to keep abreast of the movements of humanisation and seek to connect with them. However, Thomas has failed to explain how such a relational ecclesiology can be sustained only with his christocentric perspectives without having recourse to a mature theology of the Holy Spirit.

It was thus Samuel Rayan's theology/ecclesiology which is found to be satisfying on all fronts: From maintaining a decolonisation and self-critical approach, to rooting the church on Indian foundations, to addressing the socioeconomic milieu of our country to engaging the church with other religions and cultures, to be conscious of the ecological crisis with a liberative stance towards the poor, the Dalits, and the marginalised. All of these are in keeping the relational distinctive dialectics in mind which is based on *the bread and the breath*, and the Word and the Spirit, precipitating a truly porous-bordered permeable church suitable for the Indian context.

Having shown Rayan's permeable Spirit ecclesiology to be comparatively appropriate, in the forthcoming final chapter we will apply such a permeable Spirit ecclesiological model to some select issues in the Indian context. We will only explore a limited number of issues out of the issues and contexts highlighted in the preliminary chapters for want of scope and space. These three issues are ecumenism, multiple religious belonging, and interfaith relations.

# CHAPTER FIVE

# IMPLICATIONS OF A PERMEABLE SPIRIT ECCLESIOLOGY FOR SELECT ISSUES IN INDIA

Any ecclesiological model's viability should be judged in terms of concrete situations and contexts. We have argued the relevance of a permeable Spirit ecclesiology for India. Now it is time to apply it in terms of particular issues. The following pages will seek to deal with some significant issues indicated in the preliminary discussions in our book. These are ecumenical relations, multiple religious belonging, and interfaith relations.

## Ecumenical relations

Working towards ecumenical unity or ecumenical relations is not particularly fashionable at present.[1] The diversity and proliferation of churches do not seem to hold promise for the kind of union envisaged a century earlier. Theologically, there are two extreme camps: one in the evangelical and pietistic traditions that see unity as a gift of grace that we receive in Christ and cannot be actively worked out; for the second camp, ecumenism is understood in spiritual terms and expressed merely in joint prayers, study, and reflection.[2] Yet in India, ecumenical relations continue to be relevant at a different level, particularly in the face of concerns for witness in a plural and multireligious society, but more so in the face of challenges from fundamentalist groups' oppression and persecution of minorities, including Christians. Although the ecumenical fervour pre-Independence (before 1947) and after has somewhat receded,[3] ecu-

1 Paul Avis, *Reshaping Ecumenical Theology: The Church Made Whole?* (London: T&T Clark, 2010), 187.

2 Avis, *Ecumenical Theology*, 187.

3 There are no recent efforts of the type of organic unity that was first envisaged during the pre-Independence times.

menical thinking has been cast in new ways[4] and has been extended in terms of wider ecumenism.[5]

Our particular concern here is to show that a permeable Spirit ecclesiological model based on the joint action of the Spirit and the Word/Christ with its potential to hold unity and diversity in tension and upholding new ways of thinking about ecumenism is a suitable basis for the church in India. For a test case, we will be assessing the church union movement of the Church of North India (CNI). We will find that the original conceptual basis of the CNI union is inappropriate for the demands of the north Indian context, and is inadequate in the face of other upcoming challenges. In the following, therefore, we will focus on the efforts of ecumenical unity in north India, with particular reference to the motivations and theological basis behind the formation of the CNI in 1970. It will be argued that the biblical-theological basis of organic unity of the CNI, which focuses on Christ's intercessory prayer (John 17),[6] is inadequate and problematic for the particular aspect of unity desired in India, i.e., unity-in-diversity. It will be seen that unity in diversity and universality and particularity are important dialectics for north Indian unity. Although the CNI has managed to express unity-in-diversity in its original plan of union, in its constitution, and to some extent in its ministry,[7] the biblical-theological basis referred to above does not give much room for the dialectics of unity-in-diversity, universality, and particularity to be worked out and has little potential to consider ecumenism in wider ways. Jesus's prayer can simply be taken as an inspiration for united witness for mission, but is theologically problematic in understanding the kind of unity envisaged therein.

---

4 After the formation of the Church of South India (CSI) in 1947 and the Church of North India (CNI) in 1970, joint efforts have been made to bring together three denominations, the CSI, the CNI, and the Mar Thoma Church (MTC), to come together to form *The Communion of Churches in India* (this name was accepted in the year 2000), which was inaugurated in 1978. This was not a fully organic union, but an attempt to manifest oneness through a common structure while retaining autonomy of the three churches. See Sahu, *United & Uniting*, 89.

5 Newer concerns of the question of discrimination of the Dalits and tribals within the church and the question of interfaith relations and ecological concerns have forced the churches to reconsider the limits of organic unity and go beyond that including the above concerns. See Sahu, *United & Uniting*, 92.

6 Other theological arguments for unity were simply assumed, but not elaborated upon, namely the trinitarian aspect expressed in the Apostles' and Nicene Creed, and the Pauline imagery of the church as the body of Christ with many members referred mostly with regard to organic unity.

7 For example, the CNI Constitution recognises both infant and adult baptism in its union. See *The Constitution of CNI* (Delhi: ISPCK, 1987), 16.

During the formation of the CNI, the main motivations were concerns of witness in mission coupled with a nationalistic fervour. However, the question of unity and diversity, and universality and particularity were uppermost in the mind of Indian Christians. The aspect of witness through our unity inherent in Christ's prayer (John 17) is what motivated Indian Christians. As Bishop Dhirendra Kumar Sahu notes,

> The central point of argument was that the unity of believers is to lead the unbelieving world to faith in Jesus as the one sent by God. The idea of mission was based on the prayer of Jesus that all believers may be brought to the unity of the divine, that the world may see the love of the Lord embodied in them and may behold the glory.[8]

The concern for unity first arose among Christians in north India, particularly Bengal, in the nineteenth century, whose educated converts and clergy sought to determine what a united church which is Indian would look like.[9] They sought a church that is self-governed, self-supporting, and self-propagating, free from colonial control, and united in its identity as an Indian church. It was pointed out previously that denominational divisions were introduced into India by the West, and as such the historical reasons that led to such denominationalism or schisms in the West were distinctly unattractive to Indians. Indian Christians were rather interested in ecumenical unity, which would lead to an Indian church. Bishop Waller wrote about Indian Christians:

> They are convinced that the church should be one: they are duly resentful at the cleavages introduced by the foreigners. They want a national expression of Christianity—an Indian Church.[10]

Thus, the concern for ecumenical unity was always linked to the question of identity of the Indian church. This called for an ecumenical unity for the churches in India that was universal in its relation with the worldwide church, but also particular in terms of maintaining its distinct Indian identity. As Sahu notes,

> The concern in the union is to manifest the universality as well as particularity of the church, expressing its identity as the people of God. This concern has occupied an important place in the history of Christianity in India.[11]

8 Sahu, *United & Uniting*, 64–65.

9 "The General Christian Conference at Calcutta in 1855 was attended by six missionary societies and it was the first of a series of similar gatherings held at different places in East India, of which seventeen are recorded between 1855–1906." See Sahu, *United & Uniting*, 12.

10 E.H.M. Waller, *Church Union in South India* (London: SPCK, 1929), 30–31, cited in Sahu, *United & Uniting*, 62.

11 Sahu, *United & Uniting*, xii.

The Indian Christian community has always been a diverse one. It was composed of people from different religious backgrounds; Hindus, Muslims, Parsees, and Sikhs. The diversity was compounded as these people from different religious backgrounds brought their own spiritual outlook, which then combined with equally diverse denominational attitudes from the European and American continents. Coupled with that was the question of caste segregation, which troubled the church.[12] Thus, it is evident that the issue of ecumenical unity in India has to consider the dialectics of unity and diversity, and universality and particularity.

The Indian Christians continued their search for a biblical-theological basis for unity. In Bengal, the Bengali Christians started to dream of a *United Church of Bengal* on the basis of the Apostles' Creed.[13] In western India, an alliance was formed in 1871 by the name of *The Western Indian Native Christian Alliance*, which had for its basis the theological foundation of *one body, one Spirit, one Lord, one Faith, one Baptism, one God and Father of all, who is above all and in all.* They also attached great importance to Jesus's prayer in John 17.[14] Gradually, these biblical-theological bases became the background of the basis for CNI.[15]

The CNI, from the beginning of its formation, showed the importance of universality and particularity among its members. The *Plan of Church Union* that was drawn up in successive stages, which finally took shape in 1965, showed this intention.

> We are agreed in seeking a united Church which will be an integral part of the Universal Church, and yet develop the special and distinctive gifts which God has given to the people of India/Pakistan in the expression of their worship, their faith and their common life.[16]

The aspect of respecting diversity amidst the union it sought was also clearly expressed in the same Plan of Union.

---

12 Sahu, *United & Uniting*, 23.

13 Sahu, *United & Uniting*, 25–26.

14 Sahu, *United & Uniting*, 30–31.

15 It took forty years of negotiations between the churches beginning in 1929 to form the CNI in 1970.

16 *The Plan of Church Union in North India and Pakistan*, 4th rev. ed. (Madras: CLS, 1965), ix. The Church of India, Pakistan, Bangladesh, and Ceylon (CIPBC) was the Anglican counterpart in the Union. In India, the bishopric of Calcutta was established in 1813, with separate dioceses for Madras and Bombay in 1835 and 1837 respectively. The bishopric of Calcutta became autonomous in 1930 and became known as the General Council of the Church of India, Burma (Myanmar), and Ceylon (Sri Lanka) named CIBC. After independence in 1947, the Indian ecclesiastical establishment came to an end and CIBC came to be known as the Church of India, Pakistan, Burma, and Ceylon (CIPBC).

> we do not desire that any one Church shall absorb other Churches, nor that one tradition shall be imposed upon all; but rather that each Church shall bring the true riches of its inheritance into the united Church to which we look forward. We intend that it shall be a Church which, while holding to the fundamental Faith and Order of the Universal Church, shall assure to its members freedom of opinion in all other matters, and also freedom of action in such varieties of practice as are consistent with the life of the Church as one organic body.[17]

This shows that the CNI was well aware of the need for universality and particularity, and unity and diversity from the beginning of its formation. Unfortunately, the primary basis of ecumenical unity, as we will find, did not reflect the above dialectics. The primary basis of the union was enumerated in the *Plan of Church Union.*

> We are seeking union because we believe that the restoration of the visible unity of the Church on earth is the will of God, and we believe that the Holy Spirit is leading us to resolve the differences which at present separate us. Our Lord Jesus Christ prayed: ". . . that they all may be one; even as thou, Father, art in me, and I in thee, that they also may be in us, so that the world may believe that thou hast sent me."[18]

This shows that Jesus's prayer for union (John 17: 20–23) was the primary basis of the union, which was categorically accepted in the *Plan of Union*, starting from the seventh Round Table Conference in 1948.[19] Apart from this primary basis, other theological arguments were noticeable in the fourth edition of the *Plan of Union* subsequently drawn up in 1965. For example, Sahu draws attention to the theological assessment of the said plan by W.J. Marshall, which revealed that "one of the dominant insight [*sic*], which informs the Plan as a whole, is the church's dependence on God."[20] Marshall argues that this simple and obvious truth about our dependence on God for unity is often largely obscured.[21] On the other hand, the trinitarian dynamics at play in the union is highlighted in the Plan of Union in the following words:

---

17 *Plan of Church Union in North India and Pakistan*, x.

18 *Plan of Church Union in North India and Pakistan*, ix.

19 Sahu, *United & Uniting*, 65, 65.

20 J.W. Marshall, "The Church of North India/Pakistan: A Theological Assessment of the Plan of Union" (PhD diss., Dublin University, 1975). This was later published as a book entitled *Faith and Order in the North India/Pakistan Unity Plan* (Delhi: ISPCK, 1987), 19, cited in Sahu, *United & Uniting*, 60.

21 Marshall, "Church of North India/Pakistan," 60.

> Believing that God created *one* Church, a spiritual union and fellowship of those who are in Christ through the indwelling power of the Holy Spirit, we pray and seek for a visible expression of this *oneness* in the worship, life and witness of the Church here and now.[22]

The CNI also affirmed its organic unity on the fundamental principle that the "church is the body of Christ and its members are members of his body."[23] The church as Christ's body appreciates God's relationship with each of us and respects differences of opinion. The fundamental principle further upholds that,

> The Church therefore acknowledges that every member has an immediate and direct relationship to God, shown equally by the life of faith and of individual conscience in response to the indwelling of the Holy Spirit. Respect for the conscientious convictions of individual members shall be accorded by the Church, as long as they are in harmony with the mind of Christ and are not disruptive of the fellowship of His Body.[24]

The above arguments show that the primary basis of the organic union of the CNI was Christ's prayer for unity, while the CNI simply assumed the trinitarian dynamics involved and the imagery of the church as Christ's body to focus on diversity in unity.[25] The problem lies in the fact that the primary basis of unity was incompatible with the model of organic unity that is envisaged in the affirming of the church as the body of Christ. In the following, it will be shown that the union based on Christ's prayer for unity is in itself a weak basis for unity in diversity and universality and particularity required for unity in the CNI. Subsequently, it will be shown that a permeable Spirit ecclesiology is a suitable alternative model for the Indian church unity and has the openness to include newer ways of thinking about ecumenism.

## Inappropriateness of Christ's prayer as a basis for unity in diversity

Concerning Christ's prayer recorded in John 17, and particularly the verses 20–23, it can be said that the meaning of the pericope itself is debatable. Commentators disagree as to how to understand the particular notion of unity that is expressed in the passage. Raymond E. Brown notes

22 *Plan of Church Union in North India and Pakistan*, viii.

23 *Plan of Church Union in North India and Pakistan*, 2.

24 *Plan of Church Union in North India and Pakistan*, 2.

25 The image of the church as a body of Christ is from the Pauline image described in Rom 12:4; 1 Cor 12. This model has been widely accepted for organic union. According to Ernest Käsemann and Raymond E. Brown, diversity is the essential character of organic unity. See Lorelei F. Fuchs, SA, *Koinonia and the Quest for an Ecumenical Ecclesiology: From Foundations through Dialogue to Symbolic Competence for Communality* (Grand Rapids, MI: W.B. Eerdmans, 2008), 54.

that though this passage is frequently used for church unity, there are several opinions or interpretations regarding it. Brown summarises the issues thus:

> Is the unity a question of united purpose expressing itself in a common Christian mission and message (Strachan)? Is it a question of Christians harmoniously working together without dissidence (Schlatter)? Is the union of Christians with each other and with Christ patterned on the union that exists between persons, especially between husband and wife (Strathman)? Is unity achieved through the unique character of God's image in the consciousness of every believer (Holtzmann)? Is it a mystical union (B. Weiss, Bernard)? Is it a unity founded upon the unity of each Christian with the Father and the Son (Behler)? Is this unity to be related to the Eucharistic mystery (A. Hamman)? Is it a unity that manifests itself in the power to work miracles (W. Bauer; cf.xiv 11–12)? Is it a unity under the "word" that founded the community—a unity that has nothing to do with personal feeling or common purpose and is not simply brotherly harmony, nor organization, nor dogma, even though these can bear witness to unity (Bultmann)? Sooner or later, most authors say that it is a union of love. It is that; but Käsemann, has a point when he says: "We usually bypass the question at this point with edifying language by reducing unity to what we call love."[26]

Brown, of course, settles for both a mystical and visible unity, which he describes as vertical (believers with the Father and the Son) and horizontal (believers among themselves).[27] However, different ways of understanding this unity, as evident in the above summarisation, has drawn theologians in different directions. Lesslie Newbigin, who was a senior statesman for the ecumenical movement in India and played a major role in the formation of the Church of South India (CSI), was clearly in favour of both a spiritual and visible unity in terms of organic union. He disapproved of the dichotomy of the spiritual and material, and thought that unity should be expressed in both ways.[28] There are others who disagree that the passage inevitably points to an organic or visible unity for the churches of the present generation.[29]

---

26 Raymond E. Brown, *The Gospel According to John (xiii–xxi): Introduction, Translation and Notes*, The Anchor Bible (New York: Doubleday, 1970), 775–776.

27 Brown, *Gospel According to John*, 776.

28 Lesslie J.E. Newbigin, *The Household of God* (London: SCM, 1953), 49, cited in Sahu, *United & Uniting*, 63.

29 Evan T. Pollard, "That All May Be One (John 17:21) and the Unity of the Church," *Expository Times* 70, no. 5 (February 1959): 149–50, cited in Sahu, *United & Uniting*, 65.

Even if we assume that the unity expected among believers is modelled on the relationship of the Father and the Son, this is difficult to explain. What kind of unity is Jesus calling us to when he says that we can be one as Jesus and the Father are one? Is it possible to be one as Jesus and Father are one? Furthermore, do we know exactly what kind of relationship Jesus and the Father have in order to understand our union on that basis? What does Jesus mean by the terms *one* and by the phrase *in you* and *in us*? Often, existing interpretations have tried to explain the unity envisaged in the prayer in terms of "a union of wills, a union of belief in a set of articles of faith, a moral harmony, or an anachronistic plea par excellence of Jesus that Christianity be healed of its institutional divisions."[30] The question is whether the text warrants that kind of interpretation. There are others who interpret the text as a farewell discourse of Jesus to his disciples, linking it to the mission of Jesus that they are to follow.[31] Primary difficulties arise in conceptualising the Father-Son relationship that we are called to participate in or imitate. The relationship of the Father and the Son cannot simply be considered as of unity, but also as distinctive. While the Father and the Son are one, the Father is not the Son and the Son is not the Father.[32] Furthermore, the passage suggests a mutual indwelling between the Father and the Son. The question is whether our relationship with other believers can be imaged on the unity and distinctiveness of the Father and the Son, and, moreover, in their mutual indwelling. Is the perichoretic union between the Father and the Son expected of our relationship with other believers actually possible?[33] Here it will be useful to reiterate some of the counter-arguments of Kathryn Tanner regarding this element of perichoretic union which assumes Social Trinity. Tanner shows that the unity among human beings cannot be modelled on the unity among the Trinity. If we hold the perichoretic union of the Trinity as valid, which suggests an intermingling among persons of the Godhead, this cannot be true of human beings. Here, it is evident that *koinonia* among human beings cannot be the same as perichoresis in the Trinity. Furthermore, the relationship of the Father and the Son cannot be the same as the relationship between Jesus and human beings. The difference

30 Laura A. Weber, "That They May All Be One—John 17:21–23: A Plotinian Application to Unity" (PhD diss., Marquette University, Wisconsin, 1995), 18, accessed November 24, 2019, http://epublications.marquette.edu/dissertations/AAI9634107.

31 Weber, "That They May All Be One," 23; George R. Beasley-Murray, *John*. Word Biblical Commentary, vol. 36 (World Publishing, Dallas, Texas: 1987), 291–307.

32 T.E. Pollard has used John 17:21 to argue against church union. Since the unity is based on the oneness of the Father and the Son, this unity should allow for diversity. See Brown, *Gospel According to John*, 775.

33 Weber, "That They May All Be One," 18–22.

due to the otherness of God and the sinfulness of humanity makes a considerable difference between those relationships.[34] Thus, the whole question of basing our unity on this passage is essentially problematic.

## The permeable Spirit ecclesiology as an alternate model for ecumenical unity

The preceding discussion highlights some of the complex problems with regard to this passage of Scripture when used as the basis for Christian unity or unity for the churches. My present concerns, however, are particularly with the dialectics of unity and diversity, and the expansion of the idea of unity. We have found that the negotiators of the CNI were aware from the beginning of a need for unity that included diversity. However, the basis of unity in question fails to conceive of the kind of unity that north India desires. The emphasis here is on the concept of our oneness with the Father and the Son, and on the oneness of the believers whatever the nature of oneness might be. Therefore, in this model there is a conspicuous lack of the notion of diversity. Even if the distinctiveness of the trinitarian persons is emphasised over that of unity in this model, it does not follow that the same distinction in unity would apply for the believers individually or the churches. On the other hand, if it is assumed that Jesus brings us unity among ourselves and with the Father through the Spirit, it does not necessarily indicate the reason why this unity should essentially be conceived in diversity. This model does not clarify why the universality and oneness of the church should be conceived without a homogenising of its particularities. Furthermore, it does not clearly indicate what the Son's role is or what is the Spirit's role is in this process of our union with others and our union with the Father. If both the Son and the Spirit's roles are simply to unite, who is responsible for preserving our particular identities or diversities within this process of unity? The above problems essentially drive a wedge between the basis of union and the model of unity that is envisaged in the organic unity that is the church imaged as a body of Christ. It is clear that the above basis of unity modelled on Christ's prayer is incompatible with the unity in diversity image that the church as a body of Christ envisages and therefore creates conceptual problems for thinking about unity. This prayer can be taken as a pious affirmation of unity for common witness, but is unsuitable as a basis for organic unity.

Considering the above problems in the light of the particular kind of ecumenism India requires, we argue that the model of a permeable Spirit ecclesiology based on Irenaeus's two hands of the Father, the Word/Christ, and the Spirit working together in the world (also understood as

[34] See Tanner's arguments explicated in this book earlier.

*breath and bread*—Spirit and Logos Christology as in Rayan) is more appropriate for addressing the concerns of the CNI expressed in the dialectics of universality-particularity, unity-diversity. It will be found that this basis and model also has the capacity to go beyond the organic union model. In a permeable Spirit ecclesiological model, there is room for a relational-distinctive dialectics in terms of unity and diversity, universality and particularity, which we have shown so far in this project. These relational-distinctive dialectics correspond to the role of both the Spirit and Christ/Son/Word as they bring us towards unity.

In previous chapters, we articulated how both the Spirit and Christ are each responsible for maintaining unity and diversity, and universality and particularity or distinctiveness. This was shown through reference to Yong and Rayan how the Spirit's presence brings unity right from creation, turning chaos into cosmos. The Spirit brings consciousness of our unity with God and with the rest of creation. The Spirit makes us aware and conscious of the presence of God in all and how interrelated we are to others who are alike or unlike us. It was shown how the Spirit brings unity among the diverse community gathered at Pentecost. The eschatological Spirit thus poured out (Acts 2; Joel 2:28–29) brings together the young and the old, sons and daughters, slaves and free, while maintaining the identity of each by the gift of empowered speech manifested individually. In these ways, the Spirit is the Spirit of both unity and diversity, and universality and particularity. Similar unity and diversity or distinctiveness and particularity can be expressed about the Word or Christ working in the world. God's creation is through the Word or Logos. Nothing is created without the Word (John 1:1–4). In this sense, the Logos is active in creation from the beginning. The manifestation of the Logos is through the particularity of God's diverse creation. This Logos or the Word was made flesh again in the historic particularity of Jesus Christ (John 1:14). On the other hand, the presence and action of the Spirit in Jesus Christ is evidenced from his conception, baptism, ministry, his whole life, death, resurrection, ascension, and Pentecost. We have shown through engaging with Western and Indian theologians that eschatologically and pneumatologically, the particular Christ develops a universal and cosmic character drawing all creation unto him towards consummation.

When the above paradigm of a permeable Spirit ecclesiology is applied to the churches in India, they acquire features of unity and diversity, and universality and particularity both in Christ and the Spirit. This model in fact outlines both the unity of the working of Christ and the Spirit, and also highlights their distinctive roles in the process of unity. The churches can be united on the basis of affirming unity in the one Lord Jesus Christ.

Similarly, the churches are drawn into unity by the Spirit who unites us in Christ. The Spirit also baptises us into the one body of Christ with diverse members. The Spirit, who is the Spirit of diversity, also motivates the churches to preserve the distinctive identity or tradition of each church while affirming unity among them. On the other hand, the manifestation of the Word can be diverse in different churches through their particular forms of proclamation, worship, liturgy, and ministries. The Spirit urges us to respect the diversity of each denomination in terms of their cultural and local contexts. The universality of Christ through the Spirit also acknowledges the particularity of the Word manifested in each church, in each context, and therefore opens the way to include more churches in the communion. The particularity and distinctiveness envisaged in both Spirit and Christ also enables the church to focus on developing a distinct Indian character for the church. In the Spirit, it will be open to the diversities of the Indian religio-cultural context, while bringing harmony to form an Indian identity for the church. This model avoids the problem of conceiving our unity on the basis of the Father-Son relationship, which we are unsure of and that is difficult to conceive. The permeable Spirit ecclesiological model, which allows unity in diversity and universality and particularity, is therefore appropriate as a complementary model for India. The efficacy of this model lies in the compatibility it brings with the basis of union and the corresponding theological foundation that is envisaged in the image of the church as a body of Christ in terms of unity in diversity.

Furthermore, the significance of this model lies in that it offers a paradigm to move beyond organic unity towards other forms of unity. We will discuss how this is so, shortly. We have already noted earlier that post-CNI, the efforts made towards unity were more in terms of the nature of the communion of churches rather than an organic unity. In this sense the CNI, CSI, and the Mar Thoma Church are united in basic structure, but operate as autonomous churches. Lorelei Fuchs outlines different forms of unity besides organic unity that has been tried by various churches throughout the world at different stages amidst different concerns—namely, *Federal Union*, *Conciliar Fellowship*, *Unity in Reconciled Diversity*, *Communion of Communions*, and *Koinonia*.[35] It is beyond our scope here to discuss the above models; however, it shows that though organic unity is not simply dismissed, other models are required for ecumenical unity. Mention may be made here of a recent model of ecumenism known as "receptive ecumenism" which is gathering momentum in the West.

[35] Fuchs, *Koinonia and the Quest*, 53–69.

Receptive ecumenism, in the words of its founder Paul Murray from Durham University is,

> "What, in any given situation, can one's own tradition appropriately learn with integrity from other traditions?" and, moreover, to ask this question without insisting, although certainly hoping, that these other traditions are also asking themselves the same question. With this, the conviction is that if all were asking and pursuing this question, then all would be moving, albeit somewhat unpredictably, but moving nevertheless, to places where more may, in turn, become possible than appears to be the case at present. It is, as that suggests and as befits the character of Christian life, the way of hope-filled conversion.[36]

Receptive ecumenism is a valuable paradigm in so far as it nurtures a humble recognition that the other tradition has something to contribute to our learning. It is in this essential attitude of openness and humility towards other traditions that it harbours the potential of a significant movement for unity. This has the potential to maintain the dialectics of unity in diversity as diversity is made an opportunity to learn rather than becoming an obstacle. In this sense, this model of ecumenism makes sense where in India, unity in diversity is one of the main requirements.

However, the context of India, poses different problems and challenges with regard to ecumenical unity. They are not limited to the concerns for unity in diversity, or a common witness for Christ or identity as an Indian Christian. Although they still remain vital concerns, the experience of more than forty years of unity of the churches in CNI, for example, has revealed further hurdles and challenges. Sahu notes that the "joining together of different denominations meant that the church became the repository of considerable and varied groups"[37] with various goals and aspirations. On the other hand, there is a constant threat of "pressure from a caste-structured society" that prioritises the privileged over the marginalised and downtrodden, which results in continuing segregation and discrimination within the church.[38] The question of church unity in India is entangled with the concerns of disunity not merely due to inherited Western historic denominational divisions over doctrine and ministry, but due to issues of caste segregation, tribal divisions, and Christians being a miniscule minority amidst a multireligious society. The

36 Paul D. Murray, "Receptive Ecumenism and Catholic Learning—Establishing the Agenda 1," in *Receptive Ecumenism and the Call to Catholic Learning: Exploring a Way for Contemporary Ecumenism*, ed. Paul D. Murray (Oxford: Oxford University Press, 2008), 12.

37 Sahu, *United & Uniting*, 82.

38 Sahu, *United & Uniting*, 82–83.

question of unity of the church cannot be addressed without taking into consideration the above issues because they are integral to the life and the identity of the church in India. In other words, unity of the church cannot be conceived without justice and liberation of the marginalised. Sahu contends that the present church in India must include in its concerns of unity and ministry, the struggles and aspirations of the Dalit and tribal Christians and the wider society with its multicultural and multireligious character in which the Indian church has its being.[39] Therefore, the question is—Do the different models of unity mentioned so far and receptive ecumenism, in particular, have the capacity to include the issues of justice and liberation, along with unity?

Y.T. Vinayaraj, in his article on Ecumenism, *Re-defining Oikumene: A Subaltern Perspective,* argues why this kind of ecumenism is needed in India which is also consistent with the epistemic shift in the wider ecumenical movement. He shows that the change of perspectives of ecumenism was due to the changing concerns of the global and the local. Vinayaraj shows three phases in this change: He discusses that in the first phase ecumenism was basically a Christianisation programme, which affirmed the universality of Christ and the Christian gospel, cast in the essential unity of the Christian church and its universal growth. Vinayaraj argues that it was basically ecclesiocentric and anthropocentric in focus.[40] In the second phase, there was a shift in focus in the post-war situation and with the formation of decolonised nation states. The ecumenical movement began to show its concern for poverty and racism, and critiqued the hegemonic tendencies of mission strategies. Vinayaraj notes that in this phase, "the ecumenical movement re-defined its faith and theology in solidarity with the struggles of the marginalised and enlarged its geography and ethnography to the Asian-African-Pacific-Latin-American cultures and people."[41] The third phase in the 1960s and 1970s was characterised by the emergence of black, feminist, Dalit, tribal, *minjung*, ecological, and other contextual liberation theologies. It made ecumenism shift its focus from anthropocentric to a life-centred vision. It essentially was a move in the direction of a "counter-imagination of unity in the context

39 Sahu, *United & Uniting*, 83.

40 Y.T. Vinayaraj, *Ecumenism, Re-defining Oikumene: A Subaltern Perspective*, accessed November 19, 2019, http://revytvinayaraj.blogspot.co.uk/2012/01/ecumenism.html. This paper was presented at the seminar on *Edinburgh 1910 and Beyond* at Whitefield, Bangalore, on November 28, 2009, and published in "Theology of Our Times" in October 2010. Vinayaraj refers to the focus of Edinburgh (1910), Jerusalem (1928), and Tambaram (1938) conferences.

41 Vinayaraj, *Ecumenism*. Vinayaraj refers to the New Delhi (1961) and Uppsala (1968) conferences.

of fragmentation, marginalization, and globalisation."[42] This decisive shift is in "rejecting the unitary notions of modernity, like scientism, liberal humanism, and Marxism; this new epistemological shift gives special attention to the so-called "other"/"marginal"/"local"/"little"/"mission field" histories or narratives of life worlds.[43] Vinayaraj argues that it is imperative that ecumenism, therefore, focuses on revisiting the other in terms of marginalised communities, affirming the dignity and importance of difference in our notions of unity, understanding the importance of local movements, and building up of a pluriform and dialogical community.[44]

The above arguments show that ecumenism has shifted in its understanding through different phases. Ecumenism that includes the concerns of the marginalised, the other, including their particular struggles and challenges, ought to be one of the primary approaches in India. It is therefore argued that a permeable Spirit ecclesiological model has the capacity, through the presence and liberationist work of the Spirit in the world, to include the concerns and the struggles of the marginalised, and values the particularity of the other through the presence of the Logos in creation. Through the presence and work of the Spirit and Christ, a permeable church can be envisaged that goes beyond its ecclesiological borders, not in terms of a universalising hegemonic tendency of Christendom, but in honouring the particular struggles of each local community. It extends its borders through the Spirit beyond the church to people of other communities in solidarity, especially with the marginalised and with concerns of justice and peace. Here, unity of the church is essentially envisaged in solidarity and liberation. It is shown through the Spirit ecclesiology of Samuel Rayan how questions of unity and diversity, and universality and particularity are also linked with the questions of liberation. A permeable Spirit ecclesiology, therefore, holds in tension diversity in unity, particularity in universality, along with a liberationist approach that is appropriate for India.

## Multiple Religious Belonging[45]

In the previous chapters, it was indicated that in India, intermingling and transcending of boundaries between religions and cultures are quite common. Even people from the lowest rung of the society, for example Dalits, feel comfortable living in two worlds. This is also shown in the case

---

42 Vinayaraj, *Ecumenism*. Vinayaraj refers to the Canberra Conference in 1991.

43 Vinayaraj, *Ecumenism*.

44 Vinayaraj, *Ecumenism*.

45 A revised version of this topic has been published in *The Indian Journal of Theology* 60, no. 2 (2018): 48–64.

for Christian converts from other faith backgrounds who continue to be Christians while maintaining the cultures, practices, and rituals of their previous community. So, multiple religious belonging is quite common in the Indian scenario. In the following, it will be argued that a permeable Spirit ecclesiology, with its relational-distinctive dialectics, creates space for people engaged in multiple religious belonging.

The Indian context highlighted the struggle of Indian Christians living in "two worlds," seeking to negotiate boundaries between Christianity and their former religion. This has been particularly noted among the religious practices of marginalised groups of Dalits and tribals, who constitute the majority of the church in India. While considering Indian theologies, it has been highlighted that the question of transcending religious boundaries has been common in India, both in terms of actual practice and in terms of intellectual accommodation of various faiths in one's conceptual make-up and religious experience. It has been pointed out that from the early nineteenth century, efforts have been made by Christians in India who have sought to live by reconciling more than one tradition within their religiosity. For example, Brahmabandhav Upadhaya (1861–1907), a prominent Bengali convert to Catholicism, sought to identify himself as a Hindu-Catholic or Hindu-Christian.

Brahmabandhav affirms,

> We are Hindus so far as our physical and mental constitution is concerned, but in regard to our immortal souls we are Catholic. We are Hindu Catholics . . .. The test of being a Hindu cannot therefore lie in religious opinions.[46]

There were others like Manilal C. Parekh (1885–1967), who from the time of his baptism understood himself to be a Hindu-Christian although he considered Hinduism as a national and cultural entity rather than a religious one.[47] One of the best-known figures, who probably profoundly experienced, though not without difficulty, what it means to belong to two different traditions at the same time is Swami Abhishiktananda. He was a French Benedictine monk (his original name was Dom Henri Le Saux) who came to India to show the Hindu mystics, whom he admired, that there is a similar tradition of mysticism in Christianity. Together with another French priest, he established an Indian Christian monastery or *ashram* in 1950 which he named *Shantivanam*, near Tiruchirappalli, in south India. Near the end of his life, his friends in France thought that he

46 B. Animananda, *The Blade: Life and Work of Brahmabandhab Upadhyaya* (Calcutta: Roy & Son, 1947) cited in Boyd, *Indian Christian Theology*, 68.

47 Boyd, *Indian Christian Theology*, 266.

had become a Hindu while others, some of them from India, thought that he remained a Catholic. This explains the kind of dual religious identity in which Abhishiktananda lived.[48]

Multiple religious belonging is a complex phenomenon of the interplay of identity and religious belonging in different cultures. Peniel J.R. Rajkumar and Joseph P. Dayam admit that "needless to say, an amoebic and amorphous phenomenon like multiple religious belonging, which is replete with its variegated diversity and attendant complexity, holds in it more questions that we have even yet learned to ask."[49] The conceptual difficulty in understanding multiple religious belonging is somewhat minimised by the efforts of some who have tried to understand it by applying different terminologies or highlighting the differences between Western/European/American and Eastern/Asian understanding. There are others who have tried to categorise different strands of the phenomenon.

In the following, we will briefly discuss them. In terms of terminologies, various usages besides multiple religious belonging are applied—namely, *multiple religious participation (MRP)*, *hybridity*, and *liminality*.[50] John J. Thatamanil suggests that, in some instances, the term MRP is more appropriate than multiple religious belonging and highlights the difference between the two. He claims that the term MRP is the "best generic term for modes of religious life in which persons take up ideas and practices drawn from the repertoires of discrete traditions."[51] Following John Berthong, a Confucian-Christian, Thatamanil revises the definition of MRP thus:

> multiple religious participation is the conscious (and sometimes even unconscious) use of religious ideas, practices, symbols, meditations, prayers, chants, and sensibilities drawn from the repertoires of more than one religious tradition.[52]

---

48 Michael Amaladoss, "Being a Hindu-Christian: A Play of Interpretations—the Experience of Swami Abhishiktananda," in *Many Yet One: Multiple Religious Belonging*, eds. Peniel Jesudason Rufus Rajkumar and Joseph Prabhakar Dayam (Geneva: WCC, 2016), 90.

49 Peniel J.R. Rajkumar and Joseph P. Dayam, "Introduction" in Rajkumar and Dayam, *Many Yet One*, 1.

50 The terms *(in) betweenness*, *dual belonging*, and *hyphenated identities* are also used sometimes. See Rajkumar and Dayam, "Introduction," 1, and Allan Samuel Palanna, "(In) Betweenness and Being Analogical: Making Sense of Hospitable Faith," in Rajkumar and Dayam, *Many Yet One*, 149.

51 John J. Thatamanil, "Eucharist Upstairs, Yoga Downstairs: On Multiple Religious Participation," in Rajkumar and Dayam, *Many Yet One*, 10.

52 Thatamanil, "Eucharist Upstairs," 11.

He further notes that "multiple religious participation may lead to multiple religious belonging but it need not."[53] Thatamanil argues that the terms *belonging* and *identity* are more problematic than the term *participation*. The term belonging suggests actually having membership in more than one community, which is both acknowledged by the individual and the concerned communities, but he says such acknowledgement from both sides is rare. Often, the individual who acknowledges their status as such is not validated or acknowledged by the other community. In this circumstance, Thatamanil asks a pertinent question: "Must claims of double belonging receive communal authorization before they can be recognized as valid?"[54]

Thatamanil argues that even the term *identity* is complex because we can speak of multiple religious *identities* or multiple religious *identity* depending on how we understand the formation of identity of a person.[55] The term *hybridity* is also used to describe the phenomenon of multiple religious belonging. The concept of hybridity in a positive sense was actually brought into postcolonial and cultural studies by Homi Bhabha and Salman Rushdie, among others. This term denotes intermingling and fusing of cultures, as also the emergence of a new identity.[56] Another term closely associated with hybridity is *liminality*, which is used by various authors to express one of the authentic categories of "Indianness," i.e., the fact of transcending of religious boundaries.[57] Felix Wilfred writes,

> In the Indian tradition, the concept of *sandhya*-conjunction is very important. It is the *twilight zone* where night and day meet. The borders and twilight zones, or to use an anthropological terminology, the position of *liminality* [italics mine] is unique and creative.[58]

The various terms mentioned above help to highlight different aspects of the phenomenon of multiple religious belonging.

---

53 Thatamanil, "Eucharist Upstairs," 11.

54 Thatamanil, "Eucharist Upstairs," 10.

55 Thatamanil, "Eucharist Upstairs," 10.

56 See Robert J.C. Young, *Postcolonialism: An Historical Introduction* (Malden, MA: Blackwell, 2001), 349. The term was earlier used in a derogatory sense to refer to persons of mixed origins. See John Scott, "Hybridity," in *A Dictionary of Sociology*, eds. John Scott and Gordon Marshall, 4th ed. (New York: Oxford University Press, 2015). See Homi K. Bhabha, *The Location of Culture*, Routledge Classics (New York: Routledge, 2004). The above references are cited in Sunder John Boopalan, "Hybridity's Ambiguity (Gift or Threat?): Marginality as Rudder," in Rajkumar and Dayam, *Many Yet One*, 138.

57 See Young, *Postcolonialism: An Historical Introduction*, 346, cited in Rajkumar and Dayam, *Many Yet One*, 136.

58 Felix Wilfred, *Margins: Site of Asian Theologies* (Delhi: ISPCK, 2008), 171.

The Western status and understanding of multiple religious belonging differ from their counterparts in the East. Catherine Cornille notes that the West is slowly coming to terms with this phenomenon, while it is almost commonplace in the East, for example, in China, Japan, and India, to name a few.[59] Wilfred writes about the Asian situation of transcending of borders.

> One widespread experience in different parts of Asia is that people, by and large, do not hold on to rigidly demarcated borders. The borders are fluid and porous. This is even more true when it is a matter of religion and religious experience . . . the Asian cultural ethos of fluid borders is very alive and active.[60]

In the West, belonging to one religion may be the norm and multiple religious belonging the exception. In the East and in the wider history of religion, multiple religious belonging is the rule rather than the exception, at least at a popular level.[61] There is a further important distinction between the West and the East in this matter: In the West, it is more a matter of choice or selection for the individual the religion one wants to draw closer to. In the East, it may not be wholly a question of choice, but a question of one's birth in a particular community, circumstances, upbringing, sociocultural, or other factors.[62] In this context, it is important to note that the concept of religions as a monolithic entity is debatable. In North America and Europe, religious multiplicity is recognised, but it is often delegitimised as syncretistic.[63] Thatamanil draws attention to the fact that scholars like Wilfred Cantwell Smith long ago understood religious traditions as fluid and impure, which flow into each other and are not essentially "discrete, reified, and homogenous entities."[64]

To further understand the phenomenon of multiple religious belonging, Catherine Cornille's categorisations are helpful. She broadly categorises the issue into two aspects: involuntary and voluntary. In

---

59 Catherine Cornille, ed., *Many Mansions? Multiple Religious Belonging and Christian Identity*, Faith Meets Faith Series (Maryknoll: Orbis Books, 1970), 1–2.

60 Wilfred, *Margins*, 175.

61 Cornille, *Many Mansions*, 1–2.

62 See Rajkumar and Dayam, "Introduction," 2. Also see Thatamanil, "Eucharist Upstairs," 8.

63 Thatamanil explains syncretism through an example. He contends that a person who cultivates yoga practice in addition to Eucharist engages in MRP, but if the yoga practice is installed within Eucharist, it becomes syncretism. He argues that the term *syncretism* "must first serve descriptively before they are subjected to normative evaluation." See Thatamanil, "Eucharist Upstairs," 11.

64 See Wilfred Cantwell Smith, *The Meaning and End of Religion* (Minneapolis, MN: Fortress Press, 1991), cited in Thatamanil, "Eucharist Upstairs," 7.

the involuntary category, she gives the example of the situation in East Asia where being a Chinese person also means belonging to Buddhism, Taoism, or Confucianism. This is not a matter of choice, but that of cultural identity. Another aspect in the involuntary category is of persons being born into families where their parents belong to more than one religion. Such people then have to negotiate different religions during their upbringing. This refers to the external circumstance rather than an individual choice.[65] In the voluntary category, there could be occasions of crisis, need, or necessity in terms of disease or difficulty when a person chooses to turn to another religion or practise it occasionally for help. Another aspect of the voluntary category is that some people might choose to identify permanently with more than one religion because they find in that religion some resources or vitality that bring them fulfilment. Cornille talks about Raimon Panikkar who went through a similar experience, saying: "I started as a Christian, I discovered I was a Hindu, and returned as a Buddhist without ceasing to be a Christian."[66] Furthermore, there are people who have not completely identified with two religions on an equal level, in which case one of the religions continue to be more dominant than the other. There are other kinds of belonging in which a person fully initiates himself into the religion of the other. Cornille gives the example of Paul Knitter, a priest, who took vows in Buddhism. Other "borderline" cases include situations where a person identifies with the symbolic and scriptural framework of one religion and with the hermeneutical framework of the other. Cornille cites cases where Christianity is sought to be understood in terms of *Advaita* or other categories.[67]

Multiple religious belonging is understandably not without its numerous adherent problems. It also poses a significant challenge for the churches. Thatamanil in his discussion of MRP, points out three pertinent problems: *misappropriation*, *contraindication*, and profound *existential uncertainty*. In his discussion of the first issue of misappropriation, Thatamanil claims that all forms of religio-cultural-ritual borrowing might not be legitimate. While exclusive ownership of a particular religious symbol or ritual by a particular religion is a debatable issue, there can be borrowing in an asymmetrical relationship of power. Thatamanil notes that "prudent questions must be raised about who borrows from whom and under what circumstances."[68] He gives the example of the

65 Catherine Cornille, "Multiple Religious Belonging and Interreligious Dialogue," *Current Dialogue* 57 (December 2015): 4–5.

66 Cornille, "Multiple Religious Belonging," 5.

67 Cornille, "Multiple Religious Belonging," 5.

68 Thatamanil, "Eucharist Upstairs," 17.

religio-cultural relationship between native Americans and non-native Americans as a result of colonisation and missions. There were cases where religious identities of the native Americans become hybrid due to coercion, and where the non Native Americans misappropriated the cultural and ritual motifs and artefacts of the subjugated natives without giving them due honour.[69] In other cases, borrowing might be a consumerist enterprise where spiritual disciplines and ritual practices are simply taken over, sold in the market, and severed from their community of origin.[70] Therefore, Thatamanil suggests that there must be criteria to discern which form of borrowing is legitimate and not dehumanising. In this sense, he suggests an ethical criterion where "persons engaging in such activities remain in conversation with communities from whom they are borrowing. *Borrowing from* is done best when *learning with*."[71] The second problem Thatamanil highlights is that of contraindication. He asks whether the ritual or practice of a particular religion is always compatible with the different tradition into which it is borrowed. He argues that it is not always the case. He contends that care should be taken about the appropriateness of the practices and their therapeutic value before borrowing. As an example, he cites that certain kinds of meditations may not be practised in a different religious tradition without a guru.[72] The third problem has to do with anxiety and uncertainty that people might face while engaging in MRP. This is true both for mystics and scholastics as well as ordinary people. Thereby, Thatamanil raises the question of spiritual care for persons who engage in such practice and highlights the lack of expertise in that field.[73]

Rajkumar and Dayam have pointed out that multiple religious belonging also has the danger of persons engaging in it in the sense of a "bricolage spirituality" or a nonserious mix of different religious and cultural elements especially as a trend of postmodernity.[74] They agree with Cornille and Peter C. Phan that there are people who take it as a "light-hearted flirting with different religions,"[75] or "self-indulgent, free-floating,

---

69 Thatamanil, "Eucharist Upstairs," 17; see also, John B. Cobb Jr., "Multiple Religious Belonging," in Cornille, *Many Mansions*, 22.

70 Thatamanil, "Eucharist Upstairs," 17.

71 Thatamanil, "Eucharist Upstairs," 17.

72 Thatamanil, "Eucharist Upstairs," 17–18.

73 Thatamanil, "Eucharist Upstairs," 18–19.

74 Rajkumar and Dayam, "Introduction," 3.

75 Catherine Cornille, "Double Religious Belonging: Aspects and Questions," *Buddhist Christian Studies* 23 (2003): 48, cited in Rajkumar and Dayam, "Introduction," 3.

cafeteria-style potpourri of mutually incompatible religiosities."[76] Peter C. Phan admits that it is sometimes a case of the New Age movement that "represents a symbolism of unbridled consumerism, excessive individualism, and the loss of collective memory that are characteristics of modernity and its twin, globalisation."[77]

Multiple religious belonging is a significant problem for Christianity and the church. It particularly poses a problem for Abrahamic religions, Christianity, Judaism, and Islam that demand exclusive commitment on the part of their adherents.[78] Cornille axiomatically states, "The more encompassing a religion's claim to efficacy and truth, the more problematic the possibility of multiple religious belonging."[79] Phan shows through a survey of well-known personalities,[80] several complications and hurdles involved in the process of multiple religious belonging. He argues that for authentic multiple religious belonging to occur, hard and patient intellectual work is needed, otherwise, it might run the risk of shallowness. He shows that this may lead to a continuous tension in the life of the individual who engages in this phenomenon, and that the learner needs to step into the shoes of the religious experiences of others and the guidance of some teachers.[81]

While problems and hurdles abound, the reality of multiple religious belonging in relation to Christianity and the church cannot be avoided. Thus, scholars and theologians continue to grapple with the problem, so that they can understand what it means theologically and ecclesiastically. Some examples would give us an idea of how they continue to think of multiple religious belonging. John R. Cobb thinks that multiple religious belonging is rather a means to an end and looks forward to transformation of religions in the process.[82] Joseph O' Leary, for example, argues for the significance of reinterpreting Christianity in terms of Mahayana Buddhism, so that the church can answer its critiques who are against a metaphysical understanding of Christianity.[83] Cornille summaris-

76 Peter C. Phan, "Multiple Religious Belonging: Opportunities and Challenges for Theology and Church," *Theological Studies* 64 (2003): 495, cited in Rajkumar and Dayam, "Introduction," 3.

77 Phan, "Multiple Religious Belonging," 498.

78 Phan, "Multiple Religious Belonging," 498.

79 Cornille, *Many Mansions*, 2.

80 One such personality that Phan holds up as an example is Aloysius Pieris of Sri Lanka.

81 Phan, "Multiple Religious Belonging," 510–513.

82 See John B. Cobb Jr., "Multiple Religious Belonging," in Cornille, *Many Mansions*, 20–27.

83 Joseph S. O'Leary, "Toward a Buddhist Interpretation of Christian Truth," in Cornille, *Many Mansions*, 29–43.

es Raymon Panikkar's position as someone who practised a lifetime of multiple religious belonging. Panikkar thinks that the question of religious identity and belonging is not only a subjective matter, but also a question of acceptance by the group. However, the group consists of individuals who continually have to negotiate boundaries. Panikkar thinks this helps in the process of the self-understanding of our faith while going beyond boundaries of fixed identities and exclusive belonging.[84] An interesting contribution in this field is made by Jacques Dupuis who comments on the relationship of complementarity and convergence of Christianity with other religions. He proposes that this relationship is able to hold the value of any particular religion while acknowledging the salvific value of other religions within the plan of God. He explains,

> The question of a complementarity and convergence between Christianity and the other religions of the world arises in the context of a theology of religions that while holding clearly to the essential and constitutive elements of the Christian faith, attributes to the other religious traditions a positive value in the order of salvation for their members and a positive significance in the plan of God for the whole of humankind.[85]

While the above positions describe different ways of positively understanding and responding to the issue of multiple religious belonging in a wider context, it has to be stressed that in India, this phenomenon includes other dimensions which need different approaches. In the preliminary discussions on the contexts of India, the struggle faced by the Dalits and tribals was described as they attempt to live in two worlds, especially Christian Dalits and tribals after conversion. The complex processes of assimilation, transformation, and/or rejection of different religio-cultural or ritual elements in Dalit and tribal religiosity in interaction with their old religion and Christianity were highlighted. It is contended that colonial Christianity has long since driven an unrealistic wedge between different communities and uprooted the masses from their indigenous communities for which these marginalised groups still continue to struggle. For most of them, it is not an intellectual choice, but one that their context demands. It is essentially a struggle for survival spiritually and existentially. We also discussed the Dalit predicament and tribal marginalisation that occurs due to the dominant cultural hegemony of the upper castes or the powerful. These two groups continue to suffer oppression, marginalisation, and violence from which they seek liberation. Thus, the question of

84 Raimon Panikkar, "On Christian Identity: Who is a Christian?" in Cornille, *Many Mansions*, 121–141.

85 Jacques Dupuis, S.J., "Christianity and Religions: Complimentarity and Convergence," in Cornille, *Many Mansions*, 61.

legitimising or delegitimising multiple religious belonging by Christianity or the church especially in the context of Dalit and tribal marginalisation takes on a different note. Phan draws attention to the necessity of engaging in multiple religious belonging with particular attention to solidarity with the poor and marginalised and working for their emancipation without which this type of engagement can easily slip into "spiritual escapism" or "bourgeois leisure life."[86] Sunder John Boopalan argues that for the right kind of hybridity (he uses this word instead of multiple religious belonging) to occur, especially a hospitable kind of hybridity, it "needs to be perpetually disposed toward marginality and sites of oppression."[87] He argues that marginality is the ethical rudder as one steers through the ambiguity of hybridity.[88] Stephen Moore notes that hybridity disrupts the normative, which corresponds to the pure, neatly arranged, straightforward space that excludes the marginalised.[89] Hybridity also functions as a worldview that "allows disparate identities to relate to each other based on shared identity and to co-exist without needing to undermine each other."[90]

Boopalan agrees with Gayatri Chakravorty Spivak, a postcolonial theorist, that the Indian scene is mostly ruled by a "liberal pluralism of repressive tolerance,"[91] a pluralism which pretends to be hospitable by claiming to be tolerant and harmonious. Actually, this is a superficial kind of pluralism that is devoid of an analysis of power, class, caste, gender, and the plight of the marginalised.[92] Boopalan instead argues for a hybridity and plurality that is embodied, mostly expressed through various rituals and practices of different religions.[93] He reminds us that rituals have an inherent power to implicate and create alternative cultures and communities. He writes,

> rituals create alternative cultures that are not easily co-opted by dominant cultures, enabling hospitable freshness and creating nonhegemonic

86 Phan, "Multiple Religious Belonging," 513.

87 John Boopalan, "Hybridity's Ambiguity (Gift or Threat?): Marginality as Rudder," in Rajkumar and Dayam, *Many Yet One,* 136.

88 Boopalan, "Hybridity's Ambiguity," 136.

89 Stephen Moore, *Empire and the Apocalypse: Postcolonialism and the New Testament, Bible in the Modern World* (Sheffield: Sheffield Phoenix Press, 2006), 109, cited in Raj Nadella, "Motif of Hybridity in the Story of the Canaanite Woman: Its Relevance for Multifaith Relation," in Rajkumar and Dayam, *Many Yet One,* 111.

90 Nadella, "Motif of Hybridity," 111.

91 Gayatri Chakravorty Spivak, *A Critique of Postcolonial Reason: Toward a History of Vanishing Present* (Cambridge: Harvard University Press, 1999), 176, cited in Boopalan, "Hybridity's Ambiguity," 138.

92 Boopalan, "Hybridity's Ambiguity," 138.

93 Boopalan, "Hybridity's Ambiguity," 139.

> multiple belongings. They "contest the exclusivity in religious orthodoxies by redefining boundaries and reformulating the relationship between Self and Other."[94] Thus, rituals have the ability to foster hybrid identities that contest[95] and reorganize identities.[96]

Boopalan contends that rituals make use of space and time that reject the unequal elevation of the intellectual over the material. The meaning-making power of ritual embodiment elicits response from participants,[97] especially those from the marginalised. James Ponniah shows the importance of rituals in multiple religious belonging through the hybrid identities that are produced and promoted in the Christian and Muslim shrines in Tamilnadu.[98] Ponniah agrees with Selva Raj that rituals are performed "often in opposition to and defiance of institutional norms and ecclesial prescriptions that occur at the grassroots level in the arena of popular piety and rituals."[99] Hybridity is thereby grounded in rituals, which can be an alternative model of religious dialogue, "a dialogue that emanates from the epicentre of rituals, performances, and practices of the people, and differs substantially from that which emanates from the official deposit of faith of institutionalized religions."[100]

In this espousal of the critical and the embodied rituals and practices ensues the discussion of how the church can understand or appropriate the issue of multiple religious belonging especially in relation to the Dalits and tribals. Joshua Samuel highlights how the Dalits, both Hindu and Christian, themselves use hybridity to counteract the influences of oppression and how the church can stand in solidarity with them in this struggle. Samuel writes,

---

94 Alexander Henn, "Introduction: Beyond Norm, Text and Dialectics—Rituals as Social Praxis," in *Rituals in an Unstable World: Contingency-Hybridity-Embodiment*, eds. Henn and Klaus Peter Kopping (Frankfurt: Peter Lang GmbH, 2008), 13, cited in Boopalan, "Hybridity's Ambiguity," 141.

95 Pnina Werbner, "Introduction: The Dialectics of Cultural Hybridity," in *Debating Cultural Hybridity: Multi-Cultural Identities and the Politics of Anti-Racism*, eds. Pnina Werbner and Tariq Modood (Atlantic Highlands, NJ: Zed Books, 1997), 23–24, cited in Boopalan, "Hybridity's Ambiguity," 141.

96 Boopalan, "Hybridity's Ambiguity," 141.

97 Boopalan, "Hybridity's Ambiguity," 141.

98 James Ponniah, "Shrines, Ritual Hospitality, and Hybrid Identities in South Asia," in Rajkumar and Dayam, *Many Yet One*, 100.

99 Selva J. Raj, "Dialogue 'On the Ground': The Complicated Identities and the Complex Negotiations of Catholics and Hindus in South India," *Journal of Hindu-Christian Studies* 17 (2004): 41, cited in Ponniah, "Shrines, Ritual Hospitality," in Rajkumar and Dayam, *Many Yet One*, 107.

100 Raj, "Dialogue," 41.

> through hybridity the subjugated people at the bottom of the social pyramid creatively appropriate and use the religious and the cultural sources of the dominant (usually their oppressors) in order to sustain themselves through their oppressive situation.[101]

Samuel argues that this element of hybridity has helped the Dalits survive under oppression. It is this element of plurality and not being able to be limited by a particular religion that has been the strength of the Dalits.[102] In relation to the church and the acceptance of Dalits living in multiple religious belonging, Samuel asks, "rather than insisting on their 'exclusive' membership in Christianity, would it be possible to accept them as members of the body of Christ, without laying down stipulations and conditions? Would that be too un-Christian?"[103]

A relevant example is the *Kristbhakta*[104] movement, explored earlier, in north India which consists of a group of non-baptised believers who are in the liminal position of being Hindus and also having love, faith, and attachment to Jesus. This phenomenon is witnessed in north India with Matridham Ashram in Varanasi as the focal point.[105] This group of people testify to their unique experience in Jesus, but express this in terms of signs, symbols, and rituals drawn from Hinduism. They are largely from the marginalised communities, but its significance lies in being a "prophetic interrogation to the static and archaic tenets of established religions."[106] Jerome Sylvester who researched this community writes,

> The *Khristbhaktas* are at the periphery of established religion . . .. Many Christians find *Khristbhakta* Movement as a new way of spreading the Gospel and new way of being Church. The type of discipleship emerging from the *Khristbhakta* Movement is different from the conventional membership of Christian Churches. Being a disciple of Christ without being member of the Church is a reality to be faced.[107]

---

101 Joshua Samuel, "Practicing Multiple Religious Belonging for Liberation: A Reflection from a Dalit Perspective," *Current Dialogue*. 57 (December 2015): 80.

102 Samuel, "Practicing Multiple Religious Belonging," 81.

103 Samuel, "Practicing Multiple Religious Belonging," 81.

104 *Kristbhaktas* are devotees of Christ, but not members of any mainline church. They are seekers, who accept *Yesubhagavan* (God in Jesus Christ) as their *Satguru* (Teacher). *Yeshubhagavan* is their *istadevta* (personal God) according to *Bhakti* tradition. Apart from Varanasi, similar movements are seen in Bihar, Delhi, Jharkhand, Uttar Pradesh, and Madhya Pradesh. There are thousands of devout seekers who seek to follow Christ in this way. See Sylvester, *Kristbhakta Movement*, 2.

105 Felix Wilfred, "Foreword," in Sylvester, *Kristbhakta Movement*, xi–xii.

106 Sylvester, *Kristbhakta Movement*, 131.

107 Sylvester, *Kristbhakta Movement*, 135.

The experience of believing without affiliation to any institution is therefore a reality in this case not only individually but also in terms of community. This points to the fact that in India, communities as well as individuals can practise multiple religious belonging. They can belong to Christ-centred communities without being baptised. We will not explore the important related issues of baptism, conversion, and the possibility of non-baptised believers in the Indian context because we have not taken up the issue of rituals, worship, and sacraments.[108] All that is suggested here is that the *Khristbhakta* movement helps us to begin to conceptualise the church in new ways. Does it not also signify the need for a kind of church that we are arguing for with a porous or permeable borders?

Turning to the tribal Christians, we also see this group maintaining both continuity and discontinuity with their previous religions especially in terms of rituals and practices. In the preceding chapters, extensive discussion was made on how tribal Christians continue to negotiate their borders in terms of their relationship with their former *Sarna* religion and Christianity. This is especially true in east and central India among the *adivasi* (tribal) community. Lovely Awomi James argues that tribal Christians maintain hybridity in terms of their use of several customs and traditions, rituals, and practices. She shows that among tribal Christians in the northeast India, their belief in the world of the spirits, practice of totemism, practice of taboos, shamanism, and traditional feasts continue amidst their Christian faith.[109]

The above observations on multiple religious belonging and hybridity in India drive home the fact that the church cannot neglect the reality of this phenomenon. Multiple religious belonging continues to happen not only intellectually, but also concretely in the rituals, ceremonies, and religious life of individuals and communities. Multiple religious belonging is a grounded reality for many common people in India; it is not limited to religious experts as we have found. As the majority of the church in India consists of Dalits, tribals, and the marginalised groups, it is expedient that the church should recognise this situation. In this case, can there be a way

---

108 Particularly important in this field are the thoughts of M.M. Thomas. See M.M. Thomas, "Church's Mission and Post-Modern Humanism: The Church-the Fellowship of the Baptised and Unbaptised," accessed September 27, 2016, http://www.religion-online.org/showchapter.asp?title=1448&C=1274. Also see Timothy C. Tennent, "The Challenge of Churchless Christianity: An Evangelical Assessment," *International Bulletin of Missionary Research*, 29, no. 4 (October 2005): 170–177.

109 Lovely Awomi James, "North East Indian Tribal Christianity and Traditional Practices: Implications for Theology of Religions Today," *Current Dialogue* 57 (December 2015): 52–62.

out in terms of reorganisation or reconceptualisation of the boundaries of the church? Here is where the significance of a permeable Spirit ecclesiological model shows itself. A permeable Spirit ecclesiology parallels the efforts of many who practise multiple religious belonging in terms of negotiating boundaries. Essentially, a permeable Spirit ecclesiological model does the same. It enables the church to negotiate its boundaries, making it softer while not losing its distinctiveness in Christ. In the Indian context and especially through our discussions of the kind of multiple religious belonging evident in the Indian context, such an ecclesiology provides the avenues to relate to people's past and also provides occasions to witness to a particular faith. It allows the people, especially Dalits, to continue to live in multiple religious belonging for their own survival amidst oppression, and also allows them to determine their identity in their rootedness to their own culture and traditions. It works similarly in the case of tribals who will then be able to uphold their particular tradition while being Christians. A permeable Spirit ecclesiology, with its character of unity and diversity, universality and particularity, and spiritual and the concrete, could help ground the phenomenon of multiple religious belonging in the lives of common people in terms of rituals and practices. Rajkumar and Dayam point out with Stephen Barton the possibility, thereby, to live life in "creative fidelity:"

> Where fidelity involves recognisable continuity with our scriptural faith tradition, and creativity involves an openness to the Spirit for the inspiration to interpret and "perform" that tradition in ways that are life-giving.[110]

Thus, we have shown that a permeable Spirit ecclesiology does not shy away, but recognises the phenomenon of multiple religious belonging, while negotiating its borders in concrete ways both to be faithful to a particular tradition while being open to relate to the other in concrete ways towards flourishing of life and freedom.

### Interfaith relations

In both Western and Indian Christian traditions as we have found, there is the acknowledgement that the church should be in relationship with other religions or people of other faiths. It is needless to repeat the different approaches of the theologians regarding church's interfaith relations and theology of religions that have already been discussed. Instead, what we intend to do is to bring out the particular interfaith relationship a

[110] Stephen C. Barton, "The Epistles and Christian Ethics," in *The Cambridge Companion to Christian Ethics*, ed. Robin Gill, 2nd ed. (Cambridge: Cambridge University Press, 2012), 63, cited in Rajkumar and Dayam, "Introduction," 3.

permeable Spirit ecclesiology would facilitate in the sense of this dialogical relationship. In other words, we will elaborate on how such dialogical relationship is upheld by a permeable Spirit ecclesiological model. It will be argued that a particular understanding of dialogical relationship between religions is required in the context of plurality and marginalisation in India. It will be evident that a discussion of interfaith relations of the church in India cannot be carried out without considering the issue of marginalisation and oppression of Dalits and tribals, as they constitute the majority in the Indian church. In essence, what we will be arguing is that a permeable Spirit ecclesiology provides the appropriate paradigm for interfaith relations, which is not simply elitist, but where the issue of marginalisation is taken seriously. In order to explore this particular kind of dialogical relationship, it is essential to begin by briefly outlining the development of the dialogical approach through the twentieth century. This will help us understand how we entered the stage of dialogue in interfaith relations and how dialogical relations with other religions should be understood within the Indian context.

During the modern times, the church's interfaith relations were integrally connected to the mission of the church. In the eighteenth and nineteenth centuries, the Christian missionary attitude was marked by the superiority of the Christian religion and the denial of the worth of other religions. The World Missionary Conference in Edinburgh (1910) harboured many of those attitudes. Gustav Warneck used the language of military conquest to describe Christian mission.[111] Henry Venn shared in the conference the view of the Scottish missionary to India, Alexander Duff, that Western education could prepare Indians for the gospel.[112] The conference also came to learn from other missionaries from "lands of living faiths" that a superior attitude to Christianity was unwise in the context of relationship between Christianity and other religions.[113] Following the conference, a change of attitude was recognisable among theologians and missionaries. Kirsteen Kim highlights some of the reasons for this change in attitude: the First and Second World Wars, which

---

[111] See Timothy Yates, *Christian Mission in the Twentieth Century* (Cambridge: Cambridge University Press, 1994), 31–32, cited in Kirsteen Kim, *Joining in with the Spirit: Connecting World Church and Local Mission* (London: Epworth Press, 2009), 21.

[112] Andrew F. Walls, *The Cross-Cultural Process in Christian History: Studies in the Transmission and Appropriation of Faith* (Maryknoll, NY: Orbis Books), 27–28, cited in Kirsteen Kim, *Joining in with the Spirit*, 22.

[113] K.P. Aleaz, "Christian Dialogues with Hinduism," in *Interfaith Relations after One Hundred Years: Christian Mission Among Other Faiths*, ed. Marina Ngursangzeli Behera, Regnum Edinburgh 2010 Series (Edinburgh: Regnum Books, 2011), 79.

undermined European supremacy; the development of a pragmatic approach to mission work; decolonisation and growth of churches in the Global South; and complaints of proselytism from Hindus.[114] In the aftermath of the conference, different attitudes were recognisable, but most of them revealed a softened attitude towards other religions. J.N. Farquhar proposed the "fulfilment theory," where Christ was considered to be the fulfilment of Hinduism. A.G. Hogg rejected such a theory, instead highlighting the contrast between Hinduism and Christianity. Later in the second Missionary Conference at Jerusalem in 1928, there was a softer approach to other religions. Religions were beginning to be considered as allies rather than enemies. W.E. Hocking was in favour of seeing the best in other religions; he was not in favour of conversion, but of seeing the emergence of religions into a world fellowship.[115] This was challenged by a later book by Hendrik Kraemer, entitled the *Christian Message in a Non-Christian World,* written as a preparatory volume for the Third Missionary Conference held in Tambaram in 1938. It was in response to this document that the *Rethinking Group* of Indian theologians like Chenchiah and Chakkarai voiced their opposition to Kraemer and the Tambaram message, that favoured a discontinuity between Christianity and other religions. Instead, Indian thinkers upheld the value of continuity as Chenchiah argued that his Hindu background helped him to appreciate Christ and Christianity.[116] In the 1940s and 1950s, openness towards other religions gradually grew and paved the way for dialogical encounter between religions. K.P. Aleaz writes, "Wide ecumenical recognition has been given through both the World Council of Churches (WCC) and the Second Vatican Council, for this dialogical approach."[117] While the WCC established a *Department for Dialogue with People of Living Faiths and Ideologies*, the Second Vatican Council (1962–65), changed the way the Roman Catholic Church understood itself, moving from an understanding of itself as a hierarchical church to being a "people of God."[118] Since the Central Committee meeting at Addis Ababa in 1971, dialogue with other religions has occupied a prominent place in the work of the WCC. In later stages, the concept of dialogue began to be described in terms of mutuality between religions while the role of the Spirit of God is recognised. The Baar Statement of the Dialogue sub-unit of the WCC is significant enough to be quoted at length.

114 Kim, *Joining in with the Spirit*, 22–23.
115 Aleaz, "Christian Dialogues," 80.
116 Aleaz, "Christian Dialogues," 81.
117 Aleaz, "Christian Dialogues," 81.
118 Kim, *Joining in with the Spirit*, 26.

> We need to respect their religious convictions (i.e., of people of other living faiths), different as these may be from our own, and to admire the things which God has accomplished and continues to accomplish in them through the Spirit. Inter-religious dialogue is therefore a "two-way" street. Christians must enter into it in a spirit of openness prepared to receive from others, while on their part, they give witness of their own faith. Authentic dialogue opens both partners to a deeper conversion to the God who speaks to each through the other. Through the witness of others, we Christians can truly discover facets of the divine mystery which we have not yet seen or responded to. The practice of dialogue will thus result in the deepening of our own life of faith. We believe that walking together with people of other living faiths will bring us to a fuller understanding and experience of truth.[119]

The above statement shows that dialogue in the character of mutuality of religions was accepted during the 1990s. This confirms the importance of the dialogical mutuality that we argued earlier as one of the twin features of relational-distinctive dialectics of a permeable Spirit ecclesiology. This dialogical-mutuality, on the one hand, treats various religions as working grounds for the Spirit and, on the other, allows a two-way communication and mutuality between religious partners.

Particularly speaking from the Indian context, this dialogical mutuality bears the character of the rejection of the colonial supremacist position of Christianity with respect to other religions, which have been found in pioneer Indian theologians right from the nineteenth century. Although some of them can be categorised as inclusivist, they treated all religions as being equal and discarded the notion of the superiority of one religion over other.[120] Aleaz, writing on the pioneering contributions of Indian thinkers and theologians, gives the example of Krishna Mohun Banerjea (1813–1885), whose theology discarded superiority of one religion over others even earlier than his Western counterparts. Aleaz needs to be quoted at length here.

> Krishna Mohun Banerjea (1813–1885) was the first Protestant Christian to interpret Jesus Christ and Christianity in terms of Vedic thought . . .. Banerjea's exposition of Christ as *True Prajapati* was an attempt to establish the fact that Christianity is not a foreign religion but rather the

---

119 "Baar Statement," *Current Dialogue* 18 (June 1990): 7, cited in Aleaz, "Christian Dialogues," 82.

120 Aleaz gives a description of several theologians from the nineteenth century onwards who engaged in interfaith relations, especially Hindu-Christian relations. He cites H.S. Krishna Pillai, A.S. Appasamy Pillai, Brahmabandhav Upadhaya, Pandipeddi Chenchiah, Vengal Chakkari, and others. See Aleaz, "Christian Dialogues," 83–99.

> fulfilment of the Vedas. In fact, thirty eight years before J.N. Farquhar, it was Krishna Mohun Banerjea who first proposed "Fulfilment Theory" or Inclusivism in Indian Christian Theology of Religions, that again without any negative criticisms of Hinduism as are found in Farquhar's book.[121] Also some eighty-four years before Raimon Panikkar,[122] K.M. Banerjea was the first person to hint at *Prajapati* as unknown Christ of Hinduism, that again without any negative criticisms of Vedanta as are found in Panikkar's thesis. Again, sixty-three years before H. Kraemer proposed his theory of discontinuity between Revelation and religions, here is an Indian theologian in the person of Banerjea expounding a point of contact and continuity between Christianity and Hinduism.[123]

In the contemporary times, Aleaz, in his theology of religions, also shows dialogical mutuality, which combines the two-way interaction of religions while discarding the superiority of one religion over the other.

Thus, while principles of dialogical mutuality between Christianity and other religions were established early on, the churches of India have still got to implement this into actual practice. The concept of interreligious relations in the nature of dialogical mutuality seems to be guiding ecumenical institutions and academia, but it has not yet profoundly affected the church on the ground level in India. There might be two particular reasons for such a condition. One reason that we have discussed at length is the colonial captivity of the church and we need not repeat it here; on the other hand, to date, the issues of interfaith relations and theology of religions have been mostly an elitist and intellectual enterprise. Interfaith efforts and theology of religions in India have been largely done in brahmanic and vedic categories as is shown in the efforts of Krishna Mohun, Brahmabandhav Upadhyaya, and others. While interreligious dialogue at this level has considerable value and continues to be done, it has failed to influence the common life of Indian Christians. For interfaith relations to be realised among the common people of the church, it needs to be grounded in the daily life of the people in their everyday relations. Stanley Samartha's categorisation of dialogue is helpful here, where dialogue is not only understood as an intellectual or elitist enterprise, but one that relates to our lives.

121 J.N. Farquhar, *The Crown of Hinduism* (London: Oxford University Press, 1913); J.N. Farquhar, *Gita and Gospel*, 3rd ed. (Madras: CLS, 1918), cited in Aleaz, "Christian Dialogues," 84.

122 Raimundo Panikkar, *The Unknown Christ of Hinduism* (London: Darton, Longman & Todd, 1964), (rev. and enlarged ed. by the same publisher in 1981). For a summary of his thesis, cf. "Isvara and Christ as a Philosophical Problem," *Religion and Society* 6, no. 3 (October 1959): 8–16, cited in Aleaz, "Christian Dialogues," 84.

123 Aleaz, "Christian Dialogues," 84.

> (1) Dialogue of Life, in which participants are more concerned with issues that pertain to daily living and common values; (2) Dialogue of Action, which involves common work for justice and shared concerns such as HIV/AIDS and the cause of the poor; (3) Dialogue of Experience, which concerns daily spiritual experience and expressions; and (4) Dialogue of Experts, which is interested in theology and philosophy of the faith traditions.[124]

This understanding of dialogue not only engages the intellectuals and experts, but opens the way for interfaith relations to common people in the church in the context of common concerns of life. This actually broadens interfaith relations in at least two aspects: one, it brings concreteness and particularity in interfaith relations while being a dialogue of life and dialogue of experience; on the other hand, it gives a critical edge to dialogue while it is done in terms of dialogue of action, i.e., shared concerns and work for justice for the poor and the marginalised. We would like to apply the permeable Spirit ecclesiological model to this wider understanding of interfaith dialogue and show that it can uphold the dimensions mentioned by Samartha.

We have previously argued that the relational-distinctive dialectics have the capacity to uphold the relational character of the church in its dialogue with other religions through the Spirit's presence and action in them. We have emphasised plurality and diversity, and also the distinctive character in terms of the Indian-Christian identity of the church, and the critical criteria regarding itself and against the structures that perpetuate marginalisation. In the Indian context, interfaith relations cannot be separated from the issue of marginalisation and oppression since they are interrelated. Since the majority of the church is constituted of the marginalised, interfaith relations cannot bypass their perspectives while the church engages in interfaith dialogue. A permeable Spirit ecclesiology has the capacity to ground the church's dialogical relations in the concrete lives of the people. We will thus deal with interfaith relations from the perspective of the marginalised, i.e., from the position of the Dalits and tribals. Interfaith relations take on a different level of complexity when approached from the context of the marginalised in India.

---

[124] Stanley J. Samartha, *One Christ, Many Religions: Towards a Revised Christology* (Maryknoll, NY: Orbis, 1991), 88. This is a summary by Veli-Matti Kärkkäinen, "Theologies of Religions," in *Witnessing to Christ in a Pluralistic Age: Christian Mission among Other Faiths*, ed. Lalsangkima Pachuau and Knud Jørgensen, Regnum Edinburgh 2010 Series (Edinburgh: Regnum Books International, 2011), 111.

The relationship of Christian Dalits and tribals to other religions, especially Hinduism, is particularly problematic. Peniel Rajkumar explores this in his article, *Re-Cast(e)ing Conversion, Re-visiting Dialogue: Indian Attempts at an Interfaith Theology of Wholeness,* where he brings a whole new dimension to interfaith thinking from a marginalised perspective. The abstract of this article is quoted here to highlight the problem.

> In India, the Christian commitment to interfaith engagement produces a paradox. On the one hand, dialogue between Christianity and other religions, especially Hinduism in this context, is seen as an advance in redressing an earlier unjust position of assumed religious exclusivity, triumphalism, and superiority on the part of an evangelical missionary Christianity. Dialogue presumes mutuality of recognition, respect, and religious value, including freedom from coercion and freedom of personal choice. However, on the other hand, in the Indian context, the caste system presents intractable problems which, in being identified with Hinduism and thus, in the context of dialogue, to be recognised and respected as a religious value on the part of the Christian dialogue partner, then results in the Christian colluding with a manifest injustice with respect to *Dalit* and *Adivasi* (tribal) peoples for whom the caste system is oppressive and restrictive.[125]

What the above essentially means is that the aspect of Christian dialogue with Hinduism nowadays is usually taken as a development of and remedy for the previous stance of interfaith engagement which was triumphalistic. But on the other hand, the caste system creates a barrier to interfaith engagement because according to the marginalised, Hinduism is to be blamed for it. In this circumstance, dialogical relations between Christianity and Hinduism in the context of caste becomes problematic. This is the paradox of the Indian situation that is expressed here.

In India, Dalits and tribals have always sought to resist brahmanic hegemony and oppression in their opposition to Hinduism. They, especially the Dalits, have shown their dissent in various ways: Following a survival strategy of accommodation in appropriating upper caste rituals and practices; through "sub-alterations"[126] in terms of non-compliance to the worldview of the high castes, for example, in their myths of origin rejecting the doctrine of *karma*; "subversion"[127] in terms of overtly debunking old

[125] Peniel J.R. Rajkumar, *Cast(e)ing Conversion, Re-visiting Dialogue: Indian Attempts at an Interfaith Theology of Wholeness*, Abstract, *JASR* 26, no. 2 (2013): 157.

[126] Peniel J.R. Rajkumar, "The Diversity and Dialectics of Dalit Dissent and Implications," in *Dalit Theology in the Twenty-first Century: Discordant Voices, Discerning Pathways*, eds. Sathianathan Clarke, Deenabandhu Manchala, and Philip Vinod Peacock (New Delhi: Oxford University Press), 56.

[127] Rajkumar, "Diversity and Dialectics," 57.

templates and meaning systems to embracing symbols of Dalit identity.[128] Dalit theology, carried out by Dalit Christians, largely remains a countermovement against Hinduism.[129] The complexity increases when the traditional Dalit religion is included within the ambit of Hindu religion. This resemblance, however, is partly due to absorption by Hinduism, historically of Dalit and tribal rituals, gods, and symbol systems.[130] This not only led to dissolution of their religio-cultural identities, but also their socioreligious autonomy. Abraham Ayrookuzhiel writes that they

> not only lost their social autonomy and economic independence but also their religiocultural self-identity as a separate group by losing control over their gods, places of worship and the right to administer to their own people's religious needs. Furthermore, many of them internalized brahminical versions of myths relating to this historical process and voluntarily accepted demeaning ritual roles in village festivals, temple rituals, and domestic rites corresponding to a servile class in a semi-feudal economy.[131]

One of the other ways in which Dalits have responded to high caste Hindu brahmanical oppression is to convert to Christianity, Buddhism, or other religions.[132] Dalits who followed B.R. Ambedkar[133] are convinced that they cannot reclaim their identity, self-dignity, and humanity by staying within the Hindu fold.[134] This brings us to the problematic position of how conversion is seen differently by different groups and in its relation to interfaith dialogue. Rajkumar writes,

> While commitment to Hindu–Christian dialogue has demanded that Christians compromise on conversions, nevertheless, commitment to the liberation and empowerment of the *Dalits* and *Adivasis* has implied

---

128 Rajkumar, "Diversity and Dialectics," 55–58.

129 See Sathianathan Clarke, "Dalit Theology: An Introductory and Interpretive Theological Exposition," in *Dalit Theology in the Twenty-first Century: Discordant Voices, Discerning Pathways*, 20–22. Clarke discusses methodological exclusivism of Dalit theology in relation to brahmanic ideology.

130 A.M. Abraham Ayrookuzhiel, "The Dalits, Religions and Interfaith Dialogue," *Journal of Hindu-Christian Studies* 7 Art. 6 (1994): 14.

131 Ayrookuzhiel, "The Dalits," 14.

132 Numerous conversions to Buddhism occurred from the Dalit Hindu community after the conversion of Ambedkar to Buddhism in 1956.

133 Bhimrao Ramji Ambedkar (1891–1956) was a jurist, economist, politician, and social reformer who inspired the Dalit Buddhist Movement and campaigned against social discrimination against Dalits, while also supporting the rights of women and labourers. He was independent India's first law minister and one of the framers of the Constitution of India.

134 Ayrookuzhiel, "The Dalits," 14.

that Christians affirm the rights of the *Dalits* and *Adivasis* to convert to Christianity as a way of liberation from the caste system.[135]

Rajkumar argues that Christianity's colonial entanglements have to be understood in a different light when considered in connection with the liberation of the marginalised. Although colonial captivity has to be decried in different manifestations of the church and society, he contends that the contributions of the missionaries and the colonial power led to the empowerment and liberation of the oppressed Dalits and tribals in certain spheres. Rajkumar quotes Daryl Balia and Kirsteen Kim:

> These conditions of mission were seen as a liberative-transformative space by Dalit communities for self-assertion and reclamation of their place in society rather than as components of the colonizing process. Therefore, Dalit entanglements with missionaries are much more complex than patron–client or colonizer–colonized relationships. Dalit communities, which had no stake in local power, viewed those in their own country who had power as "colonizers." For them, the conversion experience of which they were the primary agents helped in their quest for freedom from oppression. In this the conditions of mission played and continue to play the role of midwife.[136]

Rajkumar contends that Hindu-Christian dialogue cannot therefore continue in terms of laying the burden of colonial guilt on Christians, and viewing Hindus as victims with respect to the marginalised.[137] Victimhood has changed sides; now the Hindus are perpetrators of discrimination and violence against Christian Dalits and tribals. Rajkumar argues that if we continue to reject conversion of Dalits and tribals on the basis of promoting interfaith dialogue, we might end up in colluding with the Hindu oppressors. Rajkumar also points out that while engaging in Hindu-Christian dialogue, we must judiciously choose partners. Considering Hinduism as a non-monolithic, non-homogenous religion, we must be careful to avoid dialogue with those Hindu oppressors who perpetuate discrimination and violence, and instead choose Hindus who are against caste and who support the dignity of life.[138]

In the preceding discussion, we have highlighted the trajectory that is involved in interfaith relations while considering it from the marginalised perspective. This kind of approach is actually a contrast to the elitist dialogical approach that is common in academic and intellectual circles. This

135 Rajkumar, *Cast(e)ing Conversion*, 158.

136 Daryl Balia and Kirsteen Kim, *Witnessing to Christ Today*, vol. 2, Edinburgh 2010 (Oxford: Regnum Books International, 2010), 15.

137 Rajkumar, *Cast(e)ing Conversion*, 164–165.

138 Rajkumar, *Cast(e)ing Conversion*, 164–165.

actually opens the way to understanding interfaith relations broadly in two different ways: one, in intellectual and institutional terms, and two, in terms of more concrete and grounded form that includes the dialogue of the marginalised including their aspirations and liberation. If we return to the different forms of interfaith dialogue as expressed by Samartha quoted earlier, we can argue that interfaith dialogue should continue at both levels, while emphasising the importance of dialogue particularly at the concrete level that includes the marginalised. We should also affirm the freedom of the marginalised to convert to whichever religion they choose.

It is therefore argued here that different facets of interfaith dialogue can be accommodated in a permeable Spirit ecclesiology. We have already shown that the dialectic of dialogical mutuality forms the basis for respect for religions and sharing and exchange between religions at an equal level. On the other hand, the dialectic of particularity and universality has its place too. While universality upholds that relationality among religions is to be upheld, no particular religion should seek to homogenise the diversity and particularity of religions. This is true in the case of the efforts of the Hindu fundamentalists to homogenise Hinduism and bring the other minority religious communities under its fold. One of interfaith relation's roles is to obstruct any such efforts towards religious hegemony. A permeable Spirit ecclesiology upholds the critical character of interfaith relations through its borders. While porosity determines passage of religious concepts and facilitates dialogue, the borders filter and determine both the dialogical partners and the critical attitude towards religions and religious establishments that perpetuate the oppression of the marginalised in the name of religion. The borders of the church here play a critical, prophetic, and liberationist role. While the Holy Spirit helps to relate to religions through the Spirit's presence and action among religious communities beyond the church, the christological criterion provides the critical and prophetic edge to engage in interfaith relations with concerns of justice and liberation. Christ's life, death, and resurrection continue to be the locus of liberation for the marginalised and a prophetic critique against structures of oppression. Thus, a permeable Spirit ecclesiology with its relational-distinctive dialectics can provide the basis for the church's interfaith relations.

## Conclusion

In the preceding discussion, we demonstrated the particular character of ecumenism, multiple religious belonging, and interfaith relations when understood in the context of India. We have been able to deal with some trajectories in these issues which are different from that of the West. In other words, it was found that in all three issues there is an additional dimension from the perspective of the marginalised that needs to be taken into account in the Indian context. We argued that a permeable Spirit ecclesiology has the potential to uphold the dynamics at play regarding these issues in this particular context. However, the question remains as to how a permeable Spirit ecclesiology can tangibly help the churches to deal with the above issues. What practical tools or resources does this theology of the church provide to work with? In this concluding section, we will turn to these questions.

To begin with, a permeable Spirit ecclesiology provides some inevitable basic methodological orientations for the churches in India to consider. These orientations are twofold: a turn towards plurality and diversity, and an emphasis on the struggles, aspirations, and liberation of the marginalised and oppressed people. The turn to plurality and diversity is facilitated by the church's recognition that the Spirit of God along with the Logos/Word are present, and are working in the church and in different Christian denominations and other religious communities. This recognition and appreciation of the reality of diversity and plurality essentially opens the door to the aspect of relationality that the Indian church should develop. Particularly in terms of ecumenical relations, this becomes far easier as a starting point rather than beginning with the affirmation that we are all one and united in Christ. It helps the churches to start from the stark reality that we are manifestly plural and diverse, while it does not provide justification for our divisions. Here, diversity is turned from a problem to be shunned or a barrier to be overcome to an opportunity for relationality and engagement. Here, unity in Christ is the goal that we work towards at the practical level, starting with our appreciation and acceptance of the other in the Spirit. This also reduces our, often unintentional, tendency to take unity for uniformity in the ministry and mission of the church. Appreciation of diversity involves learning from others and accepting the gifts that others bring into the meaning and life of the Christian community. The recognition that the Spirit values plurality and diversity might go a long way into accepting and affirming each other's ministry and mission, which would eventually pave the way for a closer relationship and, ultimately, unity.

However, in the Indian situation the issues of unity and ecumenism do not end here. A permeable ecclesiology further leads the church into understanding unity and ecumenism in terms of particularity and concreteness. What this means is that Christian unity has to be pursued at the ground level, at the local level, at the level of the people. Christian unity should be a people's movement rather than merely an institutional one. The movement of unity should start from the Christians themselves in their local context. This could, on the other hand, mean that no single model of unity could be universally applicable. While not neglecting the principle of catholicity and universality of the church, each local situation will determine what sort of unity the churches require in their context. For example, a particular area or region in India could decide what brings them together. In other words, the nature of Christian or ecclesial unity may differ in their concerns for the states of West Bengal, Orissa, or Bihar, which have negligible Christian minorities from that of some of the northeastern states like Nagaland and Mizoram which are more than ninety percent Christian, and some of the southern states like Kerala and Tamilnadu with a considerable number of Christian population. The agendas, approaches, and concerns for Christian unity would be significantly different in these two regions. For example, Christian unity in the former group could be more related to the witness it can give to the people of other faiths amidst which the churches live and work; on the other hand, for northeastern states, it could be more in terms of solving the Western denominational problems that they have inherited. Therefore, at any rate, it is for Christians of different areas in India to decide what works best for them rather than have unity thrust upon them from a higher institutional level. On a general level, however, churches could come together on issues like ministry to the poor, standing up for their own minority rights, other socio-political-economic issues, or at a deeper level in their spirituality of prayers, worship, and liturgies. However, all these are simply means to an end for further, fuller, and richer unity in Christ. Speaking from the particular context of West Bengal, an eastern state in India, churches could witness more effectively within their own diverse religio-cultural context by being concretely and particularly engaged in their own communities in unity than in a kind of unity that the wider society has no conception about. In other words, rather than trying to solve the historical denominational problems which have been imported into India and about which the wider society is hardly conscious about, Christian social engagements in the wider society have more promise for effective witness and as a means to Christian unity. However, it is not suggested that the historical denominational problems should not be dealt with. Rather, it is suggested that they cannot be our starting points. In Christian unity, relationality in terms of building relationships of trust, confidence, and friendship in each other are crucial towards any further visible unity. And, the best way to achieve it is to agree to work together in the particular society where we live, engaging in concrete struggles and issues.

However, church-unity becomes more complicated when it is understood from the perspective of the marginalised. The churches in India, divided and segregated by caste and tribal affiliations, face huge obstacles towards realisation of unity. In other words, how can unity be envisaged between the high caste Christians and Dalit Christians? How can the oppressor and the oppressed be united without questions of justice? How can unity among competing tribal Christian traditions be worked out? While engaging in unity from the perspective of the marginalised and the oppressed, what matters are the essential dimensions of solidarity with them, a critical edge and a liberationist perspective, with a desire for justice and peace. A permeable Spirit ecclesiology helps the church in India to face up to the stark reality and difficult challenge of unity amidst caste and tribal divisions in the church. Its distinctive, critical, and liberationist outlook reminds the church that questions of unity of the church cannot simply bypass the question of justice for the oppressed. This involves the issue of rights and agency for the marginalised before proper unity can be worked out. The dynamics of repentance and forgiveness in Christ are crucial dimensions before Christians in India can be justly united. A permeable Spirit ecclesiology points the churches to the fact that the Spirit of God who is for liberty (2 Cor 3:17) and Christ our liberator (through his death and resurrection) continue to work between segregated Christian communities and thus it should be our pleasure to join in. A permeable Spirit ecclesiology, through the unity and oneness in the Spirit and Christ, helps the churches to realise that unity also means solidarity with the marginalised Christians and building bridges with the other marginalised communities within the churches and beyond.

In terms of interfaith relations again, how does a permeable Spirit ecclesiology help the churches? Here also, it points out to the Indian churches that interfaith relations should not be limited to academic, elitist, or intellectual enterprise. Interfaith relations in India ought to start from the ground, from a concrete level, from the living communities themselves. Interfaith relations for the Christian minorities in India, living amidst a plural, multicultural, and multireligious environment actually begin outside the church in their daily concrete lives. Interfaith relation is essentially a dialogue of life that continues to be held every day. A permeable Spirit ecclesiology's affirmation that the Spirit and the Word continue to work jointly in various communities in everyday situations, is just the right starting point for the churches to engage in interfaith relations. A permeable Spirit ecclesiology's stress on the concrete and the particular helps develop these starting points. It provides opportunities to the common people, rather than merely the experts, to explore interfaith relationships with people from different religious backgrounds who they meet, converse with, and work with on a day-to-day basis. Essentially, a permeable Spirit ecclesiology shows the churches in India that alternative, informal spaces outside the church and outside the academy could be created that would facilitate interfaith interaction.

We have shown earlier that interfaith relations have been largely elitist and intellectual with little substantial outcome on the ecclesial and ground levels. One of the reasons, of course, is the colonial captivity of the church. There have therefore been genuine efforts throughout to remedy the situation in terms of inculturation, contextualisation, indigenisation, and other similar means. However, these efforts have not been very fruitful and are often looked upon with suspicion, if at first cordial relationships are not forged between people from different communities. While not negating the role of the ecclesial and institutional efforts, and the professional theologians or intellectuals in the task of interfaith relations, it is argued that a turn to alternative spaces can be more practically effective to forge such relationships. The organised churches themselves could create such spaces in different ways. One of the ways these alternative interfaith interactive spaces could be created is by turning to social-cultural festivities. Public sociocultural festivities draw people from all religious backgrounds to a common platform. The churches could organise such festivities inviting people from different backgrounds to interact, share, and relate, thus building friendships and relationships. The other way in which the churches can engage with other religious communities is through joint efforts towards socio-economic-political issues that affect all communities, especially the minorities. Movements for justice, peace, poverty, unemployment, and a host of other common issues can bring churches and other Christians in close relationship with other communities. These will not only better interfaith relationship, but also be occasions of witness for Christ in a non-supremacist, non-patronising, and non-proselytising manner. These will be also occasions for learning, sharing, and enriching each other through the gift of each other's rich religious resources. A permeable Spirit ecclesiology informs the church that the Spirit and the Word are present and active within the various communities in their struggles, both spiritual and secular, for dignity, justice, peace, and a decent human life. To that end, the churches can look forward to cooperation with other communities, work in solidarity and enrich each other.

However, a basic question remains as we have highlighted before. This is the question of the relationship of caste segregation and interfaith dialogue with Hinduism, especially with those Hindus who perpetuate marginalisation in the name of caste and religion. These include those fundamentalist Hindus who propagate the sectarian notion of *Hindutva*, once responsible for persecution of minorities including Christians. Should we engage in interfaith relations with them? If so, what could be the nature of such a dialogue? Or, if we shun them, do we not lose opportunities for witnessing for Christ among them? These are difficult questions. A permeable Spirit ecclesiology helps the church situate itself in the reality of the situation. On the one hand, an ecclesiology with permeable borders would encourage the church to forge relationships as the Spirit and Christ are always engaged in building relationships with not only the like-minded, but also the different and the other. Such an ecclesiology would allow the church to work critically with these communities in justice with the goal of transformation and liberation both for the oppressed and the oppressor. Practically speaking, the more cordial relationships and networks are developed with the wider religious communities, the easier it will be to counteract either caste or fundamentalism. The confidence, support, and trust of people from different religious faiths who are for justice and peace are crucial for standing up to these challenges.

As regards multiple religious belonging, a permeable Spirit ecclesiology helps the church in India to recognise its reality in the first place. This recognition is then followed by an effort at comprehension. It encourages the church to seek to understand the phenomenon in its diversity and complexity, instead of simply dismissing it as some form of syncretism. The fact that many Christians and many people belonging to different religions are consciously or unconsciously, willingly or unwillingly involved in multiple religious belonging for different reasons gives food for thought and reflection for the church. However, the prime difficulty is not in the fact that the churches might recognise the reality of the phenomenon. The problem arises in acknowledgment of the status of those people or groups who engage in multiple religious belonging. They are often misunderstood or misinterpreted by both religious communities, as we have shown previously in the case of Swami Abhishiktananda. There are also those who engage in it without any commitment to any particular religion at all. While this latter kind of spirituality has to be criticised, we have also shown that common people, including Christians, engage in multiple religious belonging through shared rituals in different shrines in India without much opposition. Thus, in the case of organised Christianity or churches finding difficulty in acknowledging or accepting persons or groups who transcend religious boundaries, a permeable Spirit ecclesiology suggests that alternative spaces could be created where such people can be appreciated or their richness of experience can be welcomed. These spaces also can become nurturing grounds for them to make commitments towards a particular religion if they find themselves so disposed at some point. In other words, a permeable Spirit ecclesiology with its negotiable and soft boundaries can provide motivation for the churches to create extra space for such people. These spaces can be fellowships of like-minded people in a non-judgemental environment while providing them with opportunities for growth and nurture in their spiritualities.

However, this complex phenomenon is rendered acute while the marginalised people practise multiple religious belonging either for their survival or as a strategy to counteract oppression, as we have earlier shown. Multiple religious belonging here does not remain only a matter of religious practice, but also a subversive posture of the marginalised. It was shown how this becomes a critique of organised, institutional religion with its strict boundaries, rituals, and practices. Here, a permeable Spirit ecclesiology with its affirmation that the Spirit and the Word work both in the centre and the periphery, in the midst and in the boundaries of people's religious and spiritual lives, offers motivations for the churches. It helps the churches to recognise that God's dealing with people cannot be confined to set institutions and practices. It shows the churches the need to create alternative, liberationist spaces where religious and spiritual creativity can flourish. It suggests that the churches should go beyond, from their narrow confines, to where God is at work even at the boundaries and outside them.

# CONCLUSION

In this book, the objective has been to develop a permeable Spirit ecclesiology in the context of India. The notion of permeability was expressed in terms of the feature of relational-distinctiveness in ecclesiology. In other words, it was argued that an Indian ecclesiology needs an orientation towards relationality affirming the diversity and plurality of other faith communities, including its own denominational diversity. On the other hand, in a dialectical relationship to the above, an Indian ecclesiology needs an orientation towards distinctiveness in terms of an Indian identity and developing an embodied community of Christ. Included in this distinctiveness is a critical stance both towards itself and the wider world and a particular liberationist turn towards the marginalised. The relational-distinctive dialectics in Indian ecclesiology is argued to be fulfiled with a dialectics of a pneumatological perspective and a christological dimension working together.

This project has led to several important insights and outcomes. The very first insight is an understanding of the Indian context, especially the challenges and struggles for the churches. The struggle for the churches in India is broadly twofold. On the one hand, the churches still struggle with colonial captivity, while they must make sense of the religio-social-cultural plurality around them; on the other hand, they must respond to the marginalisation of their members with a liberationist perspective. In other words, the first challenge is the challenge of the issue of identity of the churches. The second concerns the church's response to the Dalits, *adivasis*, tribals, and other marginalised groups.

The first struggle is essentially for the churches to be released from their colonial captivity in their structures, theology, and mission, which, as argued, requires a decolonisation approach and a dynamic approach in tension with the institutions. Included in this is the church's seeking an Indian identity in terms of situating itself within the context of India religio-culturally and sociopolitically. This implies both a discontinuity from its colonial moorings and a continuity and relationship with other communities and a dynamic relationship with emerging society. The church ought to be relational with other communities in India, correcting and eradicating the alienation caused by a colonial Christianity. Yet, it must be a distinct, embodied community in terms of its rootedness and Indian character in the particular context. The distinctive rootedness and diversity of the Christian community is argued to be a critical counter approach to fundamentalist Hindu assumptions of a homogenised and monocultural Indian identity. The distinctiveness of the church in its particular local and cultural context will both manifest its "Indian-ness" and also its diversity and particularity. The unity that the church possesses ought to be manifested in such diversity.

The other challenge is that of marginalisation of Dalits, *adivasis*, tribals, and similar groups within the church and in wider society. The challenge is to consciously forge relationships with the neglected, oppressed, and marginalised groups in the church and outside, in the wider world. This is the church's relational and universal dimension, which takes it beyond the church into the wider society. This takes the form of solidarity with the oppressed groups and seeking to develop an integral theology of life and critical witness that caters to the hopes and aspirations of such groups. It also involves a simultaneous critical approach towards those structures within the church and in the society, and even the political establishments that perpetuate such marginalisation. In this sense, the church ought to be relational in terms of integrating the concerns of these marginalised groups in its understanding of the nature, ministry, and mission. The church also ought to be distinctive in its critical approach towards its segregated character and towards those forces that perpetuate marginalisation and oppression. This approach is particularly distinctive in its emphasis on justice and liberation.

Apart from an understanding of the Indian context, the book argued that a permeable Spirit ecclesiology, characterising a relational-distinctive dialectics would help the church in India to broadly address the above-mentioned challenges. In other words, a permeable church, conceptualised in terms of an emphasis on a pneumatological perspective, coupled with a christological dimension could help maintain the above-mentioned dialectics. This is a dialectical engagement where both the Spirit and Christ would be each responsible for maintaining the relational and the distinctive dimensions. In other words, as the Spirit of God manifests relational-distinctive dialectics in terms of holding in tension universality and particularity, unity and diversity, spiritual and concrete, one and many, so does the Word/Logos or Christ.

To arrive at a permeable Spirit ecclesiology, where the Spirit and Christ jointly ensure a dialectical situation, available models of ecclesiology were considered. Several models of ecclesiology, beginning with a relational model with Jürgen Moltmann, a distinctive model with Stanley Hauerwas, and a christo-theocentric model with Kathryn Tanner, were explored. Subsequently, Amos Yong's permeable Spirit ecclesiology, based on the Irenaean metaphor of the Spirit and Christ, working as two hands of the Father was found to uphold the relational-distinctive dialectics. The previous three models did have notable strengths, but they all fail in maintaining the dialectics required. Moltmann's social trinitarian model offers considerable relationality in terms of God-church-world relationships, but fails to express this relationality in a distinctive and concrete manner. His ecclesiology, which has a pneumatological perspective and eschatological orientation, is largely conflated in terms of God-church-world relationship. He fails to maintain enough distinction between God and the world and an embodied and concrete character for the church, which is required in the Indian context. Essentially, the model of Social Trinity is problematic in imaging human relationships and the church.

Stanley Hauerwas's ecclesiocentric model is a distinctive one and places significant emphases on a number of desired characteristics: concrete and embodied community of witness to Christ with its distinctive character of virtue and discipleship, the concrete liturgy and practices of the church and a critical edge with respect to assumptions of the world, which should be relevant for any context. However, Hauerwas's ecclesiocentric approach is essentially exclusive and detrimental to building relationships with other communities on a dialogical level. While highlighting the distinctive character of the church, it is without relational potential which is crucial for the Indian context.

Tanner's christo-theocentric model is significant in terms of overcoming many of the problems found in the social trinitarian model. She offers a less complicated avenue of imaging human relationships and the church on a christological model based on Christ's relationship with the Father and Jesus's human relationships. It is a critique also of an exclusive nature of ecclesiology of the post-liberal school. On the other hand, her model based on the transcendence of God allows the Christian community to be relational towards the other while critiquing socioeconomic structures for human dignity and justice. Although she leans towards a permeable ecclesiology, it lacks a dialectics where the Spirit and the Word can work together in the economy. Tanner also lacks a developed ecclesiology in terms of the nature, ministry, and mission of the church. The relational-distinctive dialectics that we have been arguing for is not present in this model in terms of expressing how universality is related to particularity, unity to diversity, and so on and so forth. Further, Tanner does not deal with the question of how a christocentric approach only could account for relation with other religions.

After finding the above approaches inadequate, the Spirit ecclesiology of Amos Yong was explored, which is based on the Irenaean metaphor. Yong's ecclesiology is pneumatologically driven while being christologically particular. Yong shows mutuality between the Spirit and the Word, Spirit Christology, and Logos Christology as working in creation, the world, and the church. His ecclesiology shows relationality in Spirit and Christ as well as distinctiveness and particularity through the Spirit and Christ. This is expressed in the nature, ministry, and mission of the church. The nature of Spirit ecclesiology in Yong shows a dynamic, eschatological, and relational character with the possibility of holding in tension different approaches of ecclesiologies together. His understanding of the four marks of the church also demonstrates the dialectics between universality and particularity, spiritual and concrete, static and dynamic, and unity and diversity, one and many dynamics. In terms of the ministries of the church, the fact that the church is constituted by the Spirit and instituted by Christ ensures an egalitarian character where the members are equal on the basis of shared gifts of the Spirit, and the offices of the church and its hierarchy are understood as functional and derivative of the joint ministry of the Spirit and Christ. The mission of the church in Yong's ecclesiology extends to other religious communities on the basis of the presence and work of the Spirit and the Logos in them. In terms of relational expansiveness, Yong's permeable Spirit ecclesiology does not limit itself to human beings, but also is open to the rest of creation. Thus, a particular shape of a permeable Spirit ecclesiology with Amos Yong was built.

Arriving at a shape of a permeable Spirit ecclesiology was only tentative at this stage as developing any Indian ecclesiology without taking into consideration the ecclesiologies of Indian theologians would be unjustifiable. Thus, contributions from Indian theologians were sought to see whether further revisions of this model were to be required. It was found with Indian theologians like Chenchiah and Thomas, that formulating any Indian ecclesiology would require addressing the questions of colonial captivity and rigid institutionalisation of the church, and the need for a decolonisation approach. Furthermore, the Indian religio-cultural context and religio-philosophical sources should play a major role in the construction of Indian ecclesiology. There ought to be the acknowledgement of the reality of multiple religious belonging too. The Western theologians along with Yong understandably lacked these perspectives. Chenchiah and Thomas's contributions, while being significant in these terms failed to show the relational-distinctive dialectics required for our ecclesiology. Thus, the permeable Spirit ecclesiology of Samuel Rayan who combined the above particular approaches and an added theology of life and most importantly a liberationist perspective, was deemed adequate. Thus, with Rayan, a suitable shape of a permeable Spirit ecclesiology for India was developed.

Another important finding in the project refers to issues of ecumenism, multiple religious belonging, and interfaith relations. It was found that an Indian ecclesiology dealing with these issues needs an integrated approach. In other words, questions of ecumenical unity or multiple religious belonging and interfaith relations cannot bypass questions of marginalisation and liberation. The voice of the marginalised sections of the society and the church needs to be taken into account while engaging in these issues. These endeavours cannot be merely elitist, but grounded in the everyday reality and context of the people of India.

In conclusion, another important issue is to be highlighted: the question of the significance of this book in the wider ecclesiological discourse. Veli-Matti Kärkkäinen in his book *An Introduction to Ecclesiology* (2002) categorises various ecclesiological traditions and major contemporary ecclesiologists, and he also includes in his survey the category of contextual ecclesiology.[1] Kärkkäinen observes the emergence and growing significance of contextual ecclesiologies in the field of ecclesiological reflections.[2] He highlights ecclesiologies from the Asian, Latin American, African, and other Global South contexts. The present book will hope to contribute to that wider discourse about contextual ecclesiology bringing the particular voice of Indian ecclesiology. It is hoped that the Indian ecclesiological turn towards plurality or diversity and marginality proposed in this book will add to the existing discussions of the implications of being the church in a plural context and within situations of marginalisation and oppression.

Moreover, in ecclesiological discussions, an emerging trend is to explore the nature of a Third Article ecclesiology. The important aspect of understanding the church from the perspective (or lens) of the Spirit is gradually coming to the fore. Gregory Liston in his work *The Anointed Church: Toward a Third Article Ecclesiology* uses Christology and Trinity as

1 See Kärkkäinen, *Introduction to Ecclesiology.*

2 Kärkkäinen, *Introduction to Ecclesiology*, 163.

vantage points through which to examine ecclesiology pneumatologically.[3] Liston's argument is that the church essentially links with Christ and Trinity through the Spirit. In this discussion of the development of a Third Article ecclesiology, the present book highlights the importance of the Irenaean metaphor of the Spirit and the Word as two hands of the Father that could be considered. The present work also moves forward on this basis to propose the relational-distinctive dialectics required for a permeable ecclesiology and this can be taken as an added contribution.

Furthermore, this project opens the way to further reflections of the church's engagement from a pneumatological perspective with the Dalits, the *adivasis* and tribals, women's issues, and ecological crisis. Ecclesiological discourses in these arenas from a pneumatological perspective and a corresponding christological dimension in dialectical relation are still to be undertaken in a recognisable way in India. Towards that end, this book provides further motivation and direction.

Overall, it is believed that this work will encourage further reflections in the theological arena regarding how the Spirit and Christ continue to work dialectically together for building a church in India which is both Indian and Christian.

---

3 See Gregory J. Liston, *Anointed Church*; see also, Gregory J. Liston, "Where the Love of Christ is Found: Toward a Third Article Ecclesiology" in *Third Article Theology: A Pneumatological Dogmatics*, ed. Myk Habets (Minneapolis, MN: Fortress Press, 2016), 342.

# BIBLIOGRAPHY

Abraham, K.C. *Liberative Solidarity: Contemporary Perspectives on Mission.* Thiruvalla: Christava Sahitya Samithi, 1996.

Amaladoss, Michael. "Being a Hindu-Christian: A Play of Interpretations—The Experience of Swami Abhishiktananda." In *Many Yet One: Multiple Religious Belonging,* edited by Peniel Jesudason Rufus Rajkumar and Joseph Prabhakar Dayam, 89–98. Geneva: WCC, 2016.

———. *Beyond Inculturation: Can the Many Be One?* Delhi: ISPCK/Vidyajyoti, 2005.

Animananda, B. *The Blade: Life and Work of Brahmabandhab Upadhyaya.* Calcutta: Roy & Son, 1947.

Appasamy, A.J. "Pramanas." *Pilgrim* 82 (June 1949): 13–15.

Avis, Paul. *Reshaping Ecumenical Theology: The Church Made Whole?* London: T&T Clarke, 2010.

Ayrookuzhiel, A.M. Abraham. "The Dalits, Religions and Interfaith Dialogue." *Journal of Hindu-Christian Studies* 7, Art. 6 (1994): 13–19. Accessed September 14, 2016. http://dx.doi.org/10.7825/2164-6279.1094.

Baago, Kaj. *Pioneers of Indigenous Christianity.* Madras: Christian Literature Society, 1969.

Badcock, Gary D. *Light of Truth and Fire of Love: A Theology of the Holy Spirit.* Grand Rapids, MI: William B. Eerdmans, 1997.

Balasundaram, F.J.B. *Contemporary Asian Christian Theology.* Delhi: ISPCK, 1995.

Baldridge, Jason. "Reconciling Linguistic Diversity: The History and Future of Language Policy in India." University of Toledo Honours Thesis, 1996. Accessed August 23, 2016. http://www.ling.upenn.edu/~jason2/papers/natlang.htm.

Balia, Daryl M., and Kirsteen Kim, eds. *Witnessing to Christ Today, Edinburgh 2010*. Vol. 2. Oxford: Regnum Books International, 2010.

Bandopadhyay, J., and Vandana Shiva. *Chipko: India's Civilisational Crisis to the Forest Crisis*. New Delhi: INTACH, 1986.

Banerjee, Himadri, Nilanjana Gupta, and Sipra Mukherjee, eds. *Calcutta Mosaic: Essays and Interviews on the Minority Communities of Calcutta*. Anthem South Asian Studies. New Delhi: Anthem Press, 2009.

Barrett, David. *World Christianity Encyclopedia*. Nairobi: Oxford University Press, 1982.

Barton, Stephen C. "The Epistles and Christian Ethics." In *The Cambridge Companion to Christian Ethics*, edited by Robin Gill, 63–74. 2nd ed. Cambridge: Cambridge University Press, 2012.

Basham, A.L. *The Wonder That Was India*. Calcutta: Rupa, 1981.

Bauckham, Richard. "Jurgen Moltmann." In *The Modern Theologians: An Introduction to Christian Theology Since 1918*, edited by David F. Ford with Rachel Muers, 147–162. 3rd ed. Oxford: Blackwell Publishing, 2005.

Bauman, Chad M. "Identity, Conversion and Violence: Dalits, Adivasis and the 2007–08 Riots in Orissa." In *Margins of Faith: Dalit and Tribal Christianity*, edited by Rowena Robinson and Joseph Marianus Kujur, 263–286. New Delhi: SAGE, 2010.

Berkmann, John, and Michael Cartwright, eds. *The Hauerwas Reader*. Durham and London: Duke University Press, 2001.

Bhabha, Homi K. *The Location of Culture*. Routledge Classics. New York: Routledge, 2004.

Bhatia, Lakshmi. "Contradiction and Change in Mizo Church." In *Margins of Faith: Dalit and Tribal Christianity*, edited by Rowena Robinson and Joseph Marianus Kujur, 169–184. New Delhi: SAGE, 2010.

Bhattacharjee, Manash. "The Clarity of a Suicide Note." *The Hindu*, January 25, 2016. Accessed October 24, 2019. http://www.thehindu.com/opinion/op-ed/dalit-scholar-rohith-vemulas-suicide-letter-clarity-of-a-suicide-note/article8130703.ece.

Boopalan, Sunder John. "Hybridity's Ambiguity (Gift or Threat?): Marginality as Rudder. In *Many Yet One: Multiple Religious Belonging*, edited by Peniel Jesudason Rufus Rajkumar and Joseph Prabhakar Dayam, 135–148. Geneva: WCC, 2016.

Boyd, Robin H. *An Introduction to Indian Christian Theology*. Delhi: ISPCK, 2000.

———. *Beyond Captivity: Explorations in Indian Christian History and Theology*. Bangalore: CFCC, 2014.

Brown, Raymond E. *The Gospel According to John (xiii-xxi): Introduction, Translation and Notes*. The Anchor Bible. New York: Doubleday, 1970.

Caleb, Sunil M. "M.M. Thomas' Engagements with Social Theories and Ideologies." In *Reclaiming Manyness: Re-reading M.M. Thomas in the Light of Indian Christian Theologies*, edited by P.G. George and Y.T. Vinayaraj, 22–29. Serampore: SATHRI, 2015.

Carbine, Rosemary P., and Hilda P. Koster. "Introduction: The Gift of Kathryn Tanner's Imagination." In *The Gift of Theology: The Contribution of Kathryn Tanner*, edited by Rosemary P. Carbine and Hilda P. Koster, xxv–xxxix. Minneapolis, MN: Fortress Press, 2015.

Certeau, Michel de. *The Practice of Everyday Life*. Translated by Stephen Rendall. Berkeley: University of California Press, 1988.

Chatterjee, Satischandra, and Dhirendramohan Dutta. *An Introduction to Indian Philosophy*. Calcutta: Calcutta University Press, 1948.

Chenchiah, P. "Who is Jesus? A Study of Jesus in Terms of the Creative Process." *Guardian* (August 5, 1943): 364–365.

———. "Christianity and Hinduism." *NCCR* 48 (March 1928): 119–138.

———. "Indian Christian Theological Task: Review and Restatement." *Guardian* 2 (February 1947): 77–79.

———. "Christians and Yoga: A Study of the Technique of Realisation in Relation to the Aims and Objects of Christianity." *Guardian* 23 (March 1944): 136–137.

———. "Indian Christians and Co-operation with Non-Christians." *Guardian* 24 (April 1958): 165–167.

———. "Indian Christians and Co-operation with Non-Christians." *Guardian* 24 (May 1, 1958): 175–177.

———. "Indian Christians: Problems and Privileges: Community or Movement?" *The Guardian* (1942): 28–30.

———. "My Search for the Kingdom." *Guardian* (February 8, 1951): 65–66.

———. "Professor Kraemer and Syncretism." *Guardian* (April 19, 1951): 188–189.

———. "Professor Kraemer and Syncretism." *Guardian* (April 26, 1951): 200–201.

———. "The Holy Spirit: Meaning and Significance of Christianity: Bible Studies." *Guardian* 30 (June 30, 1932): 252.

———. "The Holy Spirit: Meaning and Significance of Christianity: Bible Studies." *Guardian* 30 (July 21, 1932): 287.

———. "Indian Christian Politics: The Communal Way, and the Way of the Ideal." *Guardian* 4 (October 1945): 315–317.

———. "Christian Message in a Hindu Environment." *Guardian* 9 (February 1950): 100–101.

Chenchiah, P., V. Chakkarai, and A.N. Sudarisanam, eds. *Asramas Past and Present*. Madras: CLS, 1996.

Cherian, M.T. *Hindutva Agenda and Minority Rights: A Christian Response*. Bangalore: CFCC, 2007.

Church of North India (CNI) official website. Accessed October, 2019. http://www.cnisynod.org/beginning.aspx.

"Church of South India Recognized for Protecting the Planet." *Ecumenical Water Network*. Accessed August 25, 2016. http://water.oikoumene.org/en/whatwedo/news-events/church-of-south-india-recognized-for-protecting-the-planet.

Chhuanawma, Vanlal. "A Search for Tribal Identity in North-East India: A Challenge to Formation of Tribal Theology." In *Search for a New Society: Tribal Theology for North East India*, edited by Yangkahao Vashum, Peter Haokip, and Melvil Pereira, 62–82. Guwahati: North Eastern Social Research Centre, 2012.

———. "Ecumenical Realities in Indian Context Today." In *Ecumenism in India Today: A Search for a Relevant Ecclesiology and Churches and Theological Education in India*, edited by James Massey. Bangalore: BTESSC & SATHRI, 2008.

Clarke, Sathianathan. "Dalit Theology: An Introductory and Interpretive Theological Exposition." In *Dalit Theology in the Twenty-first Century: Discordant Voices, Discerning Pathways*, edited by Sathianathan Clarke, Deenabandhu Manchala, and Philip Vinod Peacock, 19–37. New Delhi: Oxford University Press, 2010.

Clarke, Sathianathan, D. Manchala, and P.V. Peacock. "Introduction." In *Dalit Theology in the Twenty First Century: Discordant Voices, Discerning Pathways*, edited by Sathianathan Clarke, Deenabandhu Manchala, and Philip Vinod Peacock, 1–16. New Delhi: Oxford University Press, 2010.

CNI Synod. *Faith and Order in the North India/Pakistan Unity Plan*. Delhi: ISPCK, 1987.

Cobb, John B., Jr. "Multiple Religious Belonging and Reconciliation." In *Many Mansions: Multiple Religious Belonging and Christian Identity*, edited by Catherine Cornille, 20–28. Faith Meets Faith Series. Maryknoll, NY: Orbis Books, 1970.

Conger, George. "First Women Bishop of India Consecrated." *Church of England Newspaper*. October 13, 2013. Accessed October 26, 2019. http://www.churchnewspaper.com/35399/archives.

Congar, Yves. *I Believe in the Holy Spirit*. Translated by David Smith. New York: Geoffrey Chapman, 1983.

Cornille, Catherine. "Multiple Religious Belonging and Interreligious Dialogue." *Current Dialogue* 57 (December 2015): 4–5.

———, ed. *Many Mansions? Multiple Religious Belonging and Christian Identity*. Faith Meets Faith Series. Maryknoll, NY: Orbis Books, 1970.

D'Souza, Alphonsus B. "Tribal Theology in the North East: Some Suggestions from Sociology." In *Search for a New Society: Tribal Theology for North East India*, edited by Yangkahao Vashum, Peter Haokip, and Melvil Pereira. Guwahati: North Eastern Social Research Centre, 2012.

"Dalit Women in India." *International Dalit Solidarity Network*. Accessed July 22, 2016. http://idsn.org/key-issues/dalit-women/dalit-women-in-india/.

Das, Somen. *The Church and the World: Towards a Biblical-Ethical Understanding*. Delhi: ISPCK, 2006.

Dharmaraj, Jacob S. *Colonialism and Christian Mission: Postcolonial Reflections*. Delhi: ISPCK, 1999.

Dikshit, K.R. and Jutta K. Dikshit. *North East India: Land, People and Economy*. Advances in Asian-Human Environmental Research. Netherlands: Springer, 2014.

Dodson, Jakob D. "Divine Hospitality and Human Diversity." In *The Theology of Amos Yong and the New Face of Pentecostal Scholarship: Passion for the Spirit*, edited by Wolfgang Vondey and Martin William Mittelstadt. Leiden: Brill, 2013.

Dulles, Avery. *Models of the Church*. Expanded Edition. New York: Doubleday, 2002.

Dupuis, Jacques. "Christianity and Religions: Complementarity and Convergence." In *Many Mansions: Multiple Religious Belonging and Christian Identity*, edited by Catherine Cornille, 61–75. Faith Meets Faith Series. Maryknoll, NY: Orbis Books, 1970.

East, Brad. "An Undefensive Presence: The Mission and Identity of the Church in Kathryn Tanner and John Howard Yoder." *Scottish Journal of Theology* 68, no. 3 (2015): 327–344.

Engineer, Asghar Ali, ed. *Communal Riots in Post-Independent India*. 2nd ed. Hyderabad: Sangam Books, 1997.

Elst, Dr. Koenraad. "The Sarna: A Case-Study in Natural Religion." Accessed October 25, 2019. http://koenraadelst.bharatvani.org/articles/chr/sarna.html.

Evan T. Pollard. "That All May Be One (John 17:21) and the Unity of the Church." *Expository Times* 70, no. 5 (February 1959): 149–50.

Faria, Stella. "Keynote Address on Feminist Biblical Hermeneutics." In *Feminist Hermeneutics*, edited by Lalrinawmi Ralte and Evangeline Anderson-Rajkumar, 15–31. Delhi: IWIT/ISPCK, 2002.

Farquhar, J.N. *The Crown of Hinduism*. London: Oxford University Press, 1913.

Firth, C.B. *An Introduction to Indian Church History*. Indian Theological Library, revised edition. Delhi: ISPCK, 1998.

Fitzmyer, Joseph A. "The Structured Ministries of the Church in the Pastoral Epistles." *The Catholic Biblical Quarterly* I, 66 (2004): 582–596.

Frykenberg, Robert Eric. *Christianity in India: From the Beginnings to the Present*. Oxford: Oxford University Press, 2008.

Fortson IV, Benjamin, W. *Indo-European Language and Culture: An Introduction*. 2nd ed. Oxford: Blackwell Publishing, 2010.

Fuchs, Lorelei F. *Koinonia and the Quest for an Ecumenical Ecclesiology: From Foundations through Dialogue to Symbolic Competence for Communality*. Grand Rapids, MI: William B. Eerdmans, 2008.

Gadgil, M. and Ranajit Guha. *This Fissured Land: An Ecological History of India*. Berkeley: University of California Press, 2013.

Gandhi, Mohandas K. *The Story of My Experiments with Truth: An Autobiography*. Ahmedabad: Navajivan Publishing House, 1984.

Gelpi, Donald L. *The Divine Mother:A Trinitarian Theology of the Holy Spirit*. Lanham, MD: University Press of America, 1984.

Goheen, M.W. "From a Christendom to a Missionary Ecclesiology (1909–1959)." Accessed October 28, 2019. https://dspace.library.uu.nl/bitstream/handle/1874/597/c2.pdf;jsessionid=5104AA509F149547018FCA78012810B7?sequence=49.

Gnanadasan, Aruna. "Dalit Women: The Dalit of the Dalit." In *A Reader in Dalit Theology*, edited by Arvind P. Nirmal and V. Devasahayam, 129–138. Madras: Gurukul Lutheran Theological College and Research Institute, 1980.

Guha, Ramachandra. *The Unquiet Woods: Ecological Change and Peasant Resistance in the Himalaya*. Expanded Edition. Berkeley: University of California Press, 2000.

Gunton, Colin. *The One, the Three and the Many: God, Creation and the Culture of Modernity*. Cambridge: Cambridge University Press, 1993.

Habets, Myk, ed. *Third Article Theology: A Pneumatological Dogmatics*. Minneapolis: Fortress Press, 2016.

Hack, Karl. *International Encyclopedia of the Social Sciences*. Detroit: Macmillan USA, 2008.

Haight, Roger. "The Structures of the Church." *Journal of Ecumenical Studies* 30, 3–4 (Summer-Fall 1993): 403–414.

Harrison, Verna. "Perichoresis in the Greek Fathers." *St. Vladimir's Theological Quarterly* 35, 1 (1991): 53–65.

Hart, Trevor. *Regarding Karl Barth*. Carlisle: Paternoster Press, 1999.

Hartley, Melissa Marie. "The 1979 Book of Common Prayer and the Practice of the Open Table in the Episcopal Church." PhD diss., Drew University, New Jersey, 2012.

Hauerwas, Stanley. *After Christendom? How the Church is to Behave If Freedom, Justice, and a Christian Nation Are Bad Ideas*. Nashville, TN: Abingdon Press, 1991.

———. *Christian Existence Today*. Grand Rapids, MI: Brazos Press, 2001.

———. *A Community of Character: Toward a Constructive Christian Social Ethic*. Notre Dame, IN: University of Notre Dame Press, 1981.

———. *Peaceable Kingdom*. Notre Dame, IN: University of Notre Dame Press, 1983.

———. "Peacemaking: The Virtue of the Church." In *The Hauerwas Reader*, edited by John Berkmann and Michael Cartwright. Durham and London: Duke University Press, 2001.

———. *Resident Aliens: Life in the Christian Colony*. Nashville, TN: Abingdon Press, 1998.

———. *Sanctify Them in Truth: Holiness Exemplified*. Nashville, TN: Abingdon Press, 1998.

———. *Truthfulness and Tragedy: Further Investigations in Christian Ethics*. Notre Dame, IN: University of Notre Dame Press, 1977.

Hauerwas, Stanley, and William H. Willimon. *The Holy Spirit*. Nashville, TN: Abingdon Press, 2015.

Healy, Nicholas M. *Hauerwas: A (Very) Critical Introduction, Interventions*. Grand Rapids, MI: William B. Eerdmans, 2014.

Hedlund, Roger E. *Christianity/Indian: The Emergence of an Indigenous Community*. Delhi: ISPCK, 2004.

Hedlund, Roger. *Quest for Identity: India's Churches of Indigenous Origin: The Little Tradition in Indian Christianity*. Chennai/Delhi: MIIS/ISPCK, 2000.

Hoefer, Herbert, ed. *Debate on Mission*. Madras: Gurukul, 1979.

Hollenweger, Walter. *Pentecostalism: Origins and Developments Worldwide*. Peabody, MA: Hendrickson, 1997.

Holmes, Stephen. *The Holy Trinity: Understanding God's Life*. Milton Keynes, England: Paternoster Press, 2012.

Hoskins, Janet, ed. *Headhunting and Social Imagination in Southeast Asia*. Stanford, CA: Stanford University Press, 1996.

James, Lovely Awomi. "North East Indian Tribal Christianity and Traditional Practices: Implications for Theology of Religions Today." *Current Dialogue* 57 (December 2015): 52–62.

Jambhale, Roshan. "Ecumenism in India Today: Church Perspective." In *Ecumenism in India Today: A Search for a Relevant Ecclesiology and Churches and Theological Education in India*, edited by James Massey, 107–111. Bangalore: BTESSC & SATHRI, 2008.

Jathana, O.V. "Ecclesiology in Context: Reflections from an Indian Perspective in the Light of Current Ecumenical Deliberations." In *Ekklesia: Indian Conversations—A Study of the Church*, edited by Dr. Samuel George, H. Joseph Lalfakmawia, and Ajungla Jamir. Vishakapatnam/New Delhi: CWI & MCT, 2015.

John, T.K., ed. *Bread and Breath: Essays in Honour of Samuel Rayan SJ*. Jesuit Theological Forum Reflections 5. Anand, Gujarat: Gujarat Sahitya Prakash, 1991.

Job, G.V., D.M. Devasahayam, and A.N. Sudarisanam, eds. *Rethinking Christianity in India*. Madras: Sudarisanam, 1938.

Joshi, R.D. "The Church in India and its Institutions." In *Indian Church: Identity and Fulfilment*, edited by Mathai Zachariah, 64–73. Chennai/Delhi/Lucknow: CLS/ISPCK.LPH, 1971.

Joshi, Sandip. "Court Appointed Panel Highlights Misuse of AFPSA in Manipur." Accessed July 22, 2016. http://www.thehindu.com/news/national/other-states/courtappointed-panel-highlights-mis-use-of-afspa-in-manipur/article4921637.ece.

Kabir. *Bijak of Kabir*. Translated by Linda Hess and Shukhdeo Singh. Oxford: Oxford University Press, 2002.

Kadaliyil, Abraham. *Toward a Relational Spirit Ecclesiology in Asia: A Study on the Documents of the Federation of Asian Bishops' Conferences*. Germany: VDM Verlag, 2009.

Kalapura, Jose. "Margins of Faith: Dalits and Tribal Christians in Eastern India." In *Margins of Faith: Dalit and Tribal Christianity*, edited by Rowena Robinson and Joseph Marianus Kujur, 75–96. New Delhi: SAGE, 2010.

Kalita, Barnali. "Chipko Movement: A Landmark Effort in Addressing Environmental Crisis in India." *International Journal of Interdisciplinary Research and Innovations* 3, Issue 3 (July–September 2015):17–21.

Kalpavriksh. "Globalisation in India: Impacts and Alternatives." Accessed July 27, 2016. http://www.kalpavriksh.org/images/CLN/Globalisation%20Brochure.pdf.

Karkkainen, Veli-Matti. *Introduction to Ecclesiology: Ecumenical, Historical & Global Perspectives*. Madison, WI: IVP Press.

———. *Pneumatology: The Holy Spirit in Ecumenical, International, and Contextual Perspective*. Grand Rapids, MI: Baker Academic, 2002.

———. "Theologies of Religions." In *Witnessing to Christ in a Pluralistic Age: Christian Mission among Other Faiths*, edited by Lalsangkima Pachuau and Knud Jørgensen, 110–120. Regnum Edinburgh 2010 Series. Edinburgh: Regnum Books, 2011.

Kerketta, Sumit Abhay. *Adivasi Theology, Towards a Relevant Christian Theology for the Jharkhandi Adivasis*. Ranchi: ATCR/GTC, 2009.

Keshishian, Aram. *Conciliar Fellowship: A Common Goal*. Geneva: WCC Publications, 1992.

Kilby, Karen. "Perichoresis and Projection: Problems with Social Doctrines of the Trinity." First published in *New Blackfriars* 81, Issue 957 (November 2000): 432–445. Accessed November, 2015. *Wiley Online Library*. doi: 10.1111/j.1741-2005.2000.tb06456.x

Kim, Kirsteen. *Joining in with the Spirit: Connecting World Church and Local Mission*. London: Epworth Press, 2009.

———. *Mission in the Spirit: The Holy Spirit in Indian Christian Theologies*. Delhi: ISPCK, 2003.

Kothari, Ashish, and Aseem Shrivastava. *Churning the Earth: The Making of Global India*. Delhi: Penguin, 2012.

Kothari, Ashish. "Radical Ecological Democracy: A Path Forward for India and Beyond." A Great Transition Initiative (GTI) Essay: Towards a Transformative Vision and Praxis, July 2014: 7–8. Accessed July 27, 2016. http://www.greattransition.org/publication/radical-ecological-democracy-a-path-forward-for-india-and-beyond.

Kumar M., Ashok, and Rowena Robinson. "Legally Hindu: Dalit Lutheran Christians of Coastal Andhra Pradesh." In *Margins of Faith: Dalit and Tribal Christianity*, edited by Rowena Robinson and Joseph Marianus Kujur, 149–168. New Delhi: SAGE, 2010.

Kumar, Nigel Ajay. *What is Religion? A Theological Answer*. Eugene, OR: Pickwick Publications, 2013.

Kumar, Krishna. "Religious Fundamentalism in India and Beyond." *Parameters* (Autumn 2012): 17–33. Accessed July 21, 2016. strategicstudiesinstitute.army.mil/pubs/parameters/articles/.../kumar.pdf.

Kunnumpuram, Kurien. "The Beauty of the Church: An Investigation of Samuel Rayan's Ecclesiology." In *The Vision of a New Church and a New Society: A Scholarly Assessment of Dr. Samuel Rayan's Contribution to Indian Christian Theology*, edited by Kurien Kunnumpuram, 123–148. New Delhi: Christian World Imprints, 2016.

———, ed. *Jesus: The Relevance of His Person and Message for Our Times*. Vol.1 of *Selected Writings of Samuel Rayan SJ*. Bombay: St. Paul's, 2011.

———. *Nature, Women and the Church: Indian Christian Reflections on Ecology, Feminism and Ecclesiology*. Vol I, Collected Writings of Samuel Rayan SJ. Delhi: ISPCK, 2013.

Lawler, Michael G. "Perichoresis: New Theological Wine in Old Theological Wineskin." *Horizons: The Journal of the College Theological Society*, 2, Issue 1 (Spring 1995): 49–66.

Lehman, Paul. *Ethics in a Christian Context*. London: SCM Press, 1963.

Linguistic Survey of India. "2011 Our Census, Our Future." Accessed August 23, 2016. http://www.censusindia.gov.in/2011-documents/lsi/ling_survey_india.html.

Liston, Gregory J. *The Anointed Church: Toward a Third Article Ecclesiology*. Minneapolis, MN: Fortress Press, 2015.

Loder, James E. *The Logic of Spirit: Human Development in Theological Perspective*. San Francisco: Jossey-Bass Publishers, 1989.

Longchar, Wati A. *Returning to Mother Earth: Theology, Christian Witness and Theological Education: An Indigenous Perspective*. PTCA Series no. 4. Taiwan: PTCA/SCEPTRE, 2012.

———. "Tribal Identity and Theology." In *Rethinking Theology in India: Christianity in the Twenty First Century*, edited by James Massey and T.K. John. Delhi: Manohar Publishers, 2013.

Longkumer, Limatula. "Wider Ecumenism and Ecclesiology." In *Ecumenism in India Today: A Search for a Relevant Ecclesiology and Churches and Theological Education in India*, edited by James Massey. Bangalore: BTESSC/ SATHARI, 2008.

Kandilkar, M., and G. Ramachandran. "The Causes and Consequences of Particulate Air Pollution in Urban India: A Synthesis of the Science." *Annual Review of Energy and the Environment* 25 (2000): 629–684.

Maahs, Charles. "Hospitality, Power, and Mission: A Review of the Writings and Leadership of Roger W. Fjeld." *Currents in Theology and Mission* 30, no. 3 (2003): 168–72.

Madan, T.N. *Modern Myths, Locked Minds, Secularism and Fundamentalism in India*. 2nd ed. Delhi: Oxford University Press, 2010.

Majumdar, D.N. "A Study of Tribe-Caste Continuum and the Process of Sanskritization among the Bodo-Speaking Tribes of the Garo Hills." In *Tribal Situation in India*, edited by K.S. Singh. Shimla: Indian Institute of Advanced Studies, 1972.

Manorama, Ruth. "Background Information on Dalit Women in India." Accessed July 22, 2016. www.rightlivelihood.org/fileadmin/Files/PDF/Literature_Recipients/Manorama/Background_Manorama.pdf.

Marshall, J.W. "The Church of North India/Pakistan: A Theological Assessment of the Plan of Union." PhD diss., Dublin University, 1975.

Martin, Paul Chandran. "Globalisation and its Impact on Dalits: A Theological Response." In *Globalisation and its Impact on Dalits: A Theological Response*, edited by James Massey. New Delhi: Centre for Dalit/Subaltern Studies, 2004.

Massey, James. *Roots: Concise History of the Dalits*. Bangalore: CISRS, 1991.

Matthew, John V. *Advaita Vedanta Explored Towards Ecological and Dalit Theology*. New Delhi: Christian World Imprints, 2015.

Merriam-Webster Online, s.v., "permeable." Accessed October 19, 2019. https://www.merriam-webster.com/dictionary/permeable.

Michael, S.M. "Dalit Encounter with Christianity: Change and Continuity." In *Margins of Faith: Dalit and Tribal Christianity*, edited by Rowena Robinson and Joseph Marianus Kujur, 51–74. New Delhi: SAGE, 2010.

Ministry of Environment and Forests, Government of India. "Report to the People on Environment and Forests." Accessed July 26, 2016. http://moef.nic.in/downloads/public-information/Report%20 to%20the%20 People.pdf.

Minz, Nirmal. "Dalit-Tribal: A Search for Common Ideology." In *Indigenous People: Dalit Issues in Today's Theological Debate*, edited by James Massey, 134–142. Delhi: ISPCK, 1994.

———. "Missiology for Twenty First Century Tribal India." In *Missiology for the 21st Century: South Asian Perspectives*, edited by Roger E. Hedlund and Paul Joshua Bhakiaraj, 395–413. Delhi/Chennai: ISPCK/Mylapore Institute for Indigenous Studies, 2004.

———. "Theology and the Struggle of the Adivasi/Indigenous People of India." In *Rethinking Theology in India*, edited by James Massey and T.K. John, 121–150. Delhi: Manohar Publishers, 2013.

Manohar, Moses P. "Emerging Ecclesia: Societal View." In *Ecumenism in India Today: A Search for a Relevant Ecclesiology and Churches and Theological Education in India*, edited by James Massey, 93–100. Bangalore: BTESSC& SATHRI, 2008.

Moltmann, Jürgen. *The Coming of God: Christian Eschatology*. Translated by Margaret Kohl. Minneapolis, MN: Fortress, 1996.

———. *The Church in the Power of the Spirit: A Contribution to Messianic Ecclesiology*. Translated by Margaret Kohl. London: SCM, 1977.

———. *The Crucified God: The Cross of Christ as the Foundation and Criticism of Christian Theology*. Translated by R.A. Wilson and John Bowden. London: SCM, 1974.

———. *Experiences in Theology: Ways and Forms of Christian Theology*. Translated by Margaret Kohl. Minneapolis, MN: Fortress Press, 2000.

———. *The Spirit of Life: A Universal Affirmation*. Translated by Margaret Kohl. London: SCM Press, 1992.

———. "The Trinitarian Personhood of the Holy Spirit." Translated by D.L. Dabney. In *Advents of the Spirit: An Introduction to the Current Study of Pneumatology*, edited by Bradford E. Hinze and D. Lyle Dabney, 302–314. Marquette Studies in Theology 30. Milwaukee: Marquette University Press, 2001.

———. *The Trinity and the Kingdom: The Doctrine of God*. Translated by Margaret Kohl. London: SCM, 1981.

Moore, Stephen. *Empire and the Apocalypse: Postcolonialism and the New Testament: Bible in the Modern World*. Sheffield: Sheffield Phoenix Press, 2006.

Myers, Ruth A. "Who May Be Invited to the Table?" *Anglican Theological Review* 94: 2, 233–244. http://www.anglicantheologicalreview.org/static/pdf/articles/meyers_.pdf.

Nadella, Raj. "Motif of Hybridity in the Story of the Canaanite Woman: Its Relevance for Multifaith Relation." In *Many Yet One: Multiple Religious Belonging*, edited by Peniel Jesudason Rufus Rajkumar and Joseph Prabhakar Dayam, 111–120. Geneva: WCC, 2016.

Nalunnakkal, George Mathew. *Green Liberation: Towards an Integral Eco-Theology*. Delhi: ISPCK/NCCI, 1999.

"National Portal of India: Profile." Accessed July 18, 2016. https://india.gov.in/india-glance/profile.

"National Vector Borne Disease Control Programme 2007." Accessed July 26, 2016. http://www.nvbdcp.gov.in/.

Navone, John. "Divine and Human Hospitality." *New Blackfriars* 85 (2004): 329–40. *Wiley Online Library*. doi: 10.1111/j.1741-2005.2004.00034.x.

Nehru, Jawaharlal. *The Unity of India: Collected Writings 1937–1940*. New York: The John Day Company, 1942. Accessed November 19, 2019. https://ia802707.us.archive.org/13/items/unityofindiacoll006382mbp/unityofindiacoll006382mbp.pdf.

Nelavala, Surekha. "Liberation Beyond Borders: Dalit Feminist Hermeneutics." PhD diss., Drew University, New Jersey, 2008.

Neli, Linus. "Vision of a Northeast Community: Based on Peace with Justice." In *Search for a New Society: Tribal Theology for North East India*, edited by Yangkahao Vashum, Peter Haokip, and Melvil Pereira, 193–213. Guwahati: North Eastern Social Research Centre, 2012.

Neville, Robert Cummings. *A Theology Primer.* Albany, NY: State University New York Press, 1991.

Newbigin, Lesslie J.E. *The Household of God.* London: SCM, 1953.

Nirmal, A.P. "Doing Theology from a Dalit Perspective." In *A Reader in Dalit Theology*, edited by Arvind P. Nirmal, 53–70. Madras: Gurukul, 1990.

Nissiotis, Nikos A. "The Importance of the Doctrine of the Trinity for Church Life and Theology." In *The Orthodox Ethos, Essays in Honour of the Centenary of the Greek Orthodox Archdiocese of North and South America*, edited by A.J. Phillippou, 32–69. Oxford: Holy Well Press, 1964.

O'Leary, Joseph S. "Toward a Buddhist Interpretation of Christian Truth." In *Many Mansions: Multiple Religious Belonging and Christian Identity*, edited by Catherine Cornille. Faith Meets Faith Series. Maryknoll, NY: Orbis Books, 1970.

Otto, Randall. "Moltmann and the Anti-Monotheist Movement." *International Journal of Systematic Theology* 3/3 (2003): 293–308. *Wiley Online Library.* doi: 10.1111/1463-1652.00066

Palanna, Allan Samuel. "(In)Betweenness and Being Analogical: Making Sense of Hospitable Faith." In *Many Yet One: Multiple Religious Belonging*, edited by Peniel Jesudason Rufus Rajkumar and Joseph Prabhakar Dayam, 149–162. Geneva: WCC, 2016.

Pandey, Geeta. "100 Women 2014: Violence at Home is India's Failing." *BBC News India.* Accessed July 22, 2016. http://www.bbc.co.uk/news/world-asia-india-29708612.

Pandey, Ravi Bhushan. *Christianity and Tribes in India.* New Delhi: Academic Excellence, 2005.

Panikkar, Raimundo. *The Unknown Christ of Hinduism.* London: Darton, Longman & Todd, 1964.

Panikkar, Raimon. "On Christian Identity: Who is a Christian?" In *Many Mansions: Multiple Religious Belonging and Christian Identity*, edited by Catherine Cornille, 121–144. Faith Meets Faith Series. Maryknoll, NY: Orbis Books, 1970.

———. "The Dream of an Indian Ecclesiology." In *Searching for an Indian Ecclesiology*, edited by Gerwin van Leeuwen, 24–54. Bangalore: ATC, 1984.

Park, Mann. "Jurgen Moltmann's Theology of the Trinity and its Significance for Contemporary Social Questions: A Dialogical Approach." PhD diss., University of St. Michael's College, Toronto, 2000. Accessed July 20, 2019. https://tspace.library.utoronto.ca/bitstream/1807/10516/1/NQ54052.pdf

Puthanangady, Paul. "Christian Community as a Multi-cultural Reality." In *The Church in India in Search of a New Identity*, edited by Kurien Kunnumpuram, Errol D'Lima, and Jacob Parappally, 184–191. Bangalore: NBCLC, 1997).

Phan, Peter C. "Multiple Religious Belonging: Opportunities and Challenges for Theology and Church." *Theological Studies* 64 (2003): 495–519.

Philip, T.V. *Ecumenism in Asia*. New Delhi: ISPCK and CSS, 1994.

———. "Ecclesiological Discussions in India during the Last Twenty-Five Years." *Indian Journal of Theology* 25 (July–December, 1976): 3–4; 172–187. Accessed October 19, 2019. http://biblicalstudies.org.uk/pdf/ijt/25-3-4_172.pdf.

Philip, T.M. "Preface." In *M.M. Thomas Reader: Selected Texts on Theology, Religion and Society*, edited by T. Jacob Thomas, 11–13. Thiruvalla: CSS, 2002.

Pieris, Aloysius. *An Asian Theology of Liberation*. Faith Meets Faith Series. Maryknoll, NY: Orbis Books, 1988.

Pinnock, Clark H. *Flame of Love: A Theology of the Holy Spirit*. Downer's Grove, IL: IVP, 1996.

Pinto, J. Prasad. "Mission in the North Indian Context." In *Emerging Indian Missiology: Contexts and Concepts*, edited by Joseph Mattam and Joseph Valiamangalam, 121–146. Delhi: FOIM/ISPCK, 2006.

Ponniah, James. "Shrines, Ritual Hospitality, and Hybrid Identities in South Asia." In *Many Yet One: Multiple Religious Belonging*, edited by Peniel Jesudason Rufus Rajkumar and Joseph Prabhakar Dayam, 99–110. Geneva: WCC, 2016.

PTI. "Dadri: Outrage after Mob Lynches Man for Allegedly Consuming Beef." *The Indian Express*. Updated December 25, 2015. Accessed August 25, 2016. http://indianexpress.com/article/india/india-others/outrage-after-man-lynched-over-rumour-of-storing-beef-in-house/.

Presidential Order. "The Constitution (Scheduled Castes) Order, 1950, 1." Accessed August 24, 2016. http://www.lawmin.nic.in/ld/subord/rule3a.htm.

"Press Note on Poverty Estimates, 2011–12." *Government of India Planning Commission, July 2013*. Accessed July 18, 2016. http://planningcommission.nic.in/news/pre_pov2307.pdf.

Purkait, N.N. and D.K. Chakrabarty. "Pattern of Methane Emission from a Garbage Dump." *Current Science* 101 (2011): 528–531.

Radhakrishnan, Sarvepalli, and Charles A. Moore, eds. *A Source Book in Indian Philosophy*. Princeton, NJ: Princeton University Press, 1967.

Rahner, Karl. *The Trinity*. Translated by Joseph Donceel. New York: Seabury, 1974.

Raj, Selva J. "Dialogue 'On the Ground': The Complicated Identities and the Complex Negotiations of Catholics and Hindus in South India." *Journal of Hindu-Christian Studies* 17 (2004): 33–44.

Rajkumar, Peniel J.R. *Dalit Theology and Dalit Liberation: Problems, Paradigms and Possibilities*. Ashgate New Critical Thinking in Religion. Theology and Biblical Studies Series. London: Routledge, 2010.

———. "Cast(e)ing Conversion, Re-visiting Dialogue: Indian Attempts at an Interfaith Theology of Wholeness." *Journal of Academic Study of Religion* 26 no. 2 (2013): 157–171.

————. "The Diversity and Dialectics of Dalit Dissent and Implications." In *Dalit Theology in the Twenty-first Century: Discordant Voices, Discerning Pathways*, edited by Sathianathan Clarke, Deenabandhu Manchala, and Philip Vinod Peacock, 55–73. New Delhi: Oxford University Press, 2010.

Rajkumar, Peniel J. R., and Joseph Prabhakar Dayam. "Introduction." In *Many Yet One: Multiple Religious Belonging*, edited by Peniel Jesudason Rufus Rajkumar and Joseph Prabhakar Dayam, 1–4. Geneva: WCC, 2016.

Ralte, Rodinmawia. *Hindus and Hindutva, Hindu Tolerance, Hindutva Exclusivism, Emergence of Assertive Hinduism*. Taiwan: PTCA, 2014.

Ramachandra, T.V., and Shwetmala. "Emissions from India's Transport Sector: Statewise Synthesis." *Atmospheric Environment* 43 (2009): 5510–5517.

Ramakrishnan, Venkitesh. "The Reconversion Programs of the Dharam Jagaran Samity and Vishwa Hindu Parishad are Part of a Massive Expansion Plan of the Sangh Parivar." *Frontline* (January 9, 2015). Accessed October 27, 2019. http://www.frontline.in/the-nation/project-hindutva/article6715464.ece.

Rao, Aparna, ed. *The Valley of Kashmir: The Making and Unmaking of a Composite Culture*. Delhi: Manohar Publications, 2008.

Ravindranath, N.H., and R. Sukumar. "Climate Change and Tropical Forests in India." *Climatic Change* 39 (1998): 563–581.

Rayan, Samuel. "Baptism and Conversion: The Lima Text in the Indian Context." In *God's Hope Becoming Visible: Indian Christian Reflections on Some Relevant Issues of Our Times*. Vol III. Collected Writings of Samuel Rayan SJ, edited by Kurien Kunnumpuram. Delhi: ISPCK, 2013.

———. "The Challenge of the Dalit Issue: Some Theological Perspectives." In *God's Hope Becoming Visible: Indian Christian Reflections on Some Relevant Issues of Our Times*. Vol III. Collected Writings of Samuel Rayan SJ, edited by Kurien Kunnumpuram. Delhi: ISPCK, 2013.

———. "The Church-The Jesus Movement." In *Nature, Woman and the Church: Indian Christian Reflections on Ecology, Feminism and Ecclesiology*. Vol. 1 of *Collected Writings of Samuel Rayan SJ*, edited by Kurien Kunnumpuram. Delhi: ISPCK, 2013.

———. *Come Holy Spirit*. Delhi: Media House, 1998.

———. "Commonalities, Divergences and Cross-Fertilisation among Third World Theologies." In *Doing Theology: Indian Christian Reflections on Theologizing in India Today*. Vol. 2 of *Collected Writings of Samuel Rayan SJ*, edited by Kurien Kunnumpuram. Delhi: ISPCK, 2013.

———. "Decolonization of Theology." In *Doing Theology: Indian Christian Reflections on Theologizing in India Today*. Vol. 2 of *Collected Writings of Samuel Rayan SJ*, edited by Kurien Kunnumpuram. Delhi: ISPCK, 2013.

———. "Dialogue with Hinduism." In *God's Hope Becoming Visible: Indian Christian Reflections on Some Relevant Issues of Our Times*. Vol.3 of *Collected Writings of Samuel Rayan SJ*, edited by Kurien Kunnumpuram. Delhi: ISPCK, 2013.

———. "Doing Theology in India." In *Doing Theology: Indian Christian Reflections on Theologizing in India Today*. Vol II. Collected Writings of Samuel Rayan SJ, edited by Kurien Kunnumpuram. Delhi: ISPCK, 2013.

———. "The Earth is the Lord's." In *Nature, Woman and the Church: Indian Christian Reflections on Ecology, Feminism and Ecclesiology*. Vol. 1 of *Collected Writings of Samuel Rayan SJ*, edited by Kurien Kunnumpuram, SJ. Delhi: ISPCK, 2013.

———. "Ecclesiology at Work in the Indian Church Today." In *Nature, Woman and the Church: Indian Christian Reflections on Ecology, Feminism and Ecclesiology*. Vol. 1 of *Collected Writings of Samuel Rayan SJ*, edited by Kurien Kunnumpuram. Delhi: ISPCK, 2013.

———. "Ecology and Faith: The Mystery of the Earth." In *Nature, Woman and the Church: Indian Christian Reflections on Ecology, Feminism and Ecclesiology*. Vol.1 of *Collected Writings of Samuel Rayan SJ*, edited by Kurien Kunnumpuram. Delhi: ISPCK, 2013.

———. "Ecology and Theology: A Theology of Nature, a Theology of Life." In *Nature, Woman and the Church: Indian Christian Reflections on Ecology, Feminism and Ecclesiology*. Vol. 1 of *Collected Writings of Samuel Rayan SJ*, edited by Kurien Kunnumpuram. Delhi: ISPCK, 2013.

———. "Hierarchy-Religious Relationship." In *God's Hope Becoming Visible: Indian Christian Reflections on Some Relevant Issues of Our Times*. Vol.3 of *Collected Writings of Samuel Rayan SJ*, edited by Kurien Kunnumpuram. Delhi: ISPCK, 2013.

———. "How Will the Hindu Hear?" In *God's Hope Becoming Visible: Indian Christian Reflections on Some Relevant Issues of Our Times*. Vol.3 of *Collected Writings of Samuel Rayan SJ*, edited by Kurien Kunnumpuram. Delhi: ISPCK, 2013.

———. "Indian Theology and the Problem of History." In *Doing Theology: Indian Christian Reflections on Theologizing in India Today*. Vol. 3 of *Collected Writings of Samuel Rayan SJ*, edited by Kurien Kunnumpuram. Delhi: ISPCK, 2013.

———. "Interpreting Christ to India: Contributions of Roman Catholic Theological Seminaries." *Indian Journal of Theology* 23/4 (1974): 223–231.

———. "Jesus and the Poor in the Fourth Gospel." In *Jesus: Relevance of His Person and the Message for Our Times*, edited by Kurien Kunnumpuram.Vol.1. Mumbai: St. Paul's, 2011.

———. "Local Cultures: Instruments of Incarnated Spirituality." In *God's Hope Becoming Visible: Indian Christian Reflections on Some Relevant Issues of Our Times*, Vol. 3. Collected Writings of Samuel Rayan SJ, edited by Kurien Kunnumpuram, SJ. Delhi: ISPCK, 2013.

———. "New Efforts in Pneumatology," In *God's Hope Becoming Visible: Indian Christian Reflections on Some Relevant Issues of our Times.* Vol 3. *Collected Writings of Samuel Rayan*, edited by Kurien Kunnumpuram. Delhi: ISPCK, 2013.

———. "People's Theology." In *Doing Theology: Indian Christian Reflections on Theologizing in India Today.* Vol. 2 of *Collected Writings of Samuel Rayan SJ*, edited by Kurien Kunnumpuram. Delhi: ISPCK, 2013.

———. "The Praxis of Subversive Prayer." In *Jesus: Relevance of His Person and the Message for Our Times.* Vol. 1 of *Collected Writings of Samuel Rayan SJ*, edited by Kurien Kunnumpuram. Mumbai: St. Paul's, 2011.

———. "Responsibility of the Church in India Today." In *Nature, Woman and the Church: Indian Christian Reflections on Ecology, Feminism and Ecclesiology.* Vol. 1 of *Collected Writings of Samuel Rayan SJ*, edited by Kurien Kunnumpuram. Delhi: ISPCK, 2013.

———. "Seek First God's Kingdom and His Justice." In *Nature, Woman and the Church: Indian Christian Reflections on Ecology, Feminism and Ecclesiology.* Vol. 1 of *Collected Writings of Samuel Rayan SJ*, edited by Kurien Kunnumpuram, SJ. Delhi: ISPCK, 2013.

———. "Sociological Factors and the Local Church as a Eucharistic Community." In *Nature, Woman and the Church: Indian Christian Reflections on Ecology, Feminism and Ecclesiology.* Vol. 1 of *Collected Writings of Samuel Rayan SJ*, edited by Kurien Kunnumpuram. Delhi: ISPCK, 2013.

———. "Symbols of the Spirit." In *God's Hope Becoming Visible: Indian Christian Reflections on Some Relevant Issues of Our Times.* Vol.3 of *Collected Writings of Samuel Rayan SJ*, edited by Kurien Kunnumpuram. Delhi: ISPCK, 2013.

———. "Theologian as Disciple—Disciple as Theologian."In *Doing Theology: Indian Christian Reflections on Theologizing in India Today.* Vol. 2 of *Collected Writings of Samuel Rayan SJ*, edited by Kurien Kunnumpuram. Delhi: ISPCK, 2013.

———. "Theological Perspectives on the Environmental Crisis." In *Nature, Woman and the Church: Indian Christian Reflections on Ecology, Feminism and Ecclesiology*. Vol. 1 of *Collected Writings of Samuel Rayan SJ*, edited by Kurien Kunnumpuram, 78–97. Delhi: ISPCK, 2013.

———. "Theology as Art." In *Doing Theology: Indian Christian Reflections on Theologizing in India Today.* Vol. 2 of *Collected Writings of Samuel Rayan SJ*, edited by Kurien Kunnumpuram. Delhi: ISPCK, 2013.

———. "Theology of the Church." In *Nature, Woman and the Church: Indian Christian Reflections on Ecology, Feminism and Ecclesiology.* Vol. 1 of *Collected Writings of Samuel Rayan SJ*, edited by Kurien Kunnumpuram. Delhi: ISPCK, 2013.

Richardson, Alan, and John Bowden, eds. *A New Dictionary of Christian Theology*. London: SCM Press, 1983.

Robinson, Rowena, and Joseph Marianus Kujur. "Introduction." In *Margins of Faith: Dalit and Tribal Christianity*, edited by Rowena Robinson and Joseph Marianus Kujur, 1–27. New Delhi: SAGE, 2010.

Ropelt, Rowena J. "Ecclesiology of the Open Table: Intercommunion in the Church of England, A Historical and Theological Analysis." PhD diss., Catholic University of America, Washington D.C., 2003.

Sahay, K.N. *Christianity and Culture Change in India*. New Delhi: Inter India Publications, 1986.

———. *Under the Shadow of the Cross*. Calcutta: Institute of Social Research and Applied Anthropology, 1976.

Sahu, Dhirendra Kumar. *United & Uniting: A Story of the Church of North India*. Delhi: ISPCK, 2001.

Saldanha, Julian. "Patterns of Conversion in Indian Mission History." In *Mission and Conversion: A Reappraisal*, edited by Joseph Mattam and Sebastian Kim, 79–97. Fellowship of Indian Missiologists (FOIM). Mumbai: St. Paul's, 1996.

Samartha, Stanley J. *The Hindu Response to the Unbound Christ*. Madras/Bangalore: CLS/CISRS, 1974.

———. *One Christ, Many Religions: Towards a Revised Christology.* Maryknoll, NY: Orbis, 1991.

Samuel, Joshua. "Practicing Multiple Religious Belonging for Liberation: A Reflection from a Dalit Perspective." *Current Dialogue* 57 (December 2015): 78–87.

Samuel, Prasanna Kumari. *Dalit Women's Experiences: A Theological Imperative for Indian Feminist Theology*. Chennai: Gurukul, 2009.

Samuel, Thomas, and Mathew Koshy, eds. *A Theological Response to Ecological Crisis*. Punnackadu, Thiruvalla: Christava Sahithya Samithi, 2009.

Schmemann, Alexander. *Church, World, Mission: Reflections on Orthodoxy in the West*. New York: St. Vladimir's Seminary Press, 1979.

Scott, John. "Hybridity." In *A Dictionary of Sociology*, edited by John Scott and Gordon Marshall. 4th ed. New York: Oxford University Press, 2015.

Sen, Amartya. *The Argumentative Indian: Writings on Indian History, Culture and Identity*. New York: Farrar, Straus & Giroux, 2005.

Shiva, Vandana. *Staying Alive: Women, Ecology and Development*. New Delhi: Zed Books, 1989.

Singh, Navinder J., and Sumanta Bagchi. "Applied Ecology in India: Scope of Science and Policy to Meet Contemporary Environmental and Socio-Ecological Challenges—A Review." *Journal of Applied Ecology* 50 (2013): 1–11.

Smith, Wilfred Cantwell. *The Meaning and End of Religion*. Minneapolis, MN: Fortress Press, 1991.

Spivak, Gayatri Chakravorty. *A Critique of Postcolonial Reason: Toward a History of Vanishing Present*. Cambridge: Harvard University Press, 1999.

Stanislaus, L. "Dalits and Mission of the Church." In *Liberative Struggles in a Violent Society*, edited by John Vattamattam. Forum Series-1, Hyderabad, 1991. *SEDOS*, www.sedosmission.org/web/en/mission.../551-dalits-and-the-mission-of-the-church.

"Silent Rally to Demand Justice for Dalit Christians and Dalit Muslims." Accessed August 24, 2016. http://cnisynod.org/.

Subramanyam, Kadayam. "Rising Violence against Women in India: Regional Human Development View Needed." *Asia Times News & Features, South Asia* (November 11, 2015). Accessed July 22, 2016. http://atimes.com/2015/11/rising-violence-against-women-in-india-need-for-a-regional-human-development-view/.

Sylvester, Jerome. *Kristbhakta Movement: Hermeneutics of a Religio-Cultural Phenomenon*. Delhi: ISPCK, 2013.

Tanner, Kathryn. *Christ the Key*. Cambridge: Cambridge University Press, 2010.

———. "The Church and Action for the World: A Response to Amy Pauw." *Scottish Journal of Theology* 57/2 (2004): 228–232. doi: 10.1017/S0036930604000092.

———. *The Economy of Grace*. Minneapolis, MN: Augsburg Fortress, 2005.

———. "How My Mind Has Changed: Christian Claims." *Christian Century* 127, no. 4 (February 23, 2010): 40–45.

———. *The Politics of God: Christian Theologies and Social Justice*. Minneapolis, MN: Fortress Press, 1992.

———. *Theories of Culture: A New Agenda for Theology*. Guides to Theological Enquiry. Minneapolis, MN: Fortress Press, 1997.

Taylor, J.V. *The Go-Between God: The Holy Spirit & the Christian Mission*. London: SCM, 1972.

Tennent, Timothy C. "The Challenge of Churchless Christianity: An Evangelical Assessment." *International Bulletin of Missionary Research* 29, no. 4 (October 2005): 170–177.

Thangasamy, D.A. "Relevant Patterns of Church Structures." In *Indian Church: Identity and Fulfilment*, edited by Mathai Zachariah, 53–58 Chennai/Delhi/Lucknow: CLS/ISPCK.LPH, 1971.

———. *The Theology of Chenchiah with Selection from His Writings*. Bangalore: CISRS/The Literature Department of the National Council of Y.M.C.As of India, 1966.

Thatamanil, John J. "Eucharist Upstairs, Yoga Downstairs: On Multiple Religious Participation." In *Many Yet One: Multiple Religious Belonging*, edited by Peniel Jesudason Rufus Rajkumar and Joseph Prabhakar Dayam. Geneva: WCC, 2016.

*The Constitution of CNI*. Delhi: ISPCK, 1987.

*The Constitution of The Church of North India and Bye-Laws*. As Amended upto October 3, 2017. Delhi: ISPCK, 2018.

Thomas, M.M. *The Christian Response to the Asian Revolution*. Great Britain: SCM Press, 1966.

Thomas, M.M. *The Church's Mission and Post-Modern Humanism: Collection of Essays & Talks 1992–1996*. Madras/Delhi: CSS/ISPCK, 1996.

———. *A Diaconal Approach to Indian Ecclesiology*. Rome/Thiruvalla: CIIS/CSS, 1995.

———. *Ideological Quest within Christian Commitment*, 1939–1954. Madras: CLS, 1983.

———. *Man and the Universe of Faith*. Madras: CLS, 1975.

———. *Risking Christ for Christ's Sake*. Geneva: WCC, 1987.

———. *Salvation and Humanisation: Some Crucial Issues of the Theology of Mission in Contemporary India*. Madras: CLS, 1971.

Thomas, M.M. and P.T. Thomas. *Towards an Indian Christian Theology: Life and Thought of Some Pioneers*. Thiruvalla: The New Day Publications of India, 1992.

Thomson, John B. *The Ecclesiology of Stanley Hauerwas: A Christian Theology of Liberation*. Aldershot: Ashgate New Critical Thinking in Religion, Theology & Biblical Studies, 2003.

Tinker, George E. *Missionary Conquest: The Gospel and Native American Cultural Genocide*. Minneapolis, MN: Fortress Press, 1993.

"Towards a Holistic Understanding of Mission Consultation." In *Church: A Community in Mission for Justice, Peace and Integrity of Creation*, CNI Synodical Program–A Report, November 15–17, 1993, New Delhi.

Tsetsis, Georges. *Orthodox Thought: Report of Orthodox Consultations Organized by the World Council of Churches 1975–1982*. Geneva: WCC, 1983.

*United Nations FAO Global Forest Assessment Report* 2010. Accessed July 26, 2016. http://www.fao.org/forestry/fra/fra2010/en/.

Valle, Vijaya Joji Babu. "Becoming Indian: Towards an Indian Contextual Ecclesiology." PhD diss., Katholieke Universiteit Leuven, Faculty of Theology, Belgium, 2010. Accessed November 21, 2019, https://lirias.kuleuven.be/bitstream/123456789/287832/1/Valle+Thesis.pdf

Varughese, G.C., K.V. Lakshmi, A. Kumar, and N. Rana. *State of the Environment Report: India 2009*. New Delhi: Ministry of Environment and Forests, Government of India, 2009.

Vasanthakumar, Nirmala. "Role and Identity of Women in the Church." In *Feminist Hermeneutics*, edited by Lalrinawmi Ralte and Evangeline Anderson-Rajkumar. Delhi: IWIT/ISPCK, 2002.

Vinayaraj, Y.T. *Ecumenism, Re-defining Oikumene: A Subaltern Perspective*. Accessed November 19, 2019. http://revytvinayaraj.blogspot.co.uk/2012/01/ecumenism.html.

Volf, Miroslav. *After Our Likeness: The Church as the Image of the Trinity*. Grand Rapids, MI: William B. Eerdmans, 1998.

Vondey, Wolfgang, and Martin William Mittelstadt, eds. *The Theology of Amos Yong and the New Face of Pentecostal Scholarship: Passion for the Spirit*. Leiden, Netherlands: Brill, 2013.

"Wasteland Atlas." Department of Land Resources, Ministry of Rural Development, Government of India. Accessed July 26, 2016. http://dolr.nic.in/dolr/wasteland_atlas.asp.

Weber, Laura A. "That They May All Be One—John 17:21–23: A Plotinian Application to Unity." PhD diss., e-publications at Marquette. Wisconsin: Marquette University, 1995. Accessed September 24, 2016. http://epublications.marquette.edu/dissertations/AAI9634107.

Webster, John C.B. "Varieties of Dalit Christianity in North India." In *Margins of Faith: Dalit and Tribal Christianity*, edited by Rowena Robinson and Joseph Marianus Kujur, 97–118. New Delhi: SAGE, 2010.

Wilfred, Felix. "Foreward." In *Kristbhakta Movement: Hermeneutics of a Religio-Cultural Phenomenon*, by Jerome Sylvester. Delhi: ISPCK, 2013.

———. *Margins: Site of Asian Theologies*. Delhi: ISPCK, 2008.

———. *On the Banks of Ganges: Doing Contextual Theology*. Delhi: ISPCK, 2002.

Wolters, Hielke T. *Theology of Prophetic Participation: M.M. Thomas' Concept of Salvation and the Collective Struggle for Fuller Humanity in India*. Delhi/Bangalore: ISPCK/UTC, 1996.

World Council of Churches. *Baptism, Eucharist and Ministry*, Faith and Order Paper 111. Geneva: WCC, 1982.

Xaxa, V. "Tribes, Conversion and the Sangh Parivar." *Jnanadeepa* 3 (1) 2000: 23–25.

Yates, Timothy. *Christian Mission in the Twentieth Century*. Cambridge: Cambridge University Press, 1994.

Yong, Amos. *Beyond the Impasse: Toward a Pneumatological Theology of Religions*. Eugene, OR: Wipf & Stock, 2003.

———. *The Bible, Disability, and the Church: A New Vision of the People of God*. Grand Rapids, MI: William B. Eerdmans, 2011.

———. *Discerning the Spirit(s): A Pentecostal-Charismatic Contribution to Christian Theology of Religions*. England: Sheffield Academic Press, 2000.

———. *Hospitality and the Other: Pentecost, Christian Practices, and the Neighbor*. Maryknoll, NY: Orbis Books, 2008.

———. *In the Days of Caesar: Pentecostalism and Political Theology—The Cadbury Lectures 2009*. Grand Rapids, MI: William B. Eerdmans, 2010.

———. "Poured Out on All Flesh: The Spirit, World Pentecostalism, and the Renewal of Theology and Praxis in the 21st Century." *Penteco Studies* 6, no. 1 (2007): 33–34.

———. *Renewing Christian Theology: Systematics for a Global Christianity*. Waco, TX: Baylor University Press, 2014.

———. *Spirit of Love: A Trinitarian Theology of Grace*. Waco, TX: Baylor University Press, 2012.

———. *The Spirit of Creation: Modern Science and Divine Action in the Pentecostal-Charismatic Imagination*. Grand Rapids, MI: William B. Eerdmans, 2011.

———. *The Spirit Poured Out on All Flesh: Pentecostalism and the Possibility of Global Theology*. Grand Rapids, MI: Baker Academic, 2005.

———. *Spirit-Word-Community: Theological Hermeneutics in Trinitarian Perspective*. Eugene, OR: Wipf & Stock, 2002.

———. *Theology and Down Syndrome: Reimagining Disability in Late Modernity*. Waco, TX: Baylor University Press, 2007.

Young, Robert J.C. *Postcolonialism: An Historical Introduction*. Malden, MA: Blackwell, 2001.

Zachariah, Mathai. *Inside the Indian Church*. New Delhi: ISPCK, 1994.

**Websites:**

"1000 Green Schools Plan by Church of South India." *Anglican Communion News Service*. Accessed August 25, 2016. https://tinyurl.com/y5cp2lsb; https://tinyurl.com/hup2vdd.

"2011 Our Census, Our Future." *Census Info India 2011*. Accessed October 22, 2019. https://tinyurl.com/yyh3qruw.

"Census of India 2011." Accessed October 7, 2019. https://tinyurl.com/y2v3mbv4.

"Ethnic Composition of Indian Population." Accessed October 15, 2019. https://tinyurl.com/y5hacvdg.

# INDEX

## F



## G



## H



## I



## J



## K

## P



## R

## V



## W



## Y